The Medic

And

The Mama-san

Michael H. Hall

Hawkeye Publishing
Cortland, New York

This is a true story. Some names
have been changed to protect the
innocent .... and the guilty.

Library of Congress number: 93-061126
ISBN 0-9639091-0-X   Paper cover
ISBN 0-9639091-1-8   Hard cover

Printed in the United States of America,
October, 1993.
February, 1994.

Published by: Hawkeye Publishing
               37 Morningside Drive
               Cortland, N.Y. 13045

Front cover by Mari Gibbs-Pickett

For Minh

Your patience, persistence and
love made this book possible.

Mike Hall

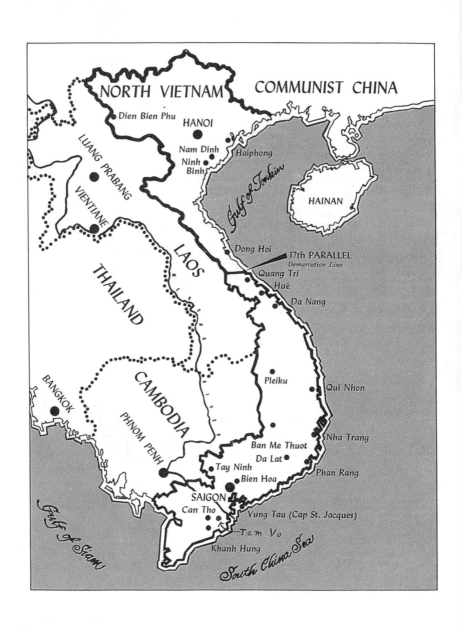

Chapter One

The stifling heat and humidity of the Mekong Delta day had given way to a cooling evening breeze. Though the temperature hovered near eighty, the gentle breeze blew over the river refreshing the parched earth and promising relief to the inhabitants of the small compound. The rude house and attached shed were set back a scant hundred feet from the rivers edge. The annual flooding in the rainy season had never reached the knoll where the farmer had constructed his home.

The walls and roof were thatched with palm leaves and a small bamboo porch faced the river. In one of the two rooms curtained off from the central living area a woman was straining in the last hours of labor. This would be her second child. There were no doctors or midwives in the vicinity but her nearest neighbor had walked the mile between their homes to assist with the birth. All went well and on the tenth of August, in 1937, a baby girl was born to Suu and Tot. Her name would be Minh. It was the year of the buffalo.

Her father Suu had also been born in the year of the buffalo and now they would need all the strength and forbearance that their namesake embodied. The fall rains were unusually heavy and the swollen river, for the first time, swallowed the land and house on the little knoll. Suu brought his small family onto his old fishing boat and for the next five years this would be their home.

The wooden sampan was sixteen feet long and six feet wide. Its depth from the gunwales was barely three and a half feet, while the width tapered to two feet at the stern. The roof and sides of the raised cabin area extended forward ten feet from the stern and were made of thatched palm leaves. The family's meager possessions were stored in the bottom of the boat beneath the tiny cabin. Fishing nets were stowed in the bow ready for use.

1

While Suu had a talent for farming, his real love was the river. He was a born fisherman. At twenty-four years of age he was lean and strong. He knew he could make a good living for his family on this river they called "Rach Cui".

These were peaceful times for Suu and Tot and their daughters, Tran and Minh. It would be three years before the Japanese invasion and Vietnam's involvement in World War II. The river was a good provider, with dozens of species of fish as well as many varieties of shrimp, crabs and lobsters. At the salt water estuary where the river emptied into the South China Sea there were many more species of marine life which could be netted and sold. The river was not a direct tributary of the mighty Mekong but was connected to it by an interlacing network of smaller streams. This watery labyrinth gave Suu access to the entire Mekong Delta area and the sea to the east. He could also row upriver to Saigon. or westward into Cambodia.

For most of the year the river was a sleeping giant, flowing languidly through reedy marshes and past dense jungle growth. Nearer to the sea there were scattered plantations of bananas, coconut palms and tobacco along the banks. Villages in the area were tiny and widely separated. The hamlets near the river were built on stilts, for in the monsoon season of April and May the river awoke, and true to its reputation, began whipping its tail like a dragon. Logs and other floating debris made this a dangerous time for small boats.

Life on the river was exciting for children. The two small girls, Tran and Minh, had the run of the boat, but learned early to respect the water and stay away from the edge of the small craft. The scenery around them was constantly changing as Suu plied the currents in his daily search for fish.

During the midday heat they would tie up under the shade of overhanging boughs, but by late afternoon Suu would ready the nets and begin to fish. Fishing was always better after dark and he would usually quit by midnight. Then the kerosene lamp would be lit and the little family would sort and clean the fish. The next day any extra fish would be sold at one of the small villages along the river. Often, there would be no money available and the fish would be bartered for cloth, thread or other necessities.

Whenever they landed each of them would scrounge for suitable wood for the cooking fire. All of the cooking was done on the boat on a fire-hardened pottery base. Some wood was converted to charcoal for more convenient cooking. At night there were homemade mosquito nets to keep out the swarms of insects. Minh's earliest memories were of sleeping on the boat at night, listening to the river and the drone of hordes of mosquitos. Rainy nights were special. Nothing sounded as good as the patter of rain on the thatched roof.

Ah, those halcyon days of childhood!

By the time she was five, Minh had been given many responsibilities. She helped wash dishes and clothing, gather firewood, sort and clean fish and helped with the rowing. Actually, the rowing was her idea.

One day as her father was at the stern, pushing the oar forward and back, Minh decided he needed some help. She nimbly scurried up onto the bow of the boat and lifted the long oar. The oar was fitted with a single loop oarlock attached to the bow, allowing enough freedom of movement to thrust the oar into the current on either side. As the long, narrow oar bit into the current the loop broke and Minh and the oar tumbled into the river. She never had time to cry out.

By some happy fortune she was swept along the side of the boat and passed almost directly beneath her father's oar. He dove into the muddy froth and was able to grab his daughter on the first try. Other than a good soaking, she was none the worse for wear. From that day, however, she never enjoyed swimming.

Their nomadic life on the river gave the family an opportunity to visit many of the villages throughout the delta region. On two occasions they made their way to Cambodia. For the first three years there were no problems finding goods for barter, but after the Japanese invasion in 1940 life became more difficult. Sometimes upon landing at a village there would be no rice or vegetables available. In those times of shortage, the only meal of the day would be a fish chowder made with whatever roots and herbs that could be gleaned from the river bank.

Several competing armies were foraging throughout the delta area by this time and Suu began to worry about his family's future. The Cao Dai and Hoa Hao were religious sects which raised large armies in the region. These armies might have had nationalistic goals at one time but they were most often used to serve the private wishes of the sects.

In addition to these militant sects there were the invading Japanese troops and the combined Vietnamese and French forces. To further complicate the scene there were Viet Minh everywhere. These were Vietnamese who wanted to remove all foreign control from their country. Their leader, Ho Chi Minh, was trying to unify them and garner whatever additional support he could. His communistic philosophies seemed well-suited to generate a spirit of nationalism among the poor rural population of Vietnam.

With so many conflicting viewpoints and armies spread throughout the country, it was small wonder that even a wandering fisherman such as Suu would be caught up in the inevitable strife. His Buddhist beliefs of peaceful existence were about to be challenged.

Shortly after Minh's fifth birthday the family arrived at the hamlet of Binh Phuoc. It was a typical delta town, with only twelve or thirteen families living there, including the family of Minh's grandfather. He was half French, his father having been a French planter who lived in the region south of Hanoi. Upon Minh's arrival she learned that her grandfather and grandmother had both died during the past year. Her father's three younger sisters had remained there after their parents deaths.

Her grandfather had owned several acres of land which he had planted to groves of fruit and nut trees. His small plantation included betel nut trees, coconut palms, oranges, mangos, bananas and several smaller fruits, all salable staples of the region. Minh's three aunts, Phai, Thiet and Hon, were unable to care for the plantation and welcomed Suu's arrival. He moved his family into the big house and prepared to settle down. His sojourn as a fisherman was over.

The house was typically one story, but that was the only thing typical about it. The construction was of masonry and wood and boasted four large interior pillars in the central living area. Another large pillar was located at each corner of the house to support the roof. The French influence was also seen in the partioned sleeping rooms which were quite unusual in most Vietnamese dwellings. The kitchen was separated from the living area by an arched doorway through the wall and a small portico. To little Minh it seemed like a palace. Her mother agreed.

4

Upon settling in, Suu immediately began to bring the plantation back into shape, and everywhere he went Minh was at his heels. Soon he had hired several neighbors to work in the fruit groves. Paths were cleared and old trees were pruned. Overgrowth was cut back and new trees were set out. Though the work was hard, life began to seem idyllic.

Minh's responsibilities once again increased. During their second year on the boat her mother had given birth to another baby. Now six, Minh was given charge of her younger sister. Her older sister, Tran, had been asthmatic and sickly from birth and was unable to help with many chores, leaving Minh with very little free time. When she wasn't watching the baby or otherwise working, she could usually be found happily climbing coconut trees, tossing down the milky fruits and sliding to the ground to be the first to split them for a refreshing drink.

Her favorite time of day was evening. She especially loved sitting on the porch, listening to the buzzing insects and the night sounds of the surrounding jungle. There were always small lizards climbing the walls and racing one another to a dark corner whenever a certain small girl tried to catch them. While the chameleons and geckos were usually too quick for her, Minh never failed in her pursuit of the crickets, which she would place in miniature bamboo cages. They were a never-ending source of amusement for her.

Minh was allowed to roam about the orchards freely but was warned about the more unfriendly denizens of the surrounding woods. Many kinds of poisonous snakes lived in the area, in addition to dozens of harmless varieties. The rule was -- avoid all of the legless crawlers. Though there were very few scorpions around, spiders and centipedes were plentiful and many of them were poisonous. It didn't take long to become accustomed to living with these creatures, and by exercising reasonable care, they were little more than a minor nuisance.

Not so the red ants!

These ferocious little warriors were attracted by the presence of food and invaded the house and grounds in true army fashion. Their bite was extremely painful and slightly poisonous. Several bites could cause a debilitating illness. The house had to be inspected daily to detect these noxious intruders. When they were found, kerosene was used as a deterrent. Despite all precautions however, the ants had time and numbers on their side. The battle to exclude them was one of the constants in this tropical existence.

During the next four years new life came to the plantation. Additional lands were cleared and new orchards begun. Tot presented Suu with his first son, a beautiful child they named Hoai. With three doting aunts, Minh could spend less time watching the babies and more time helping her father in the fields. She epitomized the word tomboy. Eight years old now, she was a big strong girl and able to keep up with anyone at whatever task she undertook.

And then tragedy struck.

Minh, her younger sister Hien, and little Hoai became ill. The chickenpox was particularly virulent and no doctor or medicine was available. The children were unable to throw off this deadly sickness and the fever began to take its toll. Suu and Tot were frantic. None of the local herbs or home medicines had an effect. Finally, unable to swallow and severely dehydrated, little Hien died. She was buried in the palm grove beside her grandparents.

Grief and anxiety ruled the house for another two weeks. Gradually Minh and Hoai recovered. Suu found solace from the death of his daughter by doubling his efforts in the fields, but Tot found the weeks of suffering and death too much to bear. She secluded herself in the house and refused to speak for days. It took a near tragedy to revive her.

One day, her aunts brought Minh to the river bank to help with the laundry. As they were scrubbing clothes on the shore Minh dropped a shirt into the water. Leaning far out to retrieve the garment, she lost her balance and tumbled into the stream. The current was not too swift at this point and Minh found herself floating on her back. She began flailing her arms, propelling herself towards the center of the river where the current was much stronger. Screaming at the top of her lungs, Aunt Phai ran to a neighbor's house looking for help.

Providentially, it was mid-afternoon and the neighbor was at home napping, waiting for the heat to subside. He ran quickly to the river and dove in without hesitation. His fast action was all that saved the young backstroker. As he pulled her to shore, gasping and sputtering, she cried over and over that she would never again go swimming. She rarely broke that promise, even in adulthood.

Upon learning of this close call, Tot left her self-imposed exile and once again took her place in the household. But the recent ordeals had taken their toll. She was changed.

From the day of her near-drowning, Minh was not allowed to leave her mother's sight. She was given so many chores it became impossible to complete them all. At the slightest hesitation to work, her mother would take a piece of firewood and beat her. The beatings became so frequent that she was covered with welts and bruises. Suu came in from the fields one night and noticed with alarm the condition of his husky young daughter. He spoke to Tot about the beatings and she deferred to him, but only for the time being.

Minh soon began to exhibit the stubborn character of her namesake, the water buffalo. During the beatings she would no longer cry. This seemed to infuriate her mother and the beatings would intensify, but Minh's will became more and more resolved and she remained silent. This bullish patience and ability to endure would strengthen her character and help her to overcome the many hardships which lay ahead.

Chapter Two

On June 6, 1943 a significant event occurred which would have an enormous impact on Minh's life. A red-headed baby boy was born to Harrison and Jean Hall in Albany, New York, U.S.A.. They named him Michael. I had arrived.

My parents had been born and raised in neighboring communities in New York's Adirondack Mountains, and had moved to Albany in 1940 when Harrison took a job with the power company. The year following my birth, Harrison, at the age of 30, enlisted in the Seabees. Jean moved back home to Olmstedville with me and lived with her parents. We remained there for the next two years while Harrison served in the South Pacific. Their wartime separation was especially difficult since they had recently lost their first-born child, Ellen, to complications of a childhood illness.

My early years were spent at Mom's knee and grandfather's heels. Pop, as Grandpa was called, owned the general store and Grandma was the post-mistress in the enclosed post office. The old ice cream fountain held a special attraction for Pop and me. We made many an evening foray to raid the luscious contents when no one was looking. Our particular targets were the round cardboard ice cream containers. The scoops couldn't remove the delicious cold treat from the rounded corners and Pop could always salvage enough for a couple of heaping dishes. Small wonder he was my favorite man at the time!

Though wartime shortages made life more difficult, Mom and I and Grandpa and Grandma Sullivan made it through the lean years, though I barely squeaked through. One evening, well before my second birthday, I crawled behind the kitchen stove, and finding a tin can of a delightful-looking liquid, quaffed the entire contents. Fortunately, the can had only two inches of kerosene in the bottom. Nevertheless, I predictably began choking and turning blue.

Grandma and Mom rushed to the rescue, found the empty can and frantically tried to make me vomit. They were only partially successful as the deadly fluid continued to wreak havoc in my stomach.

Pop warmed up the car and we began the nerve-wracking fifty mile drive to the nearest hospital. As we entered the hospital I was rigid and blue. A hastily applied stomach pump brought up the remainder of the kerosene and normal color soon returned. The burns to my throat from the volatile liquid were minor and healed within a few days. A close call all around.

When Dad returned from the war in 1946 he moved our little family to Schroon Lake, a small village about fifteen miles from Olmstedville. He continued to work for the power company and together, he and Mom raised our family there. Four more daughters were born and contributed greatly to keeping me active, or vice versa. Ginnie, Anne, Mary and Liz were hard put to stay ahead of their older sibling, but somehow they always seemed to manage. Despite the usual rivalries and squabbling, our home was filled with love.

Harrison was a strong male presence and a tireless worker. Jean was the heart of the home and always had time for her children, no matter how tired or busy she might have been. Both parents had been raised as Roman Catholics and brought a high moral fiber to the home. We children were raised to accept all people as equals, regardless of race, background or financial status. Most of the important lessons taught by Dad and Mom were imparted by their actions. They were never preachy, but believed strongly that good deeds and moral actions were the best teachers. And fortunate they were that their beliefs were held so firmly, for many of the lessons did not seem to take during their children's teen-age years. The problems were minor, however, and the fruits from those early seeds matured and flourished.

I grew up in the mountains, acquiring a deep love and respect for the natural world. While the bright lights of Lake George and Lake Placid were less than an hour away, after sampling their offerings I preferred the peace and solitude of the woods. Following my father and other mentors, I gradually acquired woodslore and an abiding conservation ethic. Hiking, camping, hunting and fishing became my overriding interests. Most of my time outside of school was spent in the woods and on the waters. That I would eventually pursue my lifework in that direction was not suspected by many, however.

Divining the future is never certain, but occasionally there are clues scattered in one's background. As a teen-ager I read <u>The Good Earth</u>, by Pearl Buck. I was deeply moved by the book and the spirit of the Chinese peasants it depicted. Who could have foreseen that one day I would have an opportunity to participate in a similar Asian drama?

Chapter Three

In the early days of 1945 in the hamlet of Binh Phuoc, life continued little changed. Suu added papayas and litchis to the plantations. Minh gathered palm leaves and rice straw for fuel. Water levels were low following the unusually dry year of 1944. Rain barrels were nearly empty and water had to be carried from ponds four miles away. Minh joined the other villagers on the slippery footpath carrying eighty pounds of water in tin cans at each end of a long flexible pole. Shoulder bruises and blisters eventually became calluses and the work became a routine daily chore. This quiet routine and the water shortage would be dramatically changed in two short months.

Unprecedented rains banished the drought. Rain barrels and ponds filled to their brims. The rice crop flourished and fruits swelled in ripeness.

And still the rains fell.

Paths washed away and farmers prayed for the rains to cease. Before their prayers were answered the river crested its banks and swept through the rice fields, gouging away much of the crop. And a poor rice harvest meant lean days ahead. Minh and her family began preparing for hard times. Food was dried and processed in clay pots. Fruits were peeled, dried and put away in storage sheds with what little grain could be salvaged. As these preparations were underway, other forces were conspiring to add to the farmers' troubles.

The Japanese surrendered in August. Just prior to ceding control, they had launched a major offensive. Thousands of French troops and Vietnamese had been captured, brutalized and slaughtered. Now, with their hated enemy no longer a threat, there was a void which many competing factions hastened to fill. Their haste and zeal began to wreak havoc among the peaceful villagers in the

11

countryside. In less than a week the quiet life of Suu and his family would be forever altered.

Three weeks after her eighth birthday Minh was hanging clothes on the line. The mid-morning sun had pushed the temperature to ninety and the day promised to be a real scorcher. As she started for the river to finish the laundry she heard a commotion down the trail. Moving forward inquisitively, she was suddenly riveted in her tracks. Directly ahead was a tall black man with hideous scars lining his face. He wore the pants of a French army uniform, but was naked from the waist up. In his hand was a long, curved knife.

Spying the young girl, he advanced towards her, flashing a grin that revealed two front teeth which had been filed to sharp points. Though she had not heard of the savage looting and raping in the villages upriver, Minh knew that her life was in peril. Without even stopping to scream, she sped down the path to her home. She raced inside and gasped her story. Aunt Phai quickly ran out the back door to call Suu. Meanwhile, Tot hid the children in the dense nippa-palms behind the house. As she started for the orchard the soldiers entered the compound at the front of the house.

Phai found Suu and his helpers working with the new papaya plantings. She had scarcely begun to relate what Minh had seen when Suu put his hand over her mouth. "Maroc", he whispered.

He had heard much of these fearsome men. The French had brought many Moroccan troops to Vietnam and their reputation for ferociousness and lack of discipline was well known. Girls of all ages were taken by the troops for their pleasure and often killed if they survived the gang rapes. Beheading was their favorite method of killing, and rumors of cannibalism only added to the terror which gripped the peasants.

Suu ran to the house as fast as he could. There, he breathed a sigh of relief. In the small courtyard were some fifty French troops with only a handful of the dreaded "Maroc". He fervently hoped that the French commander would be able to maintain control of their fierce allies.

His relief was short-lived.

The French captain gave orders for his men to search the grounds while he held Suu at gunpoint. Within a few minutes the men returned with Tot and the children.

The captain's Vietnamese interpreter began to question Suu. Was

12

he Vietminh? Was he rich? Why did he have such a large house? Was he sympathetic to the Cao Dai? The Hoa Hao? Had he helped the Japanese?

Suu realized that the fate of his family and his workers rested on his answers. Carefully, he explained that he was Buddhist and did not care for the Japanese. Neither did he favor the religious sects that were trying to gain control of the region. He merely wanted to continue working his father's farm and be left in peace.

His answers didn't satisfy the captain, who began to slap and push him. Minh watched in horror as her father was shoved against the wall of their house and five soldiers lined up with their rifles aimed at him.

He stood tall and continued to deny any association with the Vietminh. On "ready, aim, fire," five firing pins clicked on empty chambers.

Unable to coerce any more information from Suu, the captain let him go. Instead, he grabbed Tot, and the entire company headed back in the direction from which they had come. When Suu attempted to follow, a huge Maroc advanced on him with sword upraised. Thwarted for the moment, Suu retreated. He gathered his children and sisters into the house and told them to pray with him for Tot. Her life was now in Buddha's hands. Minh did as she was told, but the image of the scar-faced warriors would not leave her mind. She was sure she would never see her Mom again.

After two days of unspeakable anxiety, their prayers were answered. Tot was returned unharmed. She had been questioned, but her capture had been a ploy to give Suu time to think and perhaps change his mind. Once again the captain questioned him, and still his answers remained the same. Minh and her family were led to the side of the compound and held at gunpoint. The troops sacked the house and storage sheds, taking every bit of food that had been stored. When they were through, they piled dried palm fronds in the buildings and made Suu light them. Their home, food and dreams disappeared in the smoke.

The French left with a warning that they would return someday, and if they found that Suu or his neighbors were helping the Vietminh, everyone would suffer a most horrible death. Just as soon as the troops were out of sight, everyone began crying. Everyone, that is, except Suu and Minh. She took her father's hand, and

13

amidst the sobbing and wailing, promised to help him rebuild. In her heart she made another promise -- to seek revenge for this terrible day.

With the help of his neighbors, Suu did rebuild. Minh was by his side and helped in every way that she could. Her father possessed considerable talent and the house was soon ready to occupy. It was a much smaller home than their previous dwelling, but suitable to meet their needs. Unfortunately, the food supplies could not be replaced as quickly.

The neighboring towns to the north and south had been raided by the Japanese earlier in the year. Now, the Vietminh were becoming more active and taking what they wanted as well. There was nowhere to turn for help since the whole district was in the same plight. For most of the winter season there was only one meager meal a day. Sometimes that meal would have to last for two or three days and Minh felt not only the terrible pangs of hunger, but the awful fear of dying. Watery rice gruel with an occasional sweet potato or fish became a banquet.

Just before the end of winter, a squad of Vietminh burst into the compound and began firing their weapons into the air. Suu rushed in from the fields and found his family in grave danger once more. The leader of the communists asked for Aunt Phai by name. Somehow they had her on a list of enemies and had made a special point to come for her. Helpless, Suu watched as his sister was roughly led away, her hands bound behind her. This time, after days of prayer, no answer was forthcoming.

When spring finally arrived after the long, hungry winter, Binh Phuoc crept back to normal, and for the next year, life was seldom interrupted by the turbulent events following the Japanese occupation. Minh grew bigger and stronger every day and could work in the rice fields at the same pace as boys twice her age. Although she loved the outdoors and working with her father, most of her time was spent taking care of her younger brother. Her older sister, Tran, showed no improvement with her severe asthma and was still unable to work. Whenever tensions boiled over and squabbles erupted between the two girls, their mother would take Tran's part, and punish Minh with a beating. More and more, Minh would run off to the fields to help her father, and suffer the consequences at night. Eventually, her father saw what was happening and the beatings stopped.

Late one evening, as the family prepared to go to bed, they heard a cry outside the door. Suspiciously, Suu looked out the window. No one was in sight. Opening the door, he stepped back and gasped. There in the flickering light of the kerosene lamp was Phai. She hobbled into the house and collapsed on the floor.

The next morning she recovered enough to tell them what had happened to her during the past year. As they listened, Minh felt a rage begin rising, filling her throat with a choking, foul-tasting sensation that sent her from the room, retching.

Phai explained how she had been dragged for miles that first night. When they made camp she had been raped repeatedly until she passed out. For the next two weeks they had made their way northward until they came to a large camp in the jungle. There she was thrown into a bamboo cage and poked and teased like some kind of little animal. At that point she was sure that she would be killed.

After a week in the cage she had been questioned as to the activities of her cousin who lived in the Mekong Delta many miles from Binh Phuoc. Since she hadn't seen him in years she couldn't tell them anything they wanted to hear. Frustrated, they bound her hands and feet and placed her face down on the ground. Two men took a rough two by four board, and placing it across her back, proceeded to walk on each end of it, moving it up and down her back as they went. The excruciating pain and the sound of her bones cracking drove her into unconsciousness.

For another month she was thrown back into the cage while her back crookedly healed. And then a new man came to the camp and the questioning began all over again. This man's specialty was beating the soles of her feet with bamboo rods. After several days of the torture, they were apparently convinced that she could give them no useful information. She was released and told to find her way home alone. With her feet broken and bleeding and her back stooped, she set out into the dark jungle surrounding the camp, certain that she would never live through the night.

As her aunt finished her story, Minh felt ill again. Bravely, she remained in the room as Phai described her long, painful journey to the river, where a fisherman found her and ministered to her wounds. Months later she found her way back down the maze of rivers and backwaters until she reached home.

15

Minh looked into her aunt's eyes and quickly looked away. There was a hollow, vacant expression where once there had been laughing and dancing eyes. Minh found it hard to comprehend the cruelty men were capable of. These were not Maroc, but her own countrymen.

During the next year life once more returned to normal. Minh spent much of her time in the plantation helping her father and grew stronger still. Aunt Phai was able to get around better every day and eventually regained enough strength to help with the chores and participate in family life, but the light never returned to her eyes.

In February of 1947, less than two years after the new house was built, Minh's family was preparing for Tet, the lunar New Year and their principal holiday. It was a time of high celebration when work would be postponed and cares banished. On the eve of Tet, Minh was learning to make "banh it", a special sweet rice cake reserved for this annual holiday. The entire family was in a festive mood, anticipating the lazy days and extraordinary foods.

Just before dark, three men approached the house. Thinking that some of the neighbors were arriving early, Suu sent little Hoai to bring them in. The men entered the house unsmiling and immediately began to ask Suu political and religious questions. Suddenly, before he had a chance to answer, one of the men produced a gun and ordered Suu to leave with them. When he hesitated, the man put the gun to Hoai's head and said he would count to three. The room became deathly silent. When the gunman counted one, Suu agreed to leave. He kissed Tot and the children and made them promise not to worry. Once again, Minh watched as one of her parents was kidnapped and taken into the jungle to meet an uncertain fate.

As soon as the men had disappeared, Aunt Tiet ran to the nearest neighbor's house and spread the alarm. Moments later, friends and neighbors began to gather. In the entire village, only Suu had been taken. The kerosene lamps burned all night as Tot and her family began to cope with the realization that Suu had been taken by the Vietminh. No one knew what to expect since Vietminh activity was so unusual in the area, but Minh and her family couldn't help but think of the treatment afforded Aunt Phai at the hands of these communists.

For the next week there were friends and prayer vigils daily at

Minh's home. Soon, though, they had to return to their work and the family was left to carry on as best they could.

Minh spent all of her time in the orchards and plantations. Her grief was inconsolable. What little food she ate refused to stay down and soon she became ill. In her weakened condition she became susceptible to the many serious maladies endemic to the jungle. During the third week of her father's absence she came down with malaria.

For the next two weeks she suffered the chilling and feverish symptoms of the deadly disease. Finally her mother was able to obtain some medicine, and with the help of the medicine and her aunts' around the clock nursing care, Minh was able to break the bonds of her illness. Although she survived this close brush with death, the malaria would return to plague her intermittently for years to come.

Three long months came and went without any word from their husband and father. Anguish and desperate worry were replaced by a dull ache that never went away. Each day began with prayers that he would be released unharmed, and each day ended in the same manner, but hope was waning.

One stifling afternoon in May, three months after her father's capture, Minh was in the paddy planting rice. As she stood up to ease her aching back she saw a figure emerge from the coconut palm grove.

It was her father.

As she blinked back tears and wiped the sweat that was stinging her eyes, the apparition disappeared. She had seen this vision so often now, it seemed almost real. As she bent to her task once again the figure reappeared. It walked closer to her and called her name.

She refused to look up. How cruel, the tricks of the mind, she thought.

And then he was there, stroking her hair and kissing her. She cried as though her heart would burst. Even with all of the prayers she had never really believed that he would return. She held her father as she had never held him before. With tear-stained faces, they made their way toward the house.

That night he described what had transpired. He had a cousin in the French army and the Vietminh somehow had learned of this. They wanted to know if Suu and his cousin were both working for the French. He had assured them that he had no ties with the French whatsoever. There was a terrible irony here, considering it was the French who had burned his home. Suu had nevertheless convinced his captors that he was not working directly for the French, but could not dispel their suspicions entirely.

In the morning the family awoke to find two guards posted outside the house. For the next three days one guard remained at the house while the other accompanied Suu wherever he went. The mounting tension on the farm began to take its toll, as nerves were strained to the breaking point. Sometime in the middle of the third night, Minh awoke in a sweat.

Something was wrong!

Before her eyes could adjust to the dark she felt something move the mosquito netting above her head. She sat up and felt a hand over her mouth. A man she didn't recognize whispered, "Get your father and bring him here."

She crawled from beneath the net and hurried into her father's room. He awoke and quietly followed Minh to the room she shared with her brother and sister. The man spoke briefly to her father and then left through the open window at the rear of the house. Suu told Minh to get dressed and quietly help her brother and sister to do the same. She obeyed. A few minutes later the entire family, including her aunts, were huddled in the back room.

"That man was my cousin," whispered Suu. "He is Vietminh. He learned that I was taken for questioning because of our other cousin who is in the French army. He told me that the Vietminh are coming for me at daylight and plan to execute me. We are no longer safe here."

"What can we do?" Tot cried.

"We're going to the river," Suu answered calmly. "I want all of you to get on the boat and go down the river. I'll meet you at the army camp."

"But where will you be, Dad?" sobbed Tran.

"I'm taking a shortcut to the army camp. I'll bring them back here to meet the Vietminh with a surprise. Don't worry, just do as I say."

They crept out the back into the nippa-palm and ran through the dark forest towards the river. When they reached the path, Suu headed south for the camp while Tot and the children made for the river. Nearing the boat landing they heard voices ahead.

It was the Vietminh.

And it was Aunt Phai who saved their lives.

She pushed the children into the thick reeds and made them lie down in the shallow water. A small patrol of four or five men suddenly appeared out of the mist, padding by on bare feet, nearly stepping on Tot's hand. When all was clear, the terrified family climbed the low bank and ran along the path until they reached the river. Just as they started for the boat a light glowed briefly from the shore ahead.

There was a guard posted at the boat!

Had he not been smoking they would have been right in his lap. Tired and frightened, they moved back into the reeds. With the patrol somewhere behind them and the guard ahead, they had little choice but to remain huddled in the shallow water, enduring the swarms of insects and leeches. For a ten year old girl there was no adventure in this experience, only terror. As the giant bloodsuckers slithered across her body, Minh tried to concentrate on something enjoyable, like climbing coconut trees, or Tet. Aunt Phai had said that you could escape from the present if you only let your imagination take over. But for this young girl, the present was too overwhelming to escape.

As the first light of dawn began to filter through the mist, Tot decided to go for the boat. Her children could take no more of the mosquitoes and leeches. They would just have to take their chances with the guard. At that moment they heard shots in the direction of the plantation. Standing up, Tot glimpsed the guard sprinting along the path away from the boat. No sooner had he passed by them than the bedraggled family jumped from hiding and rushed to the boat.

"What if there are more men at the boat, Mom?" Minh asked.

Tot didn't answer. Instead, she hurried out on the rickety dock and jumped on board. Turning to Minh, she helped her over the side and the two of them lifted the rest of the family into the sturdy old craft. Casting off, they took both poles and made for the current in the center of the river. Before they had covered a hundred yards, soldiers appeared on the bank. They shouted for the women to return to shore. Tot and Tiet put their backs to the long oars and strained to reach the current.

The soldiers began firing at the boat but must have been woeful shots, as not a round struck home. Reaching the current at last, the boat floated rapidly downstream for several hundred yards until they reached a series of oxbows -- long, looping curves where the river doubled back on itself. There was little current here and the soldiers running along the shore began to gain on them. Looking ahead at more oxbows, it was apparent that the soldiers would cut them off within a few minutes. Even the children could see the hopelessness of the situation.

And then, just as in a John Wayne movie, the cavalry arrived.

From down the river came shouts and shooting. The garrison of French and Vietnamese troops, alerted by Suu, had started upriver immediately and reached them in the nick of time.

Suddenly the shoreline erupted with mortar and small arms fire. The Vietminh had also arrived in strength.

Unable to continue downriver without drawing fire, Tot and Tiet found a tiny cove along the opposite shore and tied up. They could hear the sound of bullets thudding into the solid wood of their little craft as they huddled and prayed.

The battle lasted all morning.

Finally, the shooting ceased and Suu appeared on the river bank looking for his family. He spied the boat and beckoned to them to cross the river. Jumping into his beloved fishing vessel, he was greeted by his family. They were covered with leeches and insect bites, but they were safe. With hugs and cheers, the entourage headed downriver to the army camp.

They would never return to the plantation again.

Several days later, in a final irony, Suu learned that his cousin in the Vietminh, who had risked his life to warn him of the impending danger, had been killed in the battle. He had been hiding in an underground bunker near the orchard when the regular army troops had arrived. The bunker was destroyed and Suu's brave cousin perished.

Reflecting on this tragedy, Suu came to the realization that his life as a fisherman and farmer was over. He could no longer support and protect his family as in the past. The death of his cousin was the catalyst for the biggest decision of his life. He would join the army and fight for .... what? And against whom? It was all so confusing.

A Mekong Delta home near Tam Vu

Rice paddies outside Binh Phuoc

Mekong Delta fishing boats

Rach Cui, where Minh outran the Vietminh

Chapter Four

Growing up in Schroon Lake in the 1940's and '50's was like Paradise for a young man. After school and on weekends there was endless time for a boy and his fishing pole. The lake and many streams were only a short bike ride from our house in the village. As a result, panfish, bass and trout were regular menu items in the Hall household during the summer. Providing the Friday fish was a welcome job.

In the fall, grouse, rabbit, squirrel and deer found their way into the larder. My fondest pastime in those days was riding my bike over the fifteen miles to my grandparent's house in Olmstedville. The winding, dirt road followed Trout Brook for much of the way and often provided enough fresh brook trout for a tasty meal by the time I reached their home.

On one particular day, when I was eleven, I left the bike in a handy balsam fir thicket and began to fish the tumbling creek. The small native brookies were unusually cooperative and it was not long before I was creeling my tenth trout. These silver-sided beauties with deep orange bellies and white-tipped fins lay delicately in the bottom of the ancient wicker creel, a gift from my father. As I gazed down at this treasure I could imagine my grandfather's words of praise.

And if ten trout were good, then twenty would be that much better, no matter that the daily limit was ten.

I continued to fish down the brook, taking care to check every promising pool and riffle. The trout maintained their cooperative attitude.

At the head of a long, flat run, my first cast resulted in a snagged hook. While struggling to untangle the line from a sunken log, I heard a splash just upstream. Turning to see what was going on, I slipped and landed on my hands and knees in the cold water. Fifty yards away a big black bear saw the motion and stood up on his hind legs to take a better look. The sight of this huge animal standing upright in the stream held me motionless.

My mistake!

Not being blessed with keen sight, the bear advanced towards me. At a mere fifty feet he stopped and once again stood up to sniff the air, trying to identify the dripping object ahead of him.

This was too much.

Fumbling in the creel, I withdrew a trout and threw it at the bear with a shout. Instantly the black behemoth dropped to all fours and splashed across the stream to the far shore, pausing only a few feet from one frightened fisherman.

Without a backward glance I was on my feet and legging-it for the road. A very long half hour later I was on the dirt road, walking nervously along the mile to the thicket where the bike awaited. Barely a minute passed when a car pulled up from behind me. The driver rolled down his window and offered a lift.

From the frying pan to the fire, I thought, as I recognized the good Samaritan. It was Luther Jenks, the local game warden.

"Have you had any luck?" he asked.

With beads of nervous perspiration glistening on my forehead, I responded that it had been a good day. Riding in the car with the lanky warden, my discomfort increased with each passing minute. By the time we reached the hidden bicycle, I was red-faced and sweating profusely. The greenest rookie officer would have recognized these signs of guilt, and Luther was far from new on the job. As he let me out of the car he leaned over and squeezed my shoulder.

"I wish all fishermen were as honest as you, Mike," he exclaimed. "It would sure make my job easier and insure enough fish for everyone to share. So many people keep under-sized fish and exceed the limit. It's too bad they don't stop to think of the next guy who wants to enjoy the brook."

Feeling much smaller than the three under-sized trout I had kept, I thanked the warden for the ride and started pedaling my way to Olmstedville. I never again broke a fishing law, and somewhere along the Trout Brook Road, a very wise game warden grinned broadly and hoped that his message had been received!

Throughout my teen years I continued to enjoy what I considered the good life. Our family was not well-to-do but the loving atmosphere at home and the philosophy of sharing whatever you have and not worrying about what you don't have fostered an optimistic outlook on life.

When I was fourteen, I took an interest in trapping. It was a mountain tradition which taught a man more about the woods and their inhabitants than he could ever learn through casual hiking. And pelts could be sold for good money in those days. I began trapping on my own but quickly saw that it would take forever to become an accomplished trapper without help. I approached a local man who, it was rumored, was part Indian. He was also the best trapper in the county!

Vern Kipp was a small, wiry man with sunburned, leathery skin and laughing eyes that seemed to be perpetually squinting into some unseen sun. Normally a taciturn individual, he came alive whenever I showed up for a trip into the woods. He delighted in passing on the secret techniques he had taken a lifetime to accumulate and master, though he cautioned this young apprentice to keep close the knowledge that I was gleaning.

When you find a special place where game is abundant or the fish will bite at a certain time, he would say, keep silent and enjoy the fruits, for they don't last forever, and the more people who know of them, the more imperiled they become.

This old man and boy shared many, many experiences in the Adirondack wilds. There were endless days of snowshoeing through mountain passes in search of the elusive fisher and bobcat and long nights of cramped fingers and sweet castor odors as we squatted beside a blazing campfire skinning beaver. I especially enjoyed our all night fishing trips on the shores of remote ponds or in an ice shanty on the frozen surface of Lake Champlain.

Perhaps the greatest lessons learned concerned self-reliance and confidence in dealing with the unexpected.

On a frosty March morning, with the temperature hovering just above zero, I left home alone before daylight to check a line of traps. I had laid out a seven mile circuit which could be checked by one man in a day on snowshoes.

Backing the old green 1946 Willys Jeep into a low snowdrift where it wouldn't block the narrow dirt road, I unloaded my equipment. Strapping on the trapper-style snowshoes, I slung the packbasket on my back and grabbed the ice spud. This was a large, sharp chisel mounted on the end of a five foot wooden handle. It was used for chopping holes through the ice on a pond where beaver traps were to be set.

With a few extra traps in the basket and a lilt to my step, I set off into the woods. The sun was just beginning to rise when I reached the first pond.

After chiselling out two inches of ice which had formed overnight above the trap, I leaned close to the hole and shaded my eyes. The trap and bait were untouched. I shed the wool jacket, rolled up my sleeves and deftly added an aspen twig to the bait.

Maybe tomorrow, I sighed.

I checked two more traps at the second beaver house on the pond and began the long climb up the hill leading to the next drainage. The bobcat traps along the trail were untouched. For two miles I slogged along listening to the bluejays and crows. Not many birds remained here in the north woods during the winter, and I took comfort in hearing their calls.

Breaking over the rim of the mountain, I saw the next pond. It was a large flowage created by beaver some twenty years previous. Vern had told me that by harvesting four or five beaver from the large flow each year, there would be sufficient numbers remaining to insure the continued use and growth of the pond. I hoped to be lucky enough to take two or three. Hurrying expectantly down the mountainside, I felt comfortable in the long underwear and wool pants and coat, despite the frigid temperature.

Shuffling along the snow-covered frozen surface of the pond, snowshoes clicking in rhythm, I glanced up at the sun. I'm making good time, I thought. With any luck I'll be back home well before dark. Nearing the beaver lodge, I could see the top of the pole supporting my trap canted at an odd angle.

Action?

Suddenly, with no warning, the ice beneath me gave way. Instinctively I braced the ice chisel across the front of my body. As I sank into the icy water, the chisel caught both sides of the ragged hole. I slid neck-deep into the murky pond.

Without hesitation I thrust upward like a gymnast, using the chisel handle as a horizontal bar, but the rim of ice caught the top of the packbasket, preventing me from escaping.

24

With legs numbing and face freezing with every splashing attempt, I tried again and again to free the basket. I just couldn't slip the straps without losing my precarious grip on the chisel and dared not risk sliding completely below the ice.

And then, as suddenly as it had broken through, the edge of the ice gave way and I was free.

My exhilaration lasted for only an instant. With each attempt to bring a knee up onto the ice, the snowshoes would catch on the rim and force me down again. Finally, after a dozen tries, one leg miraculously came clear. Shoving with all of my might, I cleared the other leg and rolled up onto the frozen surface.

There was no time to celebrate this triumph, as the wind chill was well below zero. The sodden clothing clung to skin that was rapidly freezing. Dropping the packbasket, I made for the shore as quickly as my numb, snowshoe-clad feet would allow.

At the edge of the woods, unable to remove the frozen leather snowshoe harnesses, I unsheathed my knife and sliced them free, realizing that a few more minutes in this condition would prove fatal.

Removing the water-logged coat, I fumbled in the pocket for a small metal tube with a paraffin seal. My waterproof matches. Would they still be dry?

Breaking the seal, I removed a wooden match, struck it on the zipper of my pants and a small plume of flame rewarded my efforts. I held the match to the scraggly bark of a white birch tree. The brief blaze warmed my fingers sufficiently to bring feeling back.

Hastily I broke dead spruce and balsam boughs from the flooded trees ringing the pond and soon had a blaze of bonfire proportions. I stripped to the skin and danced around the fire, slapping and rubbing myself to restore circulation. Standing barefoot and naked in the melting snow, I wrung out my clothing, hurriedly dressed, and tried to collect my thoughts.

The road was two miles away in a direct line, three miles if I backtracked on the old trail. I momentarily considered breaking a new trail through two feet of snow and decided it would be easier to go the longer way. Using a length of rawhide twine, I repaired the snowshoe harnesses as best I could. Without snowshoes, the trek out to the jeep would be too difficult and require much more time and energy than I had available.

Breaking into a shuffling trot, I started down my backtrail. I was forced to stop for harness adjustments several times in the first few minutes, the rawhide repairs stretching constantly.

As numbness spread over feet and legs I prayed that God would see me through this ordeal. I was sure that a Power far greater than any on earth had helped me out of the depths of the pond. If only that Power would stay with me now.

With a mile remaining, a thought began spinning through my mind. "Lie down and sleep," it whispered. "You'll be able to travel much faster after a little nap."

I had not yet learned of hypothermia and its mind-numbing symptoms, but still recognized fuzzy thinking when it surfaced. Denying the insidious suggestions, I pushed doggedly onward, praying with every step. At one point the little voice in my head told me to throw away the snowshoes, for they were only slowing my progress. Had I been able to untie the re-frozen laces I might have heeded the advice. Fortunately, or providentially, I forgot about the knife and continued to plod forward.

The jeep appeared as if in a dream. Crashing through the snow bank, I again cut the frozen harnesses free and clambered into the jeep. While it was warming up I ran up and down the road to try to restore some feeling to my feet. I was unsuccessful.

The drive home went swiftly. Upon reaching town, not wanting to alarm Mom, and perhaps fearing Dad's reaction, I headed straight for Vern's house. There I changed into dry clothing and warmed my frozen body. I would henceforth have two toes and a little finger that would be painfully sensitive to the cold as the result of frostbite. A small price to pay considering what could have been.

As my wool outerwear dried by the crackling fire, Vern and I discussed the experience. Carrying a chisel and having the presence of mind, or instinct, to brace it across the hole had been a major factor in my survival. The knife and waterproof matches which were constant companions on any trip into the woods played equal roles.

Vern was thankful that his young friend had followed the advice of his father and his mentor. Both had constantly reminded me that any expedition in the north woods, regardless of how short it was planned to be, required those two items so key to survival. A compass and map were added when traversing unfamiliar country.

What Vern couldn't understand was how I had been able to

26

overcome the best efforts of hypothermia to subdue me.

I grinned as I explained, "Well Vern, I haven't been an altar boy for the last six years for nothing. Maybe Somebody up there likes me."

Little did I know in the years to come how many times my prayers would be answered in such a swift manner.

That night, as I lay in a warm bed at home, I wondered what it would be like to live in a much warmer climate where there was no danger of falling through the ice.

Chapter Five

In the French army camp at Tham Nhien life was settling down for Minh and her family. The camp was exactly like dozens of other army camps in the Mekong Delta. Housing consisted of rows of long, dingy tin buildings, streaks of rust staining their weathered sides. The dirt streets were dusty in summer and sloppy with mud in the rainy season. Privacy was a scarce commodity.

The garrison at Tham Nhien was comprised of about six hundred French troops and four hundred Vietnamese civilian defense guards and regulars. Most of the Vietnamese troops had brought their families to live at the base with them since there was little security in the countryside. Several families were jammed into each over-crowded tin hut. Partitions of thatched palm leaves were the only separation between them.

The only well serving the base was woefully inadequate, necessitating long hikes to augment this scarce resource. Chemicals were added to both well water and river water to render them more or less potable. When it was less potable, outbreaks of dysentery were common. For people used to the spaciousness of country life the conditions were difficult. The biggest advantages were the presence of a school and the security provided by the encampment, the latter being an absolute necessity.

For three years at the camp, Minh's routine varied little. School was in session from seven a.m. until two in the afternoon, followed by household chores until evening. After supper there were more chores and school work until dark. The entire camp went to bed at dark as lamp fuel was scarce and long work days required plenty of rest at night.

Minh never cared for the structure and routine of school. She much preferred playing hookey, climbing palm trees and tall fruit trees -- sometimes spending half a day in the trees -- until school was over. She had an independent spirit and would go to great lengths to avoid studying, preferring to help the men work on a building or in the fields. It soon became known that if coconuts were needed, just call Minh and she would scramble up the tree as fast as a monkey and cut the fruit down. Her mother, of course, was not pleased by these antics. The beatings began again, but by this time Minh's stubborn nature had solidified and she remained in a test of wills with her mother.

Partly because of her tom-boy nature, Minh was often the unwilling subject of some serious teasing by the older boys. One day as she walked down the street a group of teen-age boys accosted her and playfully began spinning her around. Her shirt was accidentally torn and she ran off. An hour later she returned with a small bag slung over her shoulder and a hefty stick in her hand.

"Where are you nasty boys?" she cried out. "I have something for you."

Her taunts brought the gang on the run. As they circled around her she swung the stick in a vicious arc. Keeping their distance, the biggest boys began to call her fat and ugly. Waiting for just such a provocation, Minh reached into the bag and withdrew a handful of large stones. With great vigor, she hurled them at the boys, frequently finding the target. As the boys hesitated, she charged into the remnants of the group, her club flailing the air. Surprised and bleeding, the ruffians retreated into a nearby hootch. Minh followed them to the entrance, continuing to hurl her missiles. Missing the cowering boys, the stones broke a radio and a mirror. The occupant's cries roused the French Captain. When he learned the details of the battle he summoned Suu, and together they roared with laughter. Minh was exonerated and made an important friend.

During the three years at the camp, Tot had three more children. Two died at birth but the third, Tuong, became Minh's third sister. Minh soon found herself spending more and more time looking after her younger siblings, except during school hours. She volunteered to skip school so that she could baby-sit, but her father wouldn't hear of it. Her mother was old fashioned, believing that girls didn't need any formal education, but Suu insisted that she attend school regularly. He had a feeling that this headstrong daughter of his would someday make her mark in the world.

When Suu arrived at the camp he joined the French army as a

guide, and later, an interpreter. He was angry with the French for burning down the farm but he realized that the Vietminh were the more dangerous enemy. No one would be safe until they were defeated.

He was transferred into reconnaissance and later asked to join the intelligence branch. His quick wit and calm demeanor made him a natural for that type of work. By the end of the third year he was often away for a week or more on special assignments. He never told his family just what he did, but Tot guessed and Minh learned first-hand.

She roamed throughout the camp at every opportunity and knew everything that was happening. Her trick of biting off bottle caps made her a favorite with the French and she became privy to all of their operations. She often knew about a mission before her father was told.

One evening as she was walking behind one of the officer's huts, she heard noises inside. The open window was too much of an invitation and she peeked inside. There were three men in the room, two standing and one tied to a chair. One of the men was holding the prisoner's head back while the other poured water over his nose and mouth. They paused briefly to question the unfortunate suspect and then continued with the water. Minh heard the man gurgling, slowly drowning in the chair.

Later that night she knew why she was so upset. One of the men was her father's superior and he had mentioned her father as the man who had brought the information naming the prisoner as a Vietminh. She couldn't imagine her Dad involved in any actual torture, but he was certainly a part of the overall operation. For the first time in her life she confronted the cold reality of war, that good men were forced to do bad things.

Months later Suu received orders to move to another camp. Some of the French troops were needed further north to counter intensive communist activity and Suu would be assigned to another intelligence group. Thus, in the fall of 1950, he and his family moved to the Vietnamese army base of Tam Vu. They would remain there for the next six years.

The French troops remained at Tam Vu for only a week before they were moved still further north. Suu was ordered to remain at the base and work for the Vietnamese army. He was good at his job and given a field commission as a lieutenant. By the end of the first year he was given command of the entire intelligence unit at the base. Within five years he would be coordinating activities throughout the region. Despite his growing stature at the camp, his family earned no special privileges. Housing and other accouterments were the same as at the last camp -- the same rusty tin sheds and dusty streets.

In the first five years at this new camp Tot had five more children. Two were stillborn. Nguyet was Minh's newest sister, followed by Duc, a brother, and finally Huynh, another sister. During these years Minh continued her schooling and worked harder than ever at home. Her mother couldn't find fault with her work, but Minh's dogged persistence in expressing her individuality incurred her mother's wrath regularly.

Although there was precious little time for play or recreation, Minh secretly found time to learn to play the mandolin. She became enamored with music and contrived to meet her friend, who owned the instrument, behind the barracks for lessons. Soon, other teens joined them and before long they formed a band. Minh lived for those raucous sessions where she was free to express her talents.

It was two years before Tot learned of this "wild behavior". She beat Minh severely and made sure that she never again met with those "disreputable idlers."

Minh's outgoing nature and natural inquisitiveness soon found another outlet -- karate! Fortunately, her mother learned of this new interest almost immediately and forbade it as well. This was indeed fortunate, because with Minh's size and strength, and her short temper, it would have been only a matter of time before she hurt someone.

Despite her independent nature, Minh remained a dutiful daughter. She never shirked her family work duties and was always there to care for her brothers and sisters. She did, however, resent having to carry so much of the load. Her oldest sister was still nearly incapacitated by the chronic asthma and other related ailments, and for some unknown reason, her mother made Minh do nearly all of the work at home with little help from anyone else in the family. It may have been a case of two very strong-willed females under the same roof.

The home always seemed more peaceful when Suu was around,

but as the years went by at Tam Vu, his absences became more frequent and lasted longer. The early 1950's were unsettled times in Vietnam. The French were losing their grip on the country while the Vietminh were gaining more and more supporters. Some, through a spirit of nationalism, and most, through coercion by terrorism. The puppet government with the figurehead, Bao Dai, was in disarray. Help was being sought from America while Russia and China looked on with great interest as the small country writhed in political agonies.

Finally, in 1954, the French met their DienBienPhu. General Giap and Pham Van Dong triumphantly ended the one hundred years of French occupation. But after eight years of bitter conflict and four hundred thousand deaths, there was still untold strife and a new war waiting in the wings.

Minh was a young woman now and young men began to notice her. The mores of the times forbade boys and girls from keeping company in any way. Minh, predictably, didn't agree with such old-fashioned ideas and when a particular boy asked to see her, she readily agreed. Their relationship never went beyond stealing away to talk with one another. With so many people crowded into the camp there was no semblance of privacy for two teen-agers in a tired country.

Unfortunately for Minh, the first neighbor who saw her and her friend talking reported it to Tot. She was furious and worried. Before she beat Minh she recited a long litany of problems that could arise from talking with boys.

Some concerns, it seemed, are universal.

After this latest rebuff by her mother, Minh started to think seriously about leaving home. She had been to Saigon once with her father and remembered it as a vital, exciting city where one might find work and adventure. And then little Duc began to cry and she knew where her duty lay.

Minh still needed a break from the tough work schedule at home. Together with six neighbor women, she helped to organize a group of practical nurses. None of them had any formal medical training, but the older women had a good knowledge of herbs and their uses. The members of the group would visit households where summer flu was present or where a particular disease had caused a type of paralysis. Herb medicines were dispensed and poultices applied as needed. The victims of the paralysis were exercised and massaged much like modern day patterning of similarly afflicted individuals. The work got Minh out of the house for a break and taught her a great deal about natural herbal remedies.

Her life was hard and filled with sadness, but somewhere, just around the corner perhaps, was a glimmer of light. A glimmer that promised happiness and a chance to spread her wings and fly. That hope, and her water buffalo-inspired determination, carried her through the dark days and kept the spark of optimism alive through the trials that lay ahead.

Chapter Six

High school days in Schroon Lake were filled with the events that typified small town life in America. Studies mingled with sports, and cars competed with girls for a young man's spare time. With the nearest bowling alley twenty miles away and the movie house open only during the summer tourist season, the outdoors beckoned to me more strongly than ever.

After-school soccer in the fall was soon abandoned for extra hours in the woods. Stalking through the surrounding mountains became an obsession. The sweet smell of newly-fallen leaves in the expansive hardwood forests and the barking of gray squirrels as they foraged for beechnuts were a siren lure for this young descendent of generations of Adirondack guides.

My great-grandfather, Harrison Hall, for whom my Dad was named, had guided Theodore Roosevelt on some of his hunting trips in the big woods. In fact, Vice President Roosevelt was hiking in the High Peak wilderness when President McKinley was assassinated. Guide Harrison Hall was entrusted with the somber message and sent out to locate the Vice President and bring him out of the woods with all haste.

Hurrying over the miles of slippery trail, Hall accomplished his mission. He rushed Teddy and the rest of his party down the treacherous mountain paths and put the famous Rough Rider in a buckboard for a breakneck run to the railroad at North Creek. A waiting telegram informed him that William McKinley was dead. Roosevelt was now the President of the United States of America.

I often thought of this heritage as I carried the workworn .33 Winchester rifle given to me by my father. It was more than a family heirloom -- it was my legacy -- and I treated it with respectful care.

Hunting deer and bear with this family treasure, I felt a sense of awe as I imagined the effusive Roosevelt asking his guide for his rifle to try a shot or two. What stories the fine old walnut stock could tell.

In high school, I had enjoyed math and science, leaning toward a career in engineering, but deeper stirrings kept me from making a final decision. By the end of my senior year the nagging thoughts which had been whispering to me finally surfaced.

I decided to become a priest.

Wadhams Hall Seminary was located on New York's northern border along the St. Lawrence River. It was housed in a large Victorian mansion which had been donated to the church. A small annex used as a secondary dormitory was the only other building on the cramped grounds. The open grassy square within the shrub-covered fence served as a ball field in spring and fall and was flooded in the winter for use as a hockey rink.

The atmosphere in the seminary was conducive to quiet reflection, and academics were stressed over all else. Community prayer and service to one another were integral parts of the training, but there was always time available for personal discussions with the priests and bull sessions with the other young men.

By the time Christmas break rolled around, I had developed some truly magnificent calluses on my knees. Lest anyone develop feelings of smugness, the standing joke at Wadhams was that all seminarians were clumsy and near-sighted, and therefore spent most of their time on their hands and knees looking for objects they had dropped -- hence the calluses.

Although academics and personal development were stressed, there were diversions available to work off the tensions that inevitably develop when people spend most of their time together. To help balance the daily study and prayer, softball, football and ice hockey were encouraged. Even the priests joined in, and an occasional cross-body block or high stick to the ear did wonders for relieving the stress of cramped living.

By the end of the first year I felt happier and more fulfilled than I had ever been. I was still not completely sure that this was my ultimate vocation, but the pieces were falling into place.

During the summer break I returned to Schroon Lake to work. One weekend in mid-summer, an incident occurred which would be indelibly printed on my mind forever and help to shape my future

35

life. A priest from the seminary called to invite me on a hike. Father Cotter was a dedicated mountaineer who had climbed all forty-six Adirondack peaks over four thousand feet in elevation, earning membership in the exclusive "46ers" club. He wanted me to accompany him on a grueling ascent of two of the more challenging peaks.

I eagerly accepted the invitation to enjoy a long day with one of my favorite people. And thus, on a mild, overcast day in July, the two of us set out for the high country. The mountains Father Cotter had selected were designated as trail-less, that is, there were no marked or officially designated trails to their summits.

Using a map and compass, we made our way through the spruce and balsam fir forest covering the lower slopes of the first mountain. As we climbed higher the evergreen cover was broken by granite outcrops and long, steep rock slides.

The pace of the climb slowed markedly as we eased our way through tangled, blown-down trees interlaced with young spruce saplings reaching for the sun. By early afternoon we neared the summit. Sweating profusely, we stopped frequently to sample the refreshing, sweet water flowing in the many boulder-strewn rills which cascaded down to feed the lake. Enraptured by the rugged scenery, we failed to note the change in the weather. The temperature was falling rapidly and fog was rolling in. By the time we reached the treeless rocky crag atop the peak, visibility was zero.

Eating a hasty lunch, we decided not to attempt the climb to the adjacent mountain top, but immediately began our descent. An hour later we had covered less than a quarter mile, with another seven miles between us and the car. Our conversation was reduced to sporadic warnings about a protruding root or slippery ledge.

The fog-shrouded mountain had become a deadly trap.

One false step crossing the slippery freshets could result in a broken leg. Hidden among the dense evergreen growth were ledges with hundred foot sheer drops, certain death for a careless hiker. Unable to see more than a few feet ahead of us, we knew we were in trouble.

There were no landmarks visible to gauge our progress and we had wandered well off course in the pea soup fog, despite using the compass. Lightweight cotton shirts were no barrier to the penetrating wet and cold. The rain had become a downpour and making a fire would be an impossible task. As speech began to slur and shivering increased, Father Cotter turned to me and spoke the word that both of us were thinking -- "hypothermia".

The situation had become desperate when the wiry priest spoke again, "You know, Michael," he offered, "here we are, a priest and a seminarian in trouble, and we're trying to save ourselves, and somewhat unsuccessfully at that! I can't believe that we haven't asked for help."

Making the sign of the cross, he began to pray. After seeking forgiveness for forgetting the Lord he asked for help in resolving our predicament. We ended the prayer in Jesus' name.

Our "Amens" were lost in the wind that suddenly swept over the mountain. In less than a minute the fog was blown clear, providing two chilled hikers with a welcome view of our position.

We lost no time in taking our bearings and continuing the trek down the peak. And then, as quickly as it had arisen, the wind died completely. The fog closed in once more and we were alone with the rain and cold. But not completely alone.

With renewed confidence and energy we slowly picked our way down through the fading gray light, eventually forced to strike matches to read the compass dial, but by then we had reached the base of the mountain and the rest of the journey was routine.

Driving home that night our conversation was subdued.

"Did we witness a miracle today?" I asked.

After a moments thought Father Cotter replied, "I'm not sure, Mike. It could have been the Lord answering our prayer. If we're truly open to Him and carefully listening, we can see that all of our prayers are answered in some way. I have to admit, though, that this was without a doubt one of the most direct and spectacular answers I've ever seen."

"Well, Father," I exclaimed, "I'm convinced. There wasn't even a trace of a breeze all day and then that wind came from nowhere for just long enough to help us. You know, when I realized what happened, my hair stood up on end and my heart skipped a beat. I'll never forget this day."

And I never did.

That fall, I returned to the seminary to begin my second year of study. Classes went well but doubts began to surface, causing me to

37

spend many hours reflecting on whether I was making the right choice. A few weeks into the semester, following days of prayer and self-examination, I painfully made my decision.

Monsignor Brown, the rector of the seminary, was reluctant to meet with me. He was aware of the difficult choice I was wrestling with and had hoped that I would take more time before coming to a final decision. Nonetheless, he advised that while he thought the decision was premature, he wouldn't stand in my way. Before he dismissed me, he offered a few words of advice. These final words would sustain me in this difficult time and prove to be sanity-saving later on.

"Michael, you have prayed and reflected on this decision. When you leave here don't ever stop to second-guess yourself or agonize over it. When you take time to give your best effort to a problem and pray over it, go forward and don't look back with recriminations. They will only sadden you and become an unhealthy burden. Whatever vocation you take up in life, let your conscience be your guide, and for Heaven's sake, maintain a sense of humor."

I arrived home the day before deer season opened. Sheer coincidence, I told myself.

Following a successful season of hunting and guiding, I took a number of part-time jobs to save money for college the next fall. I entered the Environmental Science and Forestry College at Syracuse University to pursue a long-time interest -- the study of wildlife biology.

After the first year away from home I appreciated more and more the sisters and parents who were always there for me.

Ginnie had become an accomplished skater and I enjoyed watching her glide across the frozen mill pond behind Main Street. Anne was a popular student who kept busy with music and helping her mother at home. Mary and Liz enjoyed the outdoors and spent most of their free time swimming and listening to records.

Throughout my senior year in college there was a new atmosphere on campus. Demonstrations and conversations were focused on a place called Vietnam. I knew it was a small country in a part of Asia called Indochina, but beyond that it seemed of little significance. I was more interested in graduation and a job. In the summer of 1966, both arrived.

In order to pay off college loans, I returned to Schroon Lake and rejoined a consulting engineering firm supervising construction of an interstate highway through the mountains. The surveying courses paid handsome dividends as I was promoted to chief of a survey crew.

One night, as I was leaving work, a fellow surveyor offered to buy drinks at a local watering hole. Not wanting to offend this ex-Marine who had seen action in Korea, I accepted the invitation. Over a couple of beers, Bill asked me if I were worried about being drafted, since so many were being called up.

"Not really, Bill," I replied. "This road is part of the national defense highway system and working here gives me a deferment. I know some of the guys are getting married to beat the draft and I've heard some are buying deferments or heading for Canada, but that's not for me."

As the night wore on, Bill began to press, implying that I had sought out a safe job.

"Bill," I said, "I honestly didn't know anything about deferments when I took this job. I just wanted to make some good money to pay off my loans and buy a car. If I get called up, I'll go."

Bill wouldn't let the subject drop.

"Mike, the beer is getting to us but let me tell you one thing. Don't be stupid. You'd better take some time to find out just what's going on over there before you run off to get killed. Just be damned sure it's worth it, and then give it your best."

"Bill, my friend, if this is how we're going to help someone keep out the communists, then I can live with that."

"Oh sure," Bill pressed, "But can you die with that?"

"I don't plan to," I growled.

The next morning I thought back over our conversation. There had been no false bravado or whiskey-courage. I had meant everything I had said. From all that I had read, the South Vietnamese were simply trying to maintain their freedom and the U.S. was over there helping them. I couldn't recall, however, how the subject of going in the service had come up. I certainly didn't have any urge to run out and enlist.

For the next year I stayed with the highway job.

Finally, giving two weeks notice to my supervisor, I began an active search for a job as a wildlife biologist. I drove to Albany, New York, to check out the central office of the State Conservation

Department. Walking into the director's office, I asked to see the man in charge.

The Chief of the Bureau of Wildlife was a busy man, but he took time to talk with this energetic job applicant who didn't believe in making appointments. After a brief interview, he called a regional office located in the Catskill Mountains and inquired if they still had a temporary position open.

I held my breath.

The job was still available, and I was on my way to a career in my chosen field.

For three months I worked in the field as a biologist-aide, waiting for a permanent job to open anywhere in the state. The call came late one afternoon, and the next morning, after two interviews, I was hired on a permanent basis as a wildlife biologist. Five long, hard years of studying had paid off. I had finally achieved my dream.

The day before I planned to leave, my co-worker roommate brought in the mail.

"Looks like some kind of official letter here for you," Gary said.

I ripped open the envelope and stared at the letter in disbelief. It began ... "Greeting."

Chapter Seven

In the army camp at Tam Vu the family of Suu was bustling about in the sweltering afternoon heat. They were about to leave the base and move into a home of their own. Although the house was in the village and only a few blocks from the camp, the move was welcomed enthusiastically by the entire family. Minh, now nineteen, was happiest of all. She had felt so repressed in the congested army camp and longed for even a tiny amount of privacy.

Her joy was short-lived.

Barely a week after the move her mother informed her that she was to be married.

Minh was flabbergasted. Her mother's announcement had taken her completely by surprise. She tried to protest, but in her heart she knew it would do no good. This had been inevitable. Most marriages were arranged by the parents and frequently the bride and groom had never met. Minh's future bridegroom was a young soldier of twenty-five, the son of a former neighbor in the camp. Minh had never met him as he had been serving in the army north of Saigon near Tay Ninh. His family was now living in Tay Ninh and would be coming to Tam Vu for a visit in a week.

Minh threatened to run away but her father made it clear that he would lose face should that happen. Trapped by her loyalty to her father, Minh prepared for the worst.

On a sultry Friday evening, Minh's intended and his parents arrived. His name was Du.

The evening got off to a bad start when Minh refused to greet the visitors. At last her father persuaded her to at least meet the young man and pay her respects to his parents.

With great reluctance Minh entered the room. She woodenly said hello and started to withdraw to the sleeping room when Suu asked Du's parents if Minh would make a suitable wife for their son.

41

They agreed.

Before anyone could speak further, Du blurted out that he was in favor as well.

Minh turned back into the room and shouted that she didn't agree and would not be a party to any marriage, anytime, anywhere.

Tot responded that Minh's assent wasn't necessary to conclude their business and that the wedding would take place in two months.

Devastated, angry and feeling betrayed, Minh ran outside and didn't return for two days. By that time Du and his parents had left and tempers had cooled a bit. Minh plunged into her work with a ferocious vigor, trying to forget what lay ahead, but it was no use. She still felt betrayed.

Despite her objections, at the age of nineteen, Minh was married to the young soldier and left for Tay Ninh the day after the wedding.

The couple moved in with Du's family and trouble began brewing almost immediately. The household consisted of Du's parents, grandmother, older brother and his wife and baby, and six younger brothers and sisters. By custom, the new daughter-in-law was expected to take on most of the housekeeping chores. In this house, that meant that Minh was told to do everything, including the cooking, cleaning, laundry and child care.

She was overwhelmed.

Upset with the general idea of marriage in the first place, and facing the hostile demands of her new relatives, Minh lasted only a week.

Well before dawn just eight days after her marriage, Minh left Tay Ninh and started walking the ninety miles back to Tam Vu. She caught a ride with a farmer in his ox cart and made her way to Saigon. From there she cadged a ride on a sampan and reached her home two days later.

There was no welcome for the wayward wife.

Her parents had lost face. For the next month they badgered her to return to her husband. Finally, tired of all the harsh words and vilification, the beleaguered runaway gave in. Reluctantly, she accepted enough money to return to Tay Ninh by bus.

If her arrival at her father's home had been cold, the greeting she received at Du's house was positively Arctic. The family wasted no time in pushing all of the work on her until she couldn't keep up. She fell ill and took to her bed. When the doctor could find no serious illness, she was called lazy, a shirker.

For the next year life became a bitter struggle. Du seldom received a leave to visit home, and when he was able to come the fighting and tension only increased. Minh drew on all of her inner strength to survive these times.

One sister-in-law in particular was especially difficult. She went out of her way to fabricate stories about Minh and caused much trouble. Minh's sense of humor and strong will began to dissolve. She wanted so much to run away again and make a new life, but found herself pregnant.

By her eighth month, the family demands had not diminished and Minh fell ill once more. This time, the doctor pronounced her too sick to work and prescribed rest. The family listened and grudgingly took over some of her duties, but it was too little, too late.

Minh was still sick when her daughter was born and the birth was very hard. It was several weeks before Minh recovered. Meanwhile, word was sent to her husband that he had a daughter. He was able to wrangle a short leave and made it home a week after the birth. They named the girl Thu. After a few days at home Du returned to his Unit in the mountains.

Two days later he was killed.

Minh was devastated when she got the news. She hadn't been in love with her husband in any classical sense, but she had gotten used to the idea of being married.

If her life had been miserable before her man died, it became impossible thereafter. At six months of age, Thu came down with a mysterious and very serious illness. She developed a high fever which raged out of control. Her face and neck became swollen to the point where she was unable to swallow. For four days she hovered near death.

There was no money for a doctor or medicine, and little help from the relatives. Minh finally took matters into her own hands. For a week she nourished her baby by painstakingly dipping a chicken feather quill into a bowl of milk and then forcing the quill into the swollen throat to force the milk in, one drop at a time. It was a round the clock procedure which physically drained the young mother.

Miraculously, the baby survived. From the time of that early illness though, she was never able to swallow normally and eating became a chore.

Minh and Thu stayed at Du's home for the next six months. Minh was kept busy caring for her daughter most of the time and found little time to work for her in-laws. They became more abusive as the days went by, chiding Minh for not going to work outside the home in order to pay for her support. Finally reaching the limits of her patience, Minh yielded and moved out.

Completely destitute, she found room and board at a small peanut farm, where she took a job weeding. Carrying Thu with her on the job was hard work and with her strength and resistance worn low, she soon had to quit.

The farmer was a kindly man and offered to let her stay on without working. He even loaned her money, asking for no interest and telling her to pay him back someday whenever she was able. Minh thanked him and promised that she would repay his kindness as soon as she could.

The peanut farmer remained in her prayers for years.

Leaving the farm, Minh went straight to the small hospital in Tay Ninh. She stayed there with her daughter, sleeping on the floor beside her and administering the medicine which the nurses brought. The doctors did their best but there was little they could do. There was no surgery or medicine that could cure Thu. She would likely have the swallowing trouble for the rest of her life.

Alone and discouraged, Minh and Thu journeyed home to Tam Vu.

Times were rough in Suu's household as well, and two more mouths to feed would only increase the burden, but Minh was welcomed warmly. Her sisters were delighted to help with the baby and soon Minh found a job buying and re-selling ice. She also made sandwiches which she sold to students on their way to school. The pittance she earned barely covered the cost of food for herself and Thu.

For the next two years Minh remained at home, earning money when she could and caring for her daughter, who had never recovered from her illness. At the age of three she still couldn't walk or talk, and made only weak attempts to crawl. She still required help in eating and Minh began to despair of her ever walking or leading a normal life.

One day, when Thu was having difficulty breathing, Minh came to the end of her rope. She carried her tiny girl to the temple and laid her on the altar. She prayed to Buddha to heal her daughter or take her up with him forever. She could no longer bear to see her child so crippled and ill.

A monk overheard her tearful entreaty and gave Minh a small amount of herbal medicine. That night Thu began to breathe easily and the crisis was past .... but still more trouble loomed on the horizon. Tot felt sorry for her wizened little granddaughter but somehow blamed Minh for her condition. Tensions rose in the small house and one day Tot asked Minh to leave. Minh knew that she could never find a job in Tam Vu that would pay enough for her to hire a full time baby-sitter. With a heavy weight in her heart she asked her sisters to take care of Thu while she left to find a job. She hoped to find something in Saigon.

As she was preparing to leave, Tot unexpectedly told her to take Thu with her and never return. A great anger rose in Minh and all the pent-up frustrations of the past erupted. She cursed at her mother and gave full vent to her long-repressed emotions. Her sisters shrunk back in horror, for this was an unpardonable sin in the Vietnamese family. Tot stood there looking at her daughter with an open mouth. Before she could react, Minh's sisters intervened, promising to care for Thu while Minh was away. Empty now, after her outburst, Minh was deeply hurt as her mother repeated her edict. Sadly she said goodbye and turned her face northward. Saigon awaited.

Stepping off the bus on the outskirts of Saigon, Minh considered her predicament. She was broke, had no friends or acquaintances in the city and no prospects for a job. Well, she had never shrunk from a challenge before and wasn't about to now.

That night, she waited until the market place closed and lay down on a narrow wooden table where a street vendor had been selling pork. Tired and hungry, she slept profoundly and dreamed of pigs. Before dawn she was rudely awakened by the merchant and chased away. As she wandered through the streets of Cholon, the bustling Chinese market section of the city, an old woman motioned for her to come over. Her snow white hair, wrinkled face and stooped back bespoke her advanced age. Shyly, Minh approached.

"Hello, Grandmother, is there something you want?"

"Yes there is, young woman. Will you sit with me and share a bowl of rice?"

"I would, Grandmother, but I have no money to pay for the rice. Thank you for asking, though."

"Come here, girl, and eat with me," the old woman pleaded. "I only want a little company. Besides, you look like you could use a good meal."

"You have a sharp eye, Grandmother," Minh replied wearily. "I sure could use a meal .... and a job if you know of one. I came here yesterday and so far haven't had any luck."

The old woman added some pork and soy sauce to the rice and handed a bowl to Minh. She listened to her story, clicking her tongue in sympathy. When Minh had finished eating, the woman told her of a friend who lived nearby and might have a job for a hard-working girl. Taking the old woman's hands in hers, Minh thanked her profusely and hurried off down the street.

The address was easy to find. There were dozens of bolts of colored cloth hanging from a frame on the side of the street. Two tables with cutting implements were set up beside them. As Minh gathered her nerve to ask a complete stranger for a job, a man appeared in the doorway of the tiny shop. He was in his mid-twenties and well dressed. He fixed a lecherous gaze on Minh and blocked the door. She was about to turn and run away when the man walked out of the shop and crossed the street. Once again marshaling all of her courage, the shy country girl with the indomitable spirit went to the door, hesitated, and then walked inside.

The room was dark and had a strong odor of "vo soc", the all-purpose liniment used to treat everything from headaches to pneumonia. An older man came out of the shadows and smiling, asked if he could help her. Minh told him that she had been sent by the old lady down the street to inquire about a job.

The man nodded knowingly and bid her to enter his humble shop. Minh looked around as her eyes grew accustomed to the darkness. All of the man's wares were outside on the rack. She was standing in his tiny home, only part of which was used to sell cloth and make ribbons. Could this be the right place?

The man was very courteous, explaining that he and his wife made their living here, but since his wife had been ill he could really use some help. The hours would be long and she would have to work hard sewing as well as selling.

Minh eagerly accepted.

Mr. Thanh explained that she would live there with his family and help out with the younger children whenever she could. Minh could scarcely believe her luck. When she had gotten off the bus on the previous day she had passed by a Buddhist temple. Stopping in, she had prayed for her family and herself. It seemed now that Buddha had answered her prayers.

Minh stayed with the Thanh family for four years. She cooked and cleaned in addition to her store duties, but it was never a burden. The family loved her like one of their own and despite being poor, they were as generous with their goods as they were with their love. The only pall over Minh's happiness was the absence of her daughter. The money from her job didn't go far because she sent most of it home to provide for Thu. Her mother remained adamant that Minh never set foot in her house again, and Minh's stubborn streak would not allow her to return.

From her sisters' letters Minh learned that Thu began to walk when she was five years old. On hearing this welcome news Minh ached to see her little daughter, but couldn't bring herself to face her mother after the terrible words they had exchanged. Losing face within one's own family was like losing life itself. Whether learned or inherited, when this behavior was bolstered by a stubborn nature, neither Heaven nor earth could bridge the chasm.

Sometimes on balmy Saigon nights, Minh would walk along the river, drinking in the sights and sounds. The lights reflecting off the river outlined the sampans lying at rest, water lapping softly at their sides. Filled with memories of her childhood on her father's boat, she would be overcome with melancholia and sadly walk on.

Occasionally she would go to the theater to watch an opera. The glorious costumes and lilting voices never failed to stir her heart. The stories were almost always tragedies, as operas across the world are wont to be. Memorizing the songs, Minh would sing and hum for days after these rare interludes.

City life agreed with her and she soon developed a talent for evaluating people. From dealing with customers and shrewdly bargaining with the many street vendors she became street-wise, while maintaining a guileless sense of fair play. She could not pass a beggar without giving him something, though she seldom had much more herself.

Her Buddhist faith didn't require regular visits to the temple but she would stop by from time to time to say a prayer. Increasingly she missed her daughter and tried hard to overcome the powerful force keeping them apart.

Minh's nightly walks became longer and longer and she entered new parts of the city that had hitherto been unknown to her. One evening she passed by a street which had numerous bars and clubs crowded side by side. The bright lights and music attracted her. As she approached, two men reeled out of one of the bars. To avoid them, Minh ducked into an alley.

Without warning, a hand fell onto her shoulder. Before she could move, a man stepped in front of her, barring her way to the street. He started to explain how she could make a fortune by working for him at the club. Minh had never heard of such disgusting things and recoiled in horror. A feeling of total revulsion shook her. She told the man that she would rather starve than do such work. He stared at her for a long minute and then, laughing, told her to beat it.

She was gone in a flash, leaving the street and its false dreams in her dust. A week later she made a momentous decision. She was going home!

Minh arrived at her mother's door with a bag of presents in her hand and a lump in her throat. Would Thu remember her? Would Tot let her in the house? Would her beloved Dad be home?

Timidly, she knocked on the door. It swung open and Thu stood there, her tiny shoulders hunched forward, her mouth full of rice.

"Ma," she screamed, and hurled herself at the woman in the doorway.

Tears welled in Minh's eyes as she swept her daughter into her arms and hugged her. Four years fell away as nothing, as they hugged and kissed and cried.

Tot was not home but Minh's sisters and brothers were. Everyone began to talk at once. Tet was only two days away and their excitement was heightened by the unexpected visit from their long lost sister. An hour later Tot came home. She lost no time in launching into a tirade against her number two daughter. She ended by screaming that Minh had brought all of their troubles on them and on her own daughter.

Too overcome with emotion to reply, Minh took Thu into the

back room and went to bed. In the morning, on the eve of Tet, the happiest day of the year, she prepared to leave once again, but this time her daughter would be leaving with her. Before she said her good-byes, her sister Tran padded into the room. Her asthmatic condition had worsened and now she was crying, making it very difficult for Minh to understand what she was saying.

"Ma has taken Thu to a neighbors and said you are to leave without her. We've been caring for her and we can keep her here for a while longer. Ma is so angry now that I don't think you can reason with her. Why don't you come back again in a few days and get her then?"

"No way," answered Minh angrily. "She's going with me, and that's all there is to it."

"Please, Chi Ba, Ma is really upset," Tran begged, "I'm afraid she might hurt Thu to get back at you if you don't leave. Please, just think about it and come back again."

Her anger overcome by concern for Thu, Minh left.

She returned to Saigon in utter frustration. A visit to the temple didn't help this time.

For another year she remained at the shop, selling cloth and hoarding her money.

But now she had a plan.

The week before Tet, she bade a teary farewell to her kind benefactors and left the city. She caught a bus to Tay Ninh and found the kind peanut farmer who had helped her before.

"I have come back to repay your kindness," Minh told him. "My daughter is better now, and I just had to come back to thank you for all of your help. Here is the money you lent to me and a little something extra. And don't say no, because I would be terribly insulted if you didn't accept my payment."

The farmer thanked her and insisted that he knew she would return some day. He couldn't wait to tell his wife, who had not shared his faith in his fellow man.

On the day after Tet, Minh arrived without notice at her parent's home. Entering without ceremony, she gathered up her little girl and left for good. She found a boat heading north and prevailed on the crew to take her to Vung Tau. From there she traveled inland ten miles to the small fishing village of Phuoc Hai, about twenty miles from Baria. She rented a room and found a job buying fish at the wharf and re-selling the catch in the market.

She had no money to pay for a baby-sitter and was forced to keep Thu with her. With the child's poor health, there were many days when Minh couldn't get to the fishermen. Very soon there wasn't enough money to pay the rent and she was left without a place to live. Desperately searching for a new apartment, she met a man who offered to rent a room to her for a very tiny sum. She was wary of his intentions, but finally accepted.

The man was several years older than Minh, with shifty eyes and a habit of disappearing without notice for days on end. He was, however, kind to her and Thu and respected her privacy. After two months at the house he convinced her to enter into a more substantial relationship. They would be married soon, he promised. Confused and tired, and very vulnerable, she was easy prey.

A year later she was in labor.

For three days and nights she fought to give birth. For three days and nights the baby resisted. On the third night a midwife delivered her of twins. The first was stillborn, the other was a strapping, healthy boy. Minh named him Tri.

After the child was born, the man began to stay away for long periods of time. Often when he came home he would be drunk and abusive. During the next two years his absences became more frequent and his returns more violent. Minh learned from the neighbors that he was staying with many other women on his so-called business trips. She grew to detest him.

Her only solace was found by spending time with the children and helping local fishermen mend nets. She dreamed of the happy days on the river with her father and made up her mind not to let her present circumstances overwhelm her. The children were growing healthier every day in the clean air and she was able to put away a few piasters towards the future.

With a sharp business eye towards the local needs, Minh found a way to make some extra money. There always seemed to be a shortage of charcoal for cooking. She devised a plan to increase production and perhaps garner a neat profit.

She hired three villagers to help her construct charcoal burning huts and cut wood. They would be paid out of the profits from selling the finished product. Though she had never undertaken anything like this before, she was able to convince the laborers and herself that the endeavor would work.

The burning huts were six feet high, eight feet wide and domed in shape. The frames were constructed of bamboo and covered with an adobe-like mixture of mud and straw. Three vent holes were left near the bottom to aid in slow combustion.

Minh supervised and assisted in the construction and gathering of materials. After four weeks of hard work, there were eleven huts ready to go. Minh directed the crew into the woods to gather a large supply of branches and wood to burn down.

By the end of the fifth week the huts were piled full of wood and the fires were lit. It would take about ten days to burn the piles into usable charcoal. Minh didn't sleep for the first two days, worried that something would go wrong in this business venture. Finally, exhausted from her labors and worrying, she went home to bed.

On the fourth day the rains began. For two days and nights there was no let up. And then Minh's worst fears were realized .... the huts collapsed and disintegrated, ruining all of her work to that point. There was nothing left to sell -- no product with which to pay off her crew. She was in a quandary.

A man from a nearby hamlet happened by a few days later and looked over the mess. After a few pointed questions he was able to show Minh that the huts had been poorly constructed. Her laborers had been lazy and built too loose a framework and made a hasty, poor quality adobe.

Minh confronted her workers with this knowledge and they admitted to scrimping on the materials, but they demanded full payment for their work. They hadn't built those structures before and couldn't be responsible for their collapse, they reasoned.

Minh had spent most of her money on straw and bamboo, and now she had to use the rest as a down payment for the wages. She arranged to pay the balance over a period of time.

Instead of crying over the loss, Minh examined where she had made her errors in judgment and was determined not to make the same mistakes again.

One day, the man came home and took Minh and the children to a sampan. They were going downriver for a ride, he told them. Now this was very unusual behavior for him, and Minh became suspicious. A mile downstream the boat pulled in to shore and they boarded a bus. Half an hour later they were in Vung Tau, a small city on the South China Sea.

The man had taken a job there, he explained, and wanted Minh with him. Knowing how she felt about him, he had virtually kidnapped her and the children to insure their compliance. He led them to a small house which he had rented and then left for the day, promising to return later with their belongings.

The house was one of a dozen in a tiny hamlet carved out of a palm plantation just outside the city of Vung Tau. It reminded Minh of her grandfather's farm in its isolation.

Minh looked about helplessly. Her pitiful savings were in the house at Baria, and would certainly be discovered by the man. This was a real predicament.

Angry at being tricked, she started looking for a job immediately. With her two small children in tow, she spent almost a week combing the town. Every inquiry ended with the same advice, go check the American base, but she was reluctant to work at any army camp after her experiences at the French and Vietnamese bases. She sadly trudged back to her new home.

For the next week her pattern of looking for, but not finding work, continued. One sunny morning a Vietnamese patrol entered the hamlet. With them were two American army advisors. The patrol leader questioned the villagers in a rather cursory manner until he came to Minh. When he learned that she had only lived there for a few days he motioned for her to follow him. She went with the man and the entire patrol into the nearby woods. For the next several hours she was grilled by the patrol leader and the American advisors.

"Your neighbors have said that you have given food and shelter to the Vietcong. Why have you done this?" asked the lieutenant.

"Because the V.C. come at night when you are not around and demand food," Minh replied angrily. "Besides, all of the people who live here do the same thing. If we didn't, we would be killed. I don't like it, but what else can we do?"

As the questioning intensified, Minh disclosed that her father worked for the Vietnamese Army and for the French. She hesitated to do that but felt that only by being truthful would she survive. She knew all too well the methods of finding the truth and wished to avoid the harsher ones.

Finally satisfied, the patrol escorted her back home and continued on its way. Minh was more angry than scared. She vowed not to stay here for long. That night she resolved to do something about her inability to find a job.

The man had been gone since the day they arrived and the tiny palm-roofed house felt cold and foreign as she put the children to bed. Perhaps tomorrow she would have better luck, she hoped. Carefully arranging the mosquito netting around the sleeping platform, she snuggled down with the children and was asleep at once.

After what seemed only moments she sat bolt upright.

She was used to the nightly shelling and had long ago learned to sleep through it, but something made her walk outside and listen.

A muffled "crump" caught her attention as a mortar or rocket was fired. It came from a swampy area just across the small river near her house. She watched the sky and saw a flash in the direction of the American army camp. The sound of the explosion reached her shortly after.

Her heart went out to the unfortunate victims of the missile's blast. They were most likely the tall, young Americans who were here helping her country.

She had too often witnessed the tragic aftermath of these explosions and could imagine the scene at the site of the impact. Would a mother lose her son today? Would a young man lose his eyes or his arms?

Suddenly she began to cry. Huge tears rolled down her cheeks for the first time in years.

She wept for her country which hadn't seen peace in her lifetime.

She wept for all the friends and neighbors who had been killed or maimed as she grew up.

And she wept for herself. She cried softly in a quiet way, not in self-pity but for all the wrongs and injustices that were suffered by her people.

And then a baby began to cry in a house across the dirt street and she pulled herself from this soulful reverie. As she climbed back into bed a look of fierce determination crossed her face. Tomorrow she would go to the Americans and ask to work for them. There must be something in the hospital that she could do to help these strangers who had come so far to help her country.

Chapter Eight

Lightning crackled from mile-high thunder heads over the harbor at Vung Tau as Minh made her way to the American army base. The rainy season had begun and the roads were fast turning to sloughs of mud. The battered old lambretta slid to a halt outside the main gate where military police and regular army guards were busily checking a long queue of women. The rain had been expected and was shrugged off as a minor inconvenience, one more in a long parade of inconveniences suffered by these war-weary people.

Apparently the rocket attack of the previous night was blamed on information received from inside the post. All I.D. cards were being collected for an investigation. When Minh reached the gate she was asked for her U.S. identification card. Having none, she tried to explain that she was just seeking work. The Vietnamese M.P. rudely informed her that the Americans didn't need any more lackeys and that she might as well go back home.

Not one to be discouraged so easily, she determinedly repeated her inquiry. The policeman began to shout at her angrily and shoved her out of line. At that moment a young woman in a flowing white ao dai intervened.

"What's the problem?" she inquired.

Before the M.P. could answer, Minh blurted out her story. The woman coolly faced down the obnoxious policeman.

"I work on the base in the headquarters of the 36th Evacuation Hospital," she explained. "We can use some more help right now."

The M.P. tried to cut her off, but she turned to an American guard and spoke a few words in English. The guard motioned them through the gate.

Walking towards the hospital in the distance, the woman asked Minh's name. "Mine is Lieng," she said. I'm a secretary-interpreter for the Americans at their hospital. We have need of a maid who can work half a day cleaning barracks. Are you interested?"

"Well, I really wanted to work as a nurse's aide or something like that," Minh began. "I want to help the wounded soldiers and civilians, but if cleaning is the only thing open, I'll take it."

"I'll help you with the paperwork," Lieng offered. "The police background check can take quite a while, but I will try to expedite it for you."

"Thanks so much," Minh sighed. "I hope I see you soon. I really want this job."

Two weeks later Minh's new friend was at the door wearing a wide grin. Minh had the job.

Now she needed a reliable baby-sitter. An elderly neighbor came forward and soon Minh was on her way to becoming self-sufficient. The man of the house, as in Baria, was rarely home. When he was around he became increasingly abusive, threatening to beat Minh and the children. Because of his frequent absences, Minh was able to cope with his few visits. She soon found another job at the air field, cleaning barracks and doing laundry. The two jobs brought in more money than she had ever dreamed of making. She began saving as much as she could in order to become financially independent. When that day arrived, she knew that she would find a home of her own and never trust a man again.

Every morning, two hours before dawn, Minh awakened to fix food for her childrens' day. Then, to save money, she walked two miles to a point where she could catch a cheap cyclo ride to the Air Force Caribou facility. Arriving at dawn, she would do laundry for the men in the barracks and wait for them to go to work.

All the laundry was done by hand in small wash tubs. Starching and ironing was completed in the barracks, called a hootch by the airmen. When the laundry was done she would clean the hootch, sweeping, dusting and shining boots and shoes. Stopping for a noon-time meal, she would take a break with the other housemaids before walking to the hospital where she cleaned another hootch. Most days ended by washing more clothes from the second hootch and finishing up by evening. Coming home before dark, she would release the baby-sitter and enjoy her children. The work was hard but her determination to better her life and find more time to be with her children kept her going.

After a month of that rigorous schedule she found that determination was no substitute for good health. Her stamina eroded, she became ill. For two days she lay at home, barely able to get out of bed. Lieng came by on the third day to see why she hadn't been at work. One look at her friend's face brought Lieng's heart to her throat. She immediately bundled Minh and the children into a taxi and rushed to see a doctor. Suffering with chills, fever and abdominal cramps, Minh passed out on the short trip.

Following a hasty examination the doctor gave Minh an injection. Within moments she collapsed in anaphylactic shock. Realizing what must have occurred, the doctor carried Minh to his car and rushed her to Le Loi hospital. Because it was Sunday, there were no other doctors on call. With his patient gasping for breath and her fever soaring, the old physician put aside his pride and sent a young orderly to the Australian hospital for help.

The Australian doctor on duty was a middle-aged surgeon who had been up all night with a difficult delivery. He had just stretched out for a nap when the orderly arrived with his urgent request. The surgeon was tempted to send the boy back with his regrets, but something stirred him to respond. He quickly called in a back-up doctor to cover the hospital and hurried over to Le Loi.

One glance at Minh told him his trip had been in vain. Her breathing was shallow and rapid, her fever raging out of control. As he watched, she went into convulsions. He knew that a rattle of death would escape from her collapsing lungs at any moment.

He shook his head. There was no hope for the poor girl.

Lieng, standing beside her friend and holding her clammy hand, couldn't believe her eyes. One doctor had just pushed her friend to the brink of death with some unknown injection, and now a second physician was writing her off as a hopeless cause without doing anything about it. She angrily told the Aussie that if he wouldn't help her friend, she would take her up to the 36th Evac where some competent doctors would.

The weary doctor sighed and shook his head once more, giving Lieng a wry smile. Looking around him, he realized that the facilities here were inadequate for his needs. Taking the helpless Minh in his big arms, he carried her to the car, all the while silently remonstrating with himself for taking on such a clearly hopeless case.

At the Aussie hospital with his patient on the operating table, the big sandy-haired Australian tried again and again to draw a blood sample with no success. In such deep shock that her veins had collapsed, Minh drew nearer to death. Finally, cutting down to a vein in her leg, the surgeon was able to draw just enough blood to type and cross match. But then, as if her survival were not meant to be, the hospital was out of her blood type. The last of the AB negative had been used for the hemhorraging woman last night. With an I.V. of Ringers Lactate literally pouring into her and ice packed all around her, Minh lay on the table more dead than alive.

Without a word, Lieng rushed out and headed for the 36th Evac, three miles distant. She quickly located a medic whom she knew and was soon on her way back to the Australian hospital with the precious blood.

Cutting down to another leg vein, the surgeon was able to establish a second I.V. and begin to replace her dwindling life fluid. For three days Minh lay in a coma. Twice her heart stopped and only heroic efforts by the dedicated surgeon kept her alive. For three days and nights he never left her bedside. On the third night he took her wasted little body into his arms and walked around the room, loudly pleading with her to wake up, to hold on. He lightly slapped her face and pinched her toes, trying to draw some reaction.

There was none.

One the fourth morning, as the exhausted doctor slept in the bedside chair, he felt a gentle touch on his arm. Looking up, he broke into a broad grin and gave a wild Aussie war whoop. Minh was on her side, awake and smiling. She had made it.

At that moment, Lieng entered the room and he grabbed her in a great bear hug that threatened to break her bones, for he was a big, powerful man. He released Lieng and went to his patient. Gently, he felt her forehead. It was damp with perspiration and blessedly cool.

The fever had broken, the danger had passed.

Unable to pinpoint the cause of her illness, the doctor kept Minh in the hospital for another week. From the amount of hemhorraging he had suspected a miscarriage, but there was no evidence that such had occurred. Whatever the cause, he was well aware that her recovery was nothing short of miraculous.

For her part, Minh began to recover her strength as the rest and

57

nutritious food did their job. Lieng had arranged for a baby-sitter for the children to ease her mind on that account. Lying in the hospital bed, Minh began to recall fragments of what had transpired during the past few days. She vividly remembered a bright white light and a sensation of floating out of her body. As the memories became clearer she was frightened.

She clearly recalled floating above her bed, looking down on her friends and the doctor. Her pain was gone and she was totally at peace. She could hear Lieng and the doctor talking and was aware of their great concern. She wanted to comfort them and tell them that she was in a far better place, but they couldn't hear her. Other memories of the experience came to mind, but she was too disturbed to dwell on them. It would be years before she would dare to speak of this phenomenon.

A month later she had fully recovered. The man of the house had come to see her once at the hospital, scolded her for becoming ill, and then informed her that he was off to see a girlfriend. Well now, and with some money put aside, Minh gathered her meager belongings and left to find a new home, a home where she could raise her children and search for that elusive dream of happiness.

Fortune smiled on her that day. She found a two room apartment only two miles from the American base. Finding another woman to watch the children took no time at all, and soon she returned to her job at the hospital. She cut back on her work to prevent a recurrence of her illness, but still made enough money to live, with a bit put aside for an emergency.

Sundays were reserved for walks to the beach and sightseeing with the children. Life slowed down and Minh began to regain her old sense of humor and optimism. One day she stopped in to consult a seer. Fortune telling was a popular and accepted custom, and she was feeling so much better that she just had to see what might lie ahead of her.

The seer asked for her birth date and then read her palm. Consulting an astrological chart, he solemnly intoned a brief chant. Taking her hand, the old man leaned closer and in a hoarse voice, told her that she would leave her homeland. Further, she would marry a foreigner, because if she were to marry here at home, there would never be happiness in her life. Disturbed, she left the dingy room, and reflecting on the old man's words, walked slowly home.

One evening shortly thereafter, upon returning home from work, Minh noticed a neighbor behaving strangely. He locked his doors and windows, looked furtively about, and scurried off into the gathering darkness. Two more neighbors hurried into their homes and Minh heard the sound of windows being shuttered and barred. Pondering this unusual behavior, she went inside and lit the kerosene lamp. The children were asleep, probably dreaming of catching crabs in the rocks at the beach, their favorite pastime.

Suddenly, the door opened and two men strode in. They were dressed in black pajamas and wore sandals. One man had a pistol in his belt.

"You will come with us," he ordered. "Make no sound and you will not be harmed."

"I can't go anywhere," gasped Minh. "I have two very small children sleeping in the back room."

The taller of the men grabbed her arm and in a low voice warned, "If you want the children to remain sleeping, and alive, come now with no fuss."

"I can't," Minh pleaded. "Just tell me what you want."

"Move now, or the children die. It's as simple as that," the tall one growled.

With a terrible fear gripping her heart, Minh left with the men. Trembling with every step, she walked between them into the jungle. Weaving their way around several deep sloughs, they continued on for about half a mile. In a tiny clearing under a grove of betel palms they met a small group of men. A slim, middle-aged man with well-groomed hair rose to greet them. He was soft-spoken and polite, addressing Minh as Chi, or sister.

"You are working for the Americans, are you not," he asked?

"Yes, I work as a housemaid," she responded.

"You realize that they are killing your countrymen and destroying our crops with chemicals, don't you? Why then do you work for them?"

"I need the money and no other jobs are available. I don't like them, but I'll take their money." She knew better than to challenge these men.

"Well then, if you don't like them then I am sure you will help us. We only wish for you to obtain certain information while you are on the base and pass it on to us."

And then she realized for the first time what a dire predicament she was in. These were Vietcong, the new order that had evolved from the execrable Vietminh. Apprehension turned to stark terror as they continued to tell her what they wanted from her. For hours she repeated that she was only a housemaid and unable to help them.

Playing dumb didn't help.

They would settle for the most basic of information. When they again threatened her life and the lives of her children she knew they meant every word. Throughout the countryside, their reputation for ruthlessness was well earned. There was no idle boasting here. These men were all business.

Finally, Minh convinced them that because she was so new on the base she was watched at all times and under suspicion. This seemed plausible to the leader of the cadre and he agreed to let her go home.

"But make no mistake, we will return and then you will help us."

His parting words struck deeply and Minh knew that there was both threat and promise in them. The same two men escorted her back to her home before dawn. She rushed into the house and found the children still deep in innocent sleep. Breathing a sigh of relief, she collapsed into bed. Before she could fall asleep, the enormity of what had just occurred washed over her. Her children were no longer safe in this house. She would have to move.

It was a week before Minh could bring herself to tell Lieng about the incident. Her friend suggested that she move, and perhaps the two of them could share a place.

"That's a great idea," Minh responded happily. "I know an area where rents are low and people mind their own business. We should be able to find something there soon."

Lieng agreed, and before the week was out, they moved into a small house a bit closer to the base and in a much more populous area. They both realized that the V.C. would eventually locate Minh, but there was always the million to one chance that they wouldn't take the trouble to trace her.

As the days turned to weeks and weeks to months, guarded optimism returned. One night Minh returned from work early. She had stopped to shop and had some small presents for Thu and Tri. Entering the house she gave a shout for the kids.

Silence!

An ominous sense of foreboding overtook her. Where was the

sitter? She ran from the house and grabbed a passing child.

"Where is the old woman and two children from this house," she demanded?

"They left with a man about an hour ago," he answered nervously, and he pointed towards the river.

Minh was beside herself. She ran to the river and inquired of everyone she met, "Have you seen my children and their sitter?"

No one could, or would, help. With mounting anxiety, she dashed back to the house. A figure moved across the window. Someone was in the house.

Cautiously she approached the window and peered in. There in the room sat the children and their grandfather, Suu. The kids were eating sugar cane treats that Suu had bought for them. Relief cleared her mind and quickly gave way to exuberance as she rushed inside and gave her Dad a hug.

For hours, father and daughter sat and exchanged news. Minh's brother Hoai had entered the temple to prepare for the Buddhist priesthood. Her sister Tran had married and had three children. Everyone else was well and sent their greetings.

Even Ma, Minh wondered?

The unspoken question must have registered on her face for Suu began to talk about her mother. She had been sick for a long period, but was doing well now. She sent her love to Minh and asked that she come down to Tam Vu to visit. Minh nodded absently as she recalled the acrimony in their last words. She recounted her experiences of the past couple of years, but when she told of the Vietcong, Suu went white.

"They must never discover that we are related," he cautioned. "I can never be seen here with you. If they are still watching it may already be too late."

They both fell silent for awhile, considering the possibilities. It was obvious that the Vietcong would draw a connection if they were seen side by side. The family resemblance was hard to mistake. Suu tried to reassure his daughter that as yet he was undetected as a principal in the intelligence service. Still, if he was ever taken for interrogation it would be difficult to conceal his involvement. Prudence would have to govern their future visits. Perhaps Minh could get a vacation and visit the family down in the Delta.

Switching to lighter subjects, Suu asked if she had a beau. Her sharp retort was met by a mischievous grin. Male chauvinism was alive and well in Vietnam and he took his daughter's story of the man who "done her wrong" lightly. He wished her well in finding a good man and prepared to leave. As he went out the door his last words remained with her, and for some reason were most unsettling.

"My headstrong young girl, perhaps you should listen to the words of the seer and seek your destiny far from these troubled shores. I love you very much because you are so special, and for that reason I could bear not seeing you again if you were to find real happiness in another land. Only promise me that you will visit soon, and once again before you go off with some foreigner. If you had been older years ago, I would have seen you married to a Frenchman."

Suu then left for home, leaving a pensive young woman to her thoughts.

When Lieng came home that night, the two women talked for hours about men, chauvinism and the plight of an enlightened woman in an unenlightened country. When they went to bed they slept the sleep of the just.

In the morning, back on the job, Minh began to look at the tall, young Americans in a new light. No, she told herself, men are men the world over. I'll never give my heart to another as long as I draw breath.

Her stubborn attitude where males were concerned served her well. A number of G.I.'s asked her out but her response was always the same, always in the negative. She eventually grew to like a few of the men in the hootch and once in awhile stayed late to have supper, as long as they were in a group. She was called "Mama-san", as all of the local women were known. Men were "Papa-san" and children were all "Baby-san".

After three years of working at the hospital, Minh finally got her wish. She was asked to help on some of the wards. At first it was just cleaning, but she showed the nurses how quickly she learned and soon was changing bandages and assisting in many other ways. She understood very little English and the doctors and nurses knew no Vietnamese at all. Her facility with a mixture of Pidgin English and pantomime rapidly won over the doctors and corpsmen, but the nurses seemed jealous and were often hostile towards her. Reluctantly, she spent less and less time with the patients.

Many of the Vietnamese civilians who were wounded had family members staying on to help nurse them so her services weren't required there either. Whenever she did work her way through the wards she evoked smiles and laughter. Her innate sense of humor and brashness were like a breath of fresh air to the patients as they lay on their cots trying to recover from the adversities which had torn their bodies asunder.

Minh moved from bed to bed trying to bring some peace to the minds that were so troubled. Later, as she worked in the hootch or washed laundry, she couldn't get the images out of her mind. Images of men, women and children with wounds beyond description.

How could people do this to one another, she thought? Would there ever be an end to it? Every night as she kissed her children, she prayed that someday they would have an opportunity to escape the tragedies of war that surrounded them.

One of the Vung Tau beaches

Front beach - Vung Tau; old French villas in the background

Drying fish at Binh Da

Part of "shanty town" outside Vung Tau

Chapter Nine

"Greeting :"

The opening word of the letter had no connotation of friendly salutations. I knew what the letter contained without reading it. The Great Uncle in Washington had issued an invitation which brooked no refusal. At twenty-four, with college behind me and my chosen profession begun, I hadn't really expected to be drafted. True, I had consciously relinquished the deferment that went with working on the highway, and had decided that if I were called I would serve, but the letter still came as a shock.

None of my close friends were in the service. My only real knowledge of the war in Vietnam came from reading and watching the television news. What I read and saw was unsettling. Our country was enmeshed in a conflict in a small Asian country and no end was in sight. Entering the army now was certain to result in serving time in Vietnam, and in this year of 1967, the war and its casualties were both escalating rapidly.

Sinking deeper into thought, I considered my options. Canada was not among them. From all I had read, it seemed that South Vietnam was beleaguered by the North Vietnamese communists, and the United States was in Southeast Asia to help the South and stop the spread of communism before the rest of the neighboring countries fell like dominoes. At the time, without the advantage of hindsight, this reasoning appeared plausible.

And now for the real issue, I thought. In the seminary we were taught that taking human life was justifiable in three situations; in self-defense if deadly force were the only way, for capital punishment, and in a just war. Is this a just war?

The definitions of a just war were hazy in my memories.

Certainly any time a man is forced to kill to defend his life could be considered just, I thought. Still, I can't see myself aiming a rifle

64

at another person and pulling the trigger. My father taught me well the deadliness and limitations of firearms. Careful stalks and humane, one-shot kills are part of the legacy he gave to me. Lining up the sights on a human being, knowing full well from experience what happens to vital organs when they are struck by a bullet, is just too abhorrent to consider. There will have to be another way for me to serve. When I report for duty I'll request non-combatant status. That's it! Now I can notify my family and boss of my change in plans for the next two years.

No one was happy to hear that I was entering the army in such troubled times. Family and friends stood by my decision, but were saddened. My boss wished me well and told me to return safely to the job.

Following a last-minute trip to New Brunswick to say good-bye to my best friend Marc, I reported for duty, naivete personified. After testing I was told that I would be sent for training to become a warrant officer, a pilot of rotary-wing aircraft.

Whoa, I thought. That means four years instead of two, and rotary-wing sound like those helicopters that are being shot down with such deadly regularity.

"I'm sorry, but I know the draft is for two years and that's all I want," I offered. "Also, I would like to be placed as a non-combatant."

"Buddy," the testing officer explained, "if you don't accept officer training school you're cannon fodder. Your profile and test results just shout "pilot". Turn it down and I guarantee I can get you instant placement as a grunt. Take it or leave it."

"I'll still take the two years," I persisted. "And what about the non-combatant classification?"

"Son, have you registered as a conscientious objector?"

"No sir, where do I do that?"

"Buddy-boy, you have to do that a long time before you get this far. You're mine, now."

Uncertain where to turn, I took the placement paper to the first office I passed. A captain with a mountain of paper on his desk brusquely asked what the problem was. As I explained, the captain's expression changed from one of pained boredom to concern. After examining the papers he made a call and then wrote out another order. I was to report to Fort Dix, New Jersey for basic training and then to Fort Sam Houston, in San Antonio, for medical training. While there was no guarantee that I wouldn't be required to use a weapon, my primary duty would be medical in nature. That sounded good enough for me.

It would be much later that I would learn of the high casualty rate among medics.

Basic training was undertaken in the snow-covered sandy pine barrens at Fort Dix. The training was completed with few incidents, and I couldn't help but take note of the backgrounds of the draftees as the pattern was so striking. Most were from the lowest socio-economic strata and hailed from the inner cities in New York and New Jersey. Many had difficulty reading and writing, and some were there as an alternative to jail. There didn't seem to be any sons of lawyers or politicians in evidence. Apparently the selective service was very selective indeed.

With the conclusion of basic training I was sent to Fort Sam Houston in San Antonio for advanced schooling.

Most of the trainees at Fort Sam had at least a year or two of college, and some had four year degrees. The training, while maintaining early morning calisthenics, inspections, and barracks life, was heavily oriented towards classroom instruction.

By the time basic medical training ended, we had gained confidence in our abilities to perform under difficult conditions. And then, the moment of truth. The new assignment list was posted. Most of us were re-assigned to Fort Lewis, Washington, the staging area for a trip to Southeast Asia, but once again, relief flooded over my face as I found my name. I was to continue advanced medical training in Fort Sam.

The training for an operating room technician was intensive. A technician was expected to work as a scrub or circulating nurse in surgery. He would also learn to work in central material supply, sterilizing instruments and packing them in set-ups ready for specific operations.

Class work began after early morning physical training and continued until dinner. Evenings were spent studying for daily review tests. Subjects ranged from anatomy and physiology to bandaging and splinting; from medicine and drug therapy to treating victims of chemical and biological attacks. Operating room procedures were learned and practiced daily. Sterile technique, gowning and gloving, draping and many other basics became part of the daily routine. All of the equipment necessary to run an operating room had to be mastered and cleaning procedures practiced.

The most common operations were learned and the instruments needed to perform those procedures were memorized. To operate at peak efficiency, a technician had to be familiar with the procedure and be able to anticipate the surgeon's next move and need.

After several weeks of intensive training, I began the on the job phase, assisting in actual procedures in the operating room. Beginning with simple tonsillectomies and biopsies, I soon scrubbed in on more involved laparotomies and gall bladder removals.

All went well until I spent a day on the wards. Changing dressings on the burn unit was my first experience dealing with the pain borne by the patients. Finishing the day with the staff in the wing for permanently disabled veterans nearly did me in. Men with no faces and disintegrating, green bone tissue, and others with unspeakable deformities spoke eloquently of the real costs of war. These were scenes that would never be seen in the movies. Sick to my stomach, and at heart, I wondered if I would be able to handle what lay ahead. For the first time my confidence was shaken.

That night, another confidence tester was set to prepare us for the real rigors of battle. All personnel reported to the firing range at midnight in full field gear. We crawled our way through barbed wire and craters as live machine gun fire crackled just above our heads. Smoke grenades and carefully planted explosive charges added to the realism. No one panicked, but each of us privately wondered if we would do as well when the real thing came along.

A week later the training was over. And again anxious soldiers clustered around the bulletin board. Fort Lewis, the grim staging assignment, was the most common destination. And once again the euphoric sensation of reading, Hall, Michael H., Spec. 4 -- Fort Sam Houston, B.A.M.C., permanent party.

In these threatening times this was the dream assignment, second only to Tripler Hospital in Honolulu.

Still naive in the ways of the military, I celebrated my good fortune at a used car lot, investing half of my meager monthly salary in a vintage white Chevy, complete with air-conditioning and tail fins. For the next week I spent every evening in San Antonio at the Hemis-Fair which had recently opened.

67

Life was good.

Honing skills in surgery by day and sampling San Antone's diversions by night kept me busy for another two weeks. Returning from the San Antonio Zoo one Sunday afternoon, I stopped at the barracks to change clothes. Inside, the mood was somber. New orders had been posted and three men in the barracks were headed to Vietnam. I was one of them.

Life stinks, I thought.

My Asian sojourn was about to begin.

Chapter Ten

The airliner banked lazily over the South China Sea. Below, the shimmering water changed from a deep azure to pea-green in the bay at Cam Ranh. Landing on the tarmac, the Pan Am jumbo jet taxied to the end of the runway and swung sharply around. Walking down the steps, I felt like I had been shoved into a blast furnace. The combination of the 100 degree temperature and high humidity was overpowering.

A cloying, sweet odor permeated the air. Some kind of pollen or blossoms were adding their incense, producing this potent influence over the senses. By the time I reached the screened barracks, I was soaked with perspiration. Throwing my duffel bag on a cot, I stretched out for a quick nap. Perhaps it was jet lag, or the atmosphere, but I was suddenly sleepy. I was supposed to catch a C-130 cargo plane to Long Binh in a couple of hours, so it was sleep now or wait until Lord knows when.

Moments, or perhaps hours later I awoke to the sound of gunfire. Close gunfire. Nerve-shattering, goosebump-raising, very close gunfire.

Sitting up, I found myself covered with a fine layer of sand. It was in my mouth and nose and hair. Before there was time to spit, the gunfire erupted again.

A mortar round had exploded near the runway, triggering return fire. A helicopter gunship circled the hill west of the base, searching for the firing location. Long bursts of fire from the gunship probed the trees and drew a round of applause from the man on the next bunk.

"I've been here three days waiting for a plane to Long Binh," he exclaimed, "and haven't gotten a good night's rest yet. Three or four rockets come in each night and then the rest of the night is filled with flares and gunships and probing return fire. No sleep, hotter

69

than Hades and the damned sand won't quit. It blows through the screens and under the door and covers everything. And the humidity! Oh Man, it was never like this in Philly. I'm ready to go back home right now."

"I'm waiting for a ride to Long Binh myself," I offered nervously. "I take it we might be here for a while yet. They told me to report for K.P. after supper. Where is the mess hall, anyway?"

"Not far," the bleary-eyed Philadelphian replied. "And don't worry about K.P.. They told me to report too, but I haven't reported yet and I don't plan to. They're so screwed up over here that they don't really know where anyone is. I think you could spend the whole war right here trying to sleep in the sand and no one would ever know the difference."

"Yeah, well, that inspires a lot of confidence," I answered. "I think I'll go get some chow and have a look around. You take it easy, Philly."

After a leisurely supper I went back to the reception area in the small terminal and asked to see my name on the flight manifest to Long Binh. A sergeant checked a number of lists on his table and shook his head. No Spec. 4 Michael Hall appeared on any list. Thanking him I headed back to the barracks and was joined by a sergeant with a black horse insignia on his shoulder. I would be seeing a lot of those black horses in the near future.

"Are you waiting for Long Binh too?" asked the cavalryman.

"Sure am, and this doesn't look like the greatest place to wait."

"Actually, it's not too bad once you learn your way around here. But if you really want to bug out, just hang around the reception area and try to bum a ride on a chopper. Sometimes it's a whole lot quicker than waiting for a regular manifested flight."

Five o'clock the next morning found me waiting in the reception area. By six I was on a Huey helicopter heading for Long Binh. My only companions were the pilot, door gunner and a load of luggage bound for some officer's quarters. The flight was uneventful and by early afternoon I found my way to central processing in Long Binh. I was one of ten replacement medics coming in-country that day and recognized the names of four of the men I had trained with in Fort Sam.

I was assigned to the 36th Evacuation Hospital at Vung Tau. It was located about seventy miles southeast of Saigon on the South China Sea. All of the other men were being sent north to places called Tay Ninh, Pleiku and Cu Chi. Once again I had drawn a good assignment. The specialist typing the orders allowed that the fighting around Vung Tau was relatively light and there were some awesome beaches with surfin' waves. Vung Tau was used as an in-country Rest and Recuperation location.

Well, a little R. and R. wouldn't be too hard to take. With orders in hand, I headed for the sprawling airfield on the enormous base.

At the air field I was told to wait for a C-130, but this time stayed at reception and in three hours was on a chopper bound for Vung Tau, with a short stop planned for a camp near Bien Hoa, wherever that was.

Looking down, I was struck by the number of bomb craters that pock-marked the fields and paddies. The flat landscape was streaked by interlacing streams, bordered by dense jungle growth. Plantations of rubber trees and coconut palms mingled with the intensively cultivated fields. To the north there was a large expanse of trees that were obviously not cultivated. Just as I was getting comfortable the chopper banked sharply and slipped down to a scant hundred feet above the ground, heading for the jungle-like terrain to the north.

Suddenly, the chopper banked again and landed in a cleared area between a banana grove and the jungle. Two men emerged from the tree line, ran to the landing zone and unloaded a long wooden box. As quickly as they had appeared they headed back to the trees, straining at the rope handles at either end of the box. The men were dressed in civilian clothes and appeared to be Caucasian.

The pilot never looked back as he lifted off and pointed the nose of his craft toward the sea. No questions -- no explanations. I was curious but refrained from saying anything. Whatever was going on was none of my business.

It was evening when we finally circled the small city of Vung Tau. Just inland from the bay was the American base, comprised of an airfield, signal corps headquarters and hospital. South of the village was the port and small naval base. To the north was the Australian camp.

The view from the air was breathtaking. The South China Sea curled around the jutting point of land called Cape St. Jacques by the

French, and lapped at miles of white sand beaches. A small river and several smaller streams emptied into the bay. All of the spidery tributaries were fringed by dense jungle vegetation. I noted with some alarm how close they were to the base. This small delta looked like it could conceal an entire division of troops.

There was a mountain with twin camel humps rising above the American base. It was appropriately named V.C. Hill.

Inland from the beaches were miles of sand dunes covered with dense jungle vegetation. As the chopper banked for its approach, an armored personnel carrier roared over the dunes to the beach. Could there really be trouble in Paradise?

The chopper set down on a small helipad adjacent to a Quonset hut with a red cross on the curved tin roof. There were two smaller Huey helicopters with red crosses on the pad. Both of them showed evidence of past labors. Bullet holes and dents gave mute testimony that there was indeed trouble in this Paradise.

Most of the hospital buildings were tin Quonset huts, while the barracks, or hootches, were slatted wooden frames with screening on the upper half of the walls and tin roofs. Oddly, the walls from the ground up to about four feet were heavily sandbagged, while the tin roof offered no protection at all from incoming rounds. Each pair of hootches shared a sandbagged dug-out bunker.

The hospital was officially designated as semi-mobile, so rather than being a M.A.S.H. Unit, it was colloquially called a S.M.A.S.H. Unit. The Quonset hut containing the two operating rooms was the only building with air conditioning units, and these were located on the end of each room. The wards, where injured soldiers and civilians lay in rows of cots, barracks style, were "cooled" by a few fans which were woefully inadequate to combat the tropical heat and humidity.

Across the wind-blown dusty street from the hootches was the latrine. Modern showers and sinks worked fine, but the toilets were constantly out of order, consequently, field latrines consisting of halves of fifty-five gallon drums were used in out-house fashion. Periodically the drums were removed from their shelter and burned, using back-pack tanks with hand pumps filled with fuel oil. The odor hung in the air day and night and wafted throughout the camp whenever an infrequent breeze arose.

Specialist Fourth Class Michael Hall reported in to the orderly room at the 36th Evac. in early August. As I walked in the door a young Vietnamese woman came out. Her name was Minh. She took no notice of this new G.I..

After checking in I was sent to the supply tent to be issued bedding, an M14 rifle and an extra pair of jungle boots. The bedding would see the most use.

In the morning there was an orientation to the hospital. It was cut short by the sound of choppers at the helipad.

"Well, Specialist Hall," cooed Lt. Pakula, "It looks like you're about to be baptized. Follow me to the O.R. and we'll scrub in."

Just like that! No waiting period or formalities. This was the real thing at last.

Backing in through the swinging doors with scrubbed hands upraised, first glance showed that this was far different from stateside training. Instead of one table and dozens of shiny chrome machines, there were three tables and very sparse furnishings. Oxygen and nitrous oxide were supplied by steel bottles at the head of each table rather than from neat hoses protruding through walls. Even two of the Mayo stands used for spreading out instruments were made of wood instead of the familiar stainless steel.

As I was being gowned and gloved, two patients were wheeled in. They were lifted from the gurneys to the portable operating tables just a few feet apart. The operations would take place simultaneously with separate teams of surgeons and technicians.

Both victims were Vietnamese soldiers. One looked about sixteen and was probably younger. The other had taken shrapnel in the face and his age was impossible to guess. They were part of a squad of trainees who had blundered into a Vietcong ambush. Each of them had dozens of shrapnel wounds from head to foot.

I was assigned to work on the man with the more serious injuries. His face was badly damaged and a tracheotomy was the first procedure to counter the blood draining down his throat. A small incision beneath the Adam's Apple allowed the insertion of a tracheal tube which maintained the man's airway while his facial wounds were attended to. Working rapidly, the surgeon debrided the wounds, removing small fragments of metal from the face and the interior of the mouth. Several broken teeth would have to be repaired later when the patient's condition was stabilized.

The surgeon asked for the small metal emesis basin, joking that

73

he had always wanted to drop a bullet or shell fragment into one to hear the clink, just like in the old movies. Most of the fragments were concentrated in the upper body and easily removed, together with small pieces of clothing pulled into the wound by the force of the metal shards. I was amazed at the similarity of the damage to muscle tissue as compared to wild game that I had dressed and at the same time fascinated by the deftness of the surgeon in avoiding major nerves and blood vessels as he trimmed away damaged tissue and removed the foreign contaminants.

As a Penrose drain was placed in one particularly deep wound to promote drainage and minimize the danger of infection, the man's body began to buck violently and his throat emitted a gurgling sound. Suddenly he started vomiting. The airway plugged and had to be removed at once. Thirty seconds of frantic efforts cleared the throat, the airway was replaced and the operation continued, with the surgeon at the other table kibitzing about the uncooperative nature of the patient. The standing joke had the patient awakening and vomiting at the sight of such an ugly surgeon standing over him.

In truth, vomiting was commonplace since most of the wounded hadn't anticipated surgery and thus didn't refrain from eating or drinking for several hours prior to becoming casualties.

The fast-paced debriding continued. Most of the wounds were left open to close naturally. This technique, known as delayed primary closure, or D.P.C., promoted healing and reduced the chances of infection. It was also a great time saver when minutes could make the difference between life and death.

Finally, the surgeon looked up, winked at me and rotated his thumb upwards. We were finished.

In less than an hour we had cleaned no fewer than 27 wounds, including the severe facial lacerations. This man would live, thanks to the rapid evacuation to the hospital and the skilled hands of the operating team. Leaving the O.R., I glanced at the second table. The boy-soldier had lost a foot and an eye. The battle to save his life was still in progress.

Biting my lip I thought, what have I gotten into? I would soon find out.

After lunch, I was called to the orderly room. For the moment, I was told, there were enough operating room specialists to handle the load. There was, however, a temporary need for medics to crew

74

dust-off choppers. Their mission was to respond to calls from field units with casualties. Since I was the new man, I was elected. Two hours later I flew my first mission.

Again, there were no formalities. The warrant officer-pilot and door gunner were old hands. Both had been in-country for over six months and were veterans of dozens of dust-off flights. This mission was matter-of-fact for them, and to their credit, they gave encouragement to the green medic rather than initiate him with some puerile ritual.

The Huey hummed along a few hundred feet above the trees. My heart raced, keeping time with the pulsing blades of the Medevac chopper. The checkerboard pattern of paddies, dikes, creeks and jungle flashed by at that low level like a kaleidoscope of greens and browns. I tried to concentrate on the beauty of the land but to no avail. Every thicket, every stand of dense grass concealed a sniper. I was sure a rocket made in China or the U.S.S.R. would be launched at us at any moment.

Dear God, I prayed, just get us on the ground again, and gently please.

Fifteen minutes from base the radio crackled, and a short conversation later we banked sharply, guided by a plume of red smoke, and dropped straight into a tiny opening near a palm grove. The tall elephant grass had been cleared for fifty yards around. No sooner had we touched down than three soldiers hurriedly lifted a fourth into the open door of the chopper and we were on the rise, nose pointed southward.

The wounded G.I. was in excruciating pain. He had stepped on a sharpened bamboo stake, known as a punji stick, and in falling, had broken his wrist. His boot had been cut away by the platoon medic but the razor-sharp stake was still embedded in his foot. It had likely been tipped with excrement to maximize the chance for infection.

From the card pinned to the man's shirt, I noted that he had received a shot of morphine and that it was too early to administer another, despite his obvious pain. As the chopper skimmed along above the tree tops I splinted the injured wrist and did my best to comfort the wounded sergeant.

By the time we reached the hospital, the man was crying and pleading to save his foot. I tried to reassure him that he would not lose the swollen foot, but by this time there was no hope of reason prevailing.

Much later I learned that the man didn't require amputation, but it was weeks before the infection was controlled. Weeks of pain and uncertainty.

Leaving the chopper at the helipad and returning to the hootch I was drained, both physically and emotionally. Every minute on the wild chopper ride there had been an expectation of drawing ground fire, but there had been none. The morning operation and afternoon dust-off had tested me well beyond my visions of the first day. Sitting on the bunk, I realized that I had actually performed quite well. I had neither frozen nor forgotten the lessons learned back at Fort Sam. The realization of 364 more days of this had not yet sunk in. It would soon enough.

In this late summer of 1968 the pace of the war was escalating. The Tet offensive in February had signaled a shift in the communist strategy. More and more, the North Vietnamese and Vietcong were attacking in greater strengths and over a wider front, though front hardly described the real scope of the fighting. Cities and villages were bombarded with 122 mm. rockets and mortars of all description. Bombs were planted in crowded locations in cities and on American bases. Lame duck President Johnson had announced a major cut-back in bombing the North and the communist forces smelled a weakening of U.S. resolve. Accordingly, they again increased their offensives throughout the South, particularly targeting areas where the fighting had not been too intense previously.

The 36th Evac. was a beehive of activity. Every ward was filled with fresh casualties. As the number of military casualties increased, civilian wounded had to be turned away. The Vietnamese hospital, Le Loi, was already terribly overcrowded and the Australian hospital was too small to take much of the overflow. There was also a small South Korean facility which did have capable surgeons, but it too was not prepared to handle the increasing numbers of wounded.

Medical supplies and trained personnel were also in short supply. Many of the doctors drafted to serve in Vietnam came from specialty practices and had not performed the general surgery required for the vast array of battlefield wounds in years. Fortunately, old skills were generally re-learned quickly as the action mounted. Medevac choppers were landing and swinging out for more pickups day and night. Fatigue became a deadly enemy for the medical staff.

After two weeks of steady dust-offs, 24 hours a day, I was becoming accustomed to the routine. Shifts were supposed to be twelve hours on and twelve off, but seldom were. All free time was spent in the hootch, on call, due to the lack of medics. I didn't spend much time dwelling on why there was such a shortage. It was well known that the big red cross on a white field on the side of the Medevac helicopters was a coveted target. The communists' reasoning was that if soldiers saw that should they become wounded, their chance of being rescued was in jeopardy, their morale would be lowered.

The reasoning was sound.

During my third week in Vietnam, I had two significant experiences. The first began as a late afternoon call to fly north near Baria to pick up several American casualties, the result of a major attack by a large force of Vietcong. Two choppers responded -- the last two remaining at the hospital. I was in the second Huey.

Shortly before arriving at the landing zone, the L.Z., the pilot in chopper number two radioed ahead for a status report. All clear was the response. Two minutes later we were receiving heavy fire from an invisible enemy on the ground. When I saw tracer rounds arcing up towards us I broke out in a cold sweat. There was no place to duck - nothing to hide behind. I learned a new meaning for pucker.

Spotting the red smoke signaling the location of the L.Z., the pilots dropped in to pick up their loads as quickly as possible. The first chopper was back in the air in less than a minute and driving hard to the east when I heard the first rounds hit our bird. We were waiting for three more casualties who were literally being dragged across the clearing towards the gaping open doorway of the Huey. Suddenly a mortar round exploded a scant hundred yards to the rear, followed by two more just to the west. The men who were crawling and dragging their wounded buddies instantly jumped up, shouting, and dashed to the waiting chopper, half-carrying, half dragging their fallen comrades.

Spotting only Americans on the fringe of the L.Z., the door gunner could find no targets for laying out a covering fire. He helped me pull the last G.I. into the open bay. I signalled the pilot to head out and the anxious warrant officer was only too happy to oblige. Barely ten feet off the ground, there was a violent shudder and the chopper dropped to the earth with a back-wrenching slam.

With the fearsome din surrounding us, no one in the plane had heard the round which had disabled the aircraft. Later, we would learn that the Jesus nut, the massive nut that holds the rotor in place, had been hit and broken.

Before we could scramble out of the wounded bird we were surrounded by fellow G.I.s. At least a dozen men, with automatic weapons blazing, formed a rear guard, while several more assisted in removing the wounded. Grabbing the largest medical kit, I sprinted in a low crouch to a bushy clump of tall grass and nippa-palm. I had no idea where the rest of the troops had gone. Looking into the clearing I could see the downed chopper sitting alone like a helpless, wet kitten on a storm-swept green lawn. Not a soul was in sight. Amazingly, the gunfire seemed to be diminishing.

A voice behind me whispered something unintelligible.

Thank God it was an American voice, I thought. I crept backwards, all the while trying to look 360 degrees around. I would have a stiff neck for days.

Following the crawling soldier into the grass I noticed blood on my uniform. Looking down I realized that my hands were bleeding. The edges of the saw grass were like razors. Damn, I thought, it will take weeks to heal these cuts. The temperature and humidity were such that even shaving nicks took forever to heal. In addition, there were some really nasty bacteria over here that were quite resistant to many antibiotics.

A voice shouting for a medic snapped me back to reality. How could I be thinking of such trivial matters as minor cuts, I wondered? Later I would learn that retreating into insignificant thought was the mind's way of denying the stark terror of such pure experiences.

I found the field medic and together we began assessing damage. All five casualties had been brought safely from the chopper and were lying together in a small crater. Their bandages were torn and dirty from the dragging and two of them had passed out from the pain. Miraculously, there had been no further serious injuries.

As we re-bandaged the wounds a new sound could be heard approaching from the direction of the downed aircraft. Seconds later a helicopter gunship appeared from nowhere and began to hose the area down with a wicked, raking fire. The gunship was obviously in contact with someone on the ground. On their second pass over the clearing the ground fire ceased. The only sound was the chopping of the rotors.

The pilot began dropping towards the clearing. When he was within fifty feet of the ground a terrific barrage erupted. The plane shuddered once as it absorbed some kind of hit, banked away from the clearing and the stranded men, and sped out of the area.

Silence reigned. Even the insects were still. John Wayne would have said it was too quiet!

As darkness crept over the landing zone a lieutenant appeared and directed us to follow him. A group of men brought the wounded on makeshift litters. Stumbling through the darkness was a painful business. I soon learned not to grab at the grass or other plants to break my fall as we hurried in the fading light.

A few hundred feet from the L.Z. we halted. A perimeter had been established earlier and the lieutenant had assured the men that they were in a good defensive position. Not to worry.

Right, I thought. I should believe a man who had gotten us into this fix in the first place. I wonder if I should ask him if he's the gibonni who told us it was all clear below? Better not, since most officers would do the same thing. They want their men to know that their commander will bring in swift medical help and get them back to a hospital in a jiffy. Hmm, this might have something to do with that shortage of medics.

Despite all the assurances, we got no sleep that night. The wounded needed attention and more morphine to keep them from crying out and attracting unwanted attention. Their wounds were all serious but none were life-threatening if they reached a hospital soon. The most vulnerable was a black sergeant who had been walking point, well ahead of the rest of the platoon. He had multiple fragment wounds, two of them especially worrisome as they were in line with a kidney and internal hemmhorage was a possibility.

All of the men needed fluid replacement. The problem was, all of the plasma and ringers lactate was on the downed chopper. The exposed position of the Huey made any type of sortie to retrieve the fluids far too dangerous to risk. No one knew how many Vietcong were in the ambush group and reconnaissance in the dark was out of the question.

The night dragged on and still the insects remained quiet. Muffled explosions far in the distance indicated a B-52 strike.

Closer by some kind of lizards or frogs began to call. And then a rooster crowed. Could dawn be far behind?

As the sun knifed through the morning fog I cautiously stood up to stretch, surprisingly alert after a sleepless night. Adrenalin has that effect, I found. And for some strange reason, the mosquitoes had not been a major problem overnight. Liberal doses of G.I. bug repellent had been more than sufficient to keep the winged menace at bay. No one in the platoon had ever seen that happen before.

A sharp cry caught my attention. The sergeant with the possible kidney wound was in extreme distress. One glance at the man's face told me that the relief choppers couldn't arrive too soon. And then the sound of pulsating blades reached our straining ears.

A tiny bubble observation helicopter flew directly over us, followed by two Medevac Hueys and a gunship. This gunship sported a mini-gun which could spew thousands of rounds a minute. Circling our position several times, it drew no fire. The waiting Medevacs darted to the ground in the clearing as the big gunship patrolled above. Still no hostile fire.

There was no conversation as we quickly loaded the wounded onto the waiting choppers. The strain of waiting all night for an attack that never came was etched on every face. I exchanged a look with the field medic and our eyes expressed the unspoken thoughts. One of us was returning to the relative safety of the base while the other remained in the field. How were our lots chosen? What desk-bound clerk had casually typed in the assignments? Assignments that could mean the difference between life and death. Assignments that carried such different odds of survival.

Moments later I joined two of the wounded in one ship and we took off. The second chopper was right behind. Our lift-off was uneventful and as we flew south, a giant sky-crane chopper could be seen heading for the clearing to salvage the damaged plane. Breathing easily for the first time in hours, I started an I.V. in the most seriously wounded soldier. Moments later the man trembled violently and suddenly lay still. I felt for a carotid pulse. Nothing!

Putting my face above the man's mouth I checked for respiration. Again, nothing.

I fumbled for a plastic-covered wedge and placed it beneath the limp neck. Prying open the man's mouth I breathed deeply and sent a rush of air to the collapsed lungs. Alternately switching to compress the chest, I continued C.P.R..

Still no response.

With a silent prayer I struck the sternum sharply with the side of my fist. Too sharply, I thought, from the loud crack that resulted. Blowing into the mouth once more I thought I saw the chest rise slightly. And then again, and again.

He was breathing on his own. Oh God, Hallelujah, I thought. As color returned to the soldier's face I sat back weakly and broke into a cold sweat.

"Nice job, Doc," offered the door gunner. "Couldn't have done better myself." Grinning, he turned and continued to scan the ground that was slipping by so fast below.

I adjusted the I.V. drip and checked on our other casualty, silently wishing that there had been another medic available to help. What if I had screwed up? What if the man had died? What if ....? And then I remembered the words of Monsignor Brown on that last day at the seminary. Don't second guess yourself. Do your best and put it behind you. The words had sounded hollow then, and even a little preachy. But now .... how much I would need those words in the months ahead!

Landing at the Evac., we rushed the wounded into the pre-op corridor for an initial evaluation. My patient went to the table immediately. His sternum was unhurt, but he had a cracked rib where the life-restoring blow had re-started his heart, for which I was reprimanded. And the soldier did indeed have a perforated kidney with internal bleeding. His surgery, though, was a success and he was soon shipped to Japan for follow-up treatment. As with most of the casualties we worked on, I never learned if there was a full recovery.

After this harrowing experience, I expected my colleagues in the hootch to be full of questions and sympathy. Neither was forthcoming. I had come to the 36th alone, not with a full replacement company. Everyone was more concerned about his own safety and friendships took time to develop. Besides, everyone here was overworked and free time was spent in the beer tent or sleeping. Mostly sleeping!

During the following four days I flew three more dust-offs, two of them at night. On the second night flight I watched as tracers streamed up at us from the vicinity of a tiny village. We weren't hit, but from the radio messages we knew that the village came under an intensive retaliatory strike. It was during this four day stretch that the second significant event occurred.

One evening, some of the medics, nurses and doctors held an informal party behind the hootch. Tired but thirsty, I joined in the festivities. One of the nurses was rotating stateside, back to the world, and this was the first of the good-bye bashes. I met many of my co-workers who had previously been mere blurs in green scrub suits and masks as they bustled in and out of the emergency room and the O.R.'s. I also learned through the very well informed grapevine that tomorrow I was off chopper duty and assigned to the operating room full time. I would be replacing Lieutenant Stratton, the departing scrub nurse. Actually, I was told, I could never really replace all of her functions, particularly her special liaisons with two of the surgeons.

With an understanding nod I made my way through the small group of revelers and climbed to the roof of the hootch. Many nights had been spent here watching the light shows. It seemed that a night could not pass without at least two or three incoming rounds from rockets and mortars situated in the dense jungle of V.C. Hill. These were inevitably followed by flares, which would drift slowly down on small parachutes, illuminating the perimeter of the base.

In the brilliance of the flares the outline of gunships, including those with "Puff the Magic Dragon", could be seen circling and firing withering bursts, lines of tracers lighting their paths. The sound of B-52's dropping their deadly cargo in the distance added bass as counterpoint to the staccato machine gun fire and mini-gun burps.

Tonight, however, was a respite from the usual harassment. Looking down over the roof, I spotted a slim figure in baggy, white silk pants. She was cleaning up around the edges of the party. I was hypnotized, watching her move, admiring her grace. A sergeant from the neighboring hootch caught my eye.

"None of that, now," he warned, slurring his words. "She's our Mama-san and we all look out for her."

"No problem, Sarge," I rejoined with a grin, "I'm just looking. She certainly is nice to look at, though."

"Well, Pal, why don't you come down and I'll introduce you. She won't have anything to do with you anyway."

82

On the ground, I took a closer look at this girl who was poetry in motion. She appeared to be in her early twenties and had a soft, round face with the most inviting lips I had ever seen. Can there be anything so beautiful in the midst of all this carnage, I thought? I was staring at her openly and she boldly returned the look.

Sergeant Ski made the introductions and told us to get to know one another. He chuckled as he walked away and I soon found out why. Her name was Minh, she spoke almost no English and she had absolutely no interest in becoming friendly with any G.I., especially one who seemed a bit unsteady on his feet and slurred the occasional word.

She was polite, but firm. She thought that all G.I.'s were "dien-ki-dau" and "sai" too much. I later learned that that meant crazy and drunk, and not necessarily in the order.

Despite the language barrier, I continued to talk with her. Neither of us understood much when the other spoke, but neither of us minded. For some unknown reason there was an attraction between us. When the young woman had to leave for her home in Vung Tau, I leaned forward and kissed her good night. She drew back, but smiled as she said, "See you, G.I..."

Watching her walk away into the darkness, I whispered back, "See you, Mama-san."

Medevac helipad at the 36th Evac Hospital

Our crackerbox ambulance, V.C. Hill in the background

Minh on the 36th Evac company street

Mike and Minh in hootch no. 11

Chapter Eleven

In hootch number 9, Minh was troubled as she went about her work. The image of a young American with a big smile kept her from concentrating. He seemed different from the other G.I.'s. He hadn't asked to come home with her or even to see her again. The others were always bothering her, but she had never let any of them follow her downtown. The guard at the main gate, a friend of Lieng's, would hold anyone on her request.

Now this G.I. with the funny name of "Mak" just wouldn't leave her mind. Well, she thought, if he stops by today perhaps I'll talk with him again. Maybe I can learn more about America from him.

As she busied herself cleaning the hootch she wondered why any G.I. would want to go out with a Vietnamese girl when all the American women were so much more beautiful. At least all of the girls in those magazines the G.I.'s had were so good looking, though they certainly had low morals to pose the way they did. Still, it was a very wealthy country and no one was starving there. Maybe someday I will see America and judge for myself, she dreamed.

The morning after the party began one of the most intensive weeks ever for the surgical teams at the 36th Evac.. There was a major offensive in progress to the north and fresh casualties streamed in both day and night. For two days and nights no one left the operating area. Sleep was stolen in half hour breaks every few hours. The five operating tables in two rooms were never empty for more than a few minutes.

Most of the wounded were Vietnamese soldiers and civilians. The triage room resembled a crowded market place more than a hospital. Entire families with an injured member trailed into the room and encamped. The wounded were placed on litters suspended on metal frames three feet above the floor. When the litters were full more casualties were left on stretchers scattered on the floor wherever space allowed.

With only one interpreter available it was next to impossible to get histories and details of the injuries. Hysterical family members wailed and wept and were constantly underfoot, sometimes barging into the operating rooms in their concern. I vowed to learn enough Vietnamese to at least communicate with the relatives and comfort them; also, to help with diagnoses and dealing with the patients.

Midway through the second night of this long week, one of the old cracker-box ambulances rumbled up to the pre-op door, disgorging a load of fresh casualties. The first litter in the door bore a woman in her eighth month of pregnancy. She had been shot in the leg and abdomen by a Russian-made A.K.47, a high velocity automatic rifle commonly used by the Vietcong and North Vietnamese regular army. Bleeding profusely, the woman was already in shock and critical. Unfortunately, all five tables were occupied, and even more critical was the fact that there were only five anesthesiologists assigned to the unit and they were all busy. As I bent over the woman to clean her wounds and apply new pressure dressings the head nurse knelt beside me.

"Specialist Hall," she said softly, "I need you over by the door right away."

"I'll be right there. Just as soon as I get through here."

"You are through here, Specialist. Move it now, and that's an order. This is triage and the woman you're working on has no chance of making it. We have to stabilize others who will have a chance."

About to argue the case, I looked squarely into Major Mahoney's eyes. The look she returned would be in my memory for the rest of my life. That same look would burn out of my own eyes more than once before this tour of duty was completed. It was the look that I had once seen in the eyes of a mortally wounded deer. The animal had looked up with what could only be a terrible, hopeless sense of resignation. It was a look that spoke so profoundly there could be no reply, no comment. There were no words in any language which could adequately address that countenance.

I moved woodenly to the door and began to help assess the severity of the injuries to these latest victims. The training at Fort Sam must have been superbly designed for I automatically scanned wounds, evaluated vital signs and assigned a rating for admission to surgery. Tourniquets and pressure dressings were efficiently applied and I.V.'s established. For the rest of the night, moving from litter to litter, I couldn't keep from glancing to the corner where the pregnant woman rested. No one could believe she had lasted so long.

Finally, her turn came to enter the O.R.. With everything under control in pre-op, I asked to scrub in on the case. My best friend Doug had just completed a grueling ten hour marathon in O.R. and was only too happy to be relieved. He didn't know that I had spent the entire day in the second operating room, only to go on immediate duty in pre-op as the flood of casualties continued.

The gas man, as the anesthetists were called, hesitated to put the woman to sleep. Her vital signs indicated that her condition was so serious that she had no chance of surviving the anesthesia. I told the doctor that the woman's husband had been at her side all night long praying, not understanding why she had to wait so long. With that, she was put to sleep and the hopeless task commenced.

No fetal heartbeat had been detected in triage and it was assumed that the baby had not survived the wound. Nevertheless, a laparotomy was directed towards the womb and by some miracle beyond medical explanation, the baby was still alive. She was delivered by C-section and placed on another table to attend to the bullet wound through her leg. She was a very tiny baby and the wound proved too much for her. She died in a nurses arms.

The quiet in the room was deafening. Half an hour later, despite the surgeon's best efforts, her mother expired as well. The trauma had been too extensive. The doctor remarked that given the time between the shooting and her arrival at the hospital, he didn't know how she had survived as long as she had.

There were a dozen more patients with relatively minor wounds waiting in pre-op. Leaving the O.R. for a quick cup of coffee, I bumped into Major Mahoney. She was a small, feisty woman with a no-nonsense attitude when it came to running the operating theater. She had earned the respect of every person in the unit with tireless work alongside her nurses and her willingness to talk person-to-person with anyone, regardless of rank, when off duty.

Tonight, the tough Major looked like the wreck of the Hesperus, her face streaked with sweat and wisps of hair protruding Medusa-like from beneath her scrub cap.

"Specialist Hall," she sighed, "Haven't I seen you here for quite a long while?"

"Yes Ma'am, you have. I spent yesterday in the O.R. and last night in pre-op. We just finished with the woman who was pregnant."

"Well, you won't be any good to me in your condition so you'd better go get some sleep. We may need you later. You were supposed to be relieved last night, but thanks for hanging in. It's been rough. I ... hope you understand why we had to delay that woman. If we had more tables and people we wouldn't have to make decisions like that. It tears me up every time. By the way, it's almost noon. Easy to lose track of time in here under the lights."

"That's for sure, Ma'am. By the way, you've been here as long as I have and probably longer. You look like you could do with some shut-eye too."

"Hall, if you're saying I look as bad as you do, those are court martial words," she barked, good naturedly.

"No Ma'am, you're still the second best looking Irishman in this camp. I'll be heading into the arms of Morpheus for awhile now, so keep the choppers away."

"And who's the best looking ..... ah yes. You did mention in your first day interview that there's a Sullivan in your background. Someday we'll have to sit down and discuss it with my good friend, Mr. Hennesey. Now get off with you and get some sleep."

After wolfing down a heaping platter of scrambled almost-eggs in the mess tent, I collapsed on my bunk. Four hours later I was in surgery again, up to my elbows in blood.

A bomb had exploded in downtown Vung Tau and dozens of people had been injured. The most serious was the two hundred ninety pound sergeant lying on the table before me. Most of the surgeons had gone back to the villa, the officer's quarters located off base several miles away on the far side of the city. Of the two doctors remaining, one was busy in O.R. 2 and the other was across the table from me, trying to repair a lacerated liver. By coincidence, he too was from upstate New York. Captain Ibach hailed from Massena, a small city on the St. Lawrence River, just upstream from Ogdensburg where I had spent my seminary days.

"Mike, I know you haven't been trained for this, but I need your help if we're going to insure that this well-fed sergeant gets another meal. There has been some damage to one of the hepatic ducts and some ruptured vessels. I can't get to the abdominal bleeding for a long time and we don't have a long time, do we Sam," he asked the gas-passer from Seattle?

Sam shook his head.

"All right then, Mike, I want you to run the bowel to look for any punctures or nicks. I can smell a problem down there. You don't have to cut away any mesenteries, just loop the bowel out through your hands and eyeball each inch for a cut. This guy has enough shrapnel in him to keep me in fishing sinkers for a year!"

I directed the circulating technician to go find someone to scrub in to help us out, and then began the painstaking task of checking out several dozen feet of intestines.

At first I was slow and clumsy, but ten feet into the job began to show some proficiency. When the first hole was found it was a slight nick that had barely penetrated the small intestine, but was more than enough to exude some of the inner contents and cause peritonitis. Under the Captain's guidance I put in two stitches to close the wound. I was about to reach for the Mayo scissors to snip off the trailing suture ends when a hand appeared and slapped the scissors into my glove. There was Doug, wearing a grin so wide it escaped from both sides of his mask.

"O.K. hotshot, how do you rate?" he demanded. "You're getting to do more in your first month here than I've done in four."

"Specialist, hand me a sponge please," I chortled, gloating wickedly.

With the bowel nearly finished, a steady stream of blood poured from a torn vein. Unable to perform the delicate work necessary to repair the vessel, I lightly clamped off the bleeder and waited for Dr. Ibach. With a waiting line for the table, little time was spent in the niceties of fine suturing to reduce scars. Meatball surgery meant saving as many lives as possible in a short time. In this case the sergeant would survive.

This had been my first taste of work outside our standard training, but it would not be the last. And not all would end as favorably.

Meanwhile, Minh was having problems of her own. She hadn't seen "Mak" again and had relegated him to the deep recesses of her mind. Obviously she had been mistaken about him. In the light of day he apparently had no interest in her. She had no way of knowing that he was spending nearly the entire week out straight in the operating room.

At home, Tri's father had found her new address and was stopping around to bother her. She made it clear that she wanted nothing to do with him, but he became persistent in his pursuit. Once again, Minh was forced to move.

This time she ran into trouble with the baby sitter. The only woman suitable, who was willing to work long hours, turned out to be completely unreliable. Needing her job, Minh was desperate to find a replacement. Enter the cavalry!

Suu arrived at his daughter's door when she needed him most. He had retired from the army and had come to Vung Tau to find work as a carpenter. Sizing up the situation at a glance, he suggested that Minh take some time off to visit the family in Tam Vu. She was easily convinced and with Lieng's help, managed to get a week off. A day later, she and the two children were aboard a bus heading south.

This time, her arrival home was greeted with open arms. Even her mother seemed to have mellowed. The week passed all too quickly. Her family couldn't get enough of her two young children and tried to convince Minh to stay in Tam Vu. Minh wavered, but knew that there was nothing here for her. Her destiny lay to the north.

Though Suu had left for Vung Tau to find work, Minh's mother and sisters and brother were staying behind in the Delta. Her Mom declared that she had moved for the last time. She also declared that she wanted to see much more of her grandchildren, and offered to watch them for a time while Minh worked. Minh was leery of this offer, but it would surely solve her problem for the time being.

At last she accepted and returned to Vung Tau with her father. He would stay with her while his building jobs lasted. And, he would take care of any trouble with Tri's father should he discover Minh's new home.

As it happened, Suu found work in a village some distance from Vung Tau and made arrangements to stay away for weeks at a time until the jobs were completed.

Back at work, Minh had all but forgotten the young G.I. with the smiling eyes. She was busier than ever, having taken on some additional laundry for some replacement troops. She also began to spend more time on the wards, helping as needed. With street-smarts learned in Saigon and her natural propensity for stubbornness, Minh soon became the representative for all of the other housemaids. Whenever they had a problem, she would take their case to the orderly room and take the bull by the horns.

Usually the bull was a master sergeant who enjoyed the brash little Mama-san with the big mouth. Though he never understood her, with the help of Lieng's translations he always got the gist of her efforts. On occasion, when she was particularly upset by the mistreatment of one of her co-workers, the top sergeant was sure that Lieng didn't dare give him a literal translation. He thanked the Heavens that she had never heard of a union, for she would have been one hell of an organizer.

The sergeant's admiration for Minh's activism stood her in good stead whenever she ran afoul of the company commander. He was a recently transferred Captain in the 101st Airborne, the Screaming Eagles, and he was not happy to be stuck with command of a hospital unit with all of the draftees and their un-military, irreverent attitudes. Minh certainly didn't help his attitude when she referred to the eagle on his shoulder patch as a chicken!

"Hey Chicken-Guy," she would yell as she crossed the compound. With her old sense of humor back, she was not one to pass up a chance to exchange friendly barbs with anyone, least of all anyone with such a pompous demeanor who offered such a ripe target. Her specialty was deflating egos.

Two weeks after the party behind her hootch, she was hanging clothes when she saw a familiar face. "Mak" was leaning against the fence, watching her.

"Hey G.I.," she shouted, "What you do?"

"Hey Mama-san, what you do?" I replied. "I came here to see you. For two weeks I have been so busy and I missed you. Sorry."

"I no understand, G.I.. You talk-talk but you no come. Maybe you go downtown and "ba muoi lam" some bar girl."

"No Mama-san, I no flirt with bar girl. I work too much, like bac-si, doctor. We have been very, very busy. Now, I don't want to call you Mama-san so please tell me your name."

"I am called Minh. And you are Mak. You see, I remember

your name but you no remember mine."

"I'm sorry Minh. I won't forget again. But if we're going to get to know each other I am going to teach you some English and you are going to teach me some Vietnamese. I must learn so I can talk to the wounded Viets and their families. They are so scared when they come here and I want to make them feel better. And please, call me Mike, not Mak. O.K.?"

"Sure G.I., no sweat! How are you today, Mike .... not Mak? Is that O.K.?"

"That's just perfect, Minh. Do you ever get a day off? If we don't get a really big load of wounded I have next Sunday free. Would you like to show me the beach?"

"O.K. Mike. Sunday at main gate at noon."

I grinned. Her English was not too good, but at least I could understand her. And it was far better than the five or six words of Vietnamese that I knew. This would be my first chance to leave the base since my arrival. I had been on first or second call and unable to see anything since chopper duty. I prayed that night for a lull in the action and a clear day Sunday. God listened!

True to her word, Minh was outside the main gate at noon on Sunday. When she spotted me she waved me over to share a loaf of fresh-baked French bread and a cup of coconut milk.

After tasting the warm coconut milk I ordered a Coke. No sense going native too soon, though the long loaf of golden-crusted bread was delicious.

We caught one of the many smoky, three-wheeled cyclos, called lambrettas, and bounced down the rough mile of road to the city. Minh ordered the driver to detour through the main streets for a little sight-seeing. One street was remarkably clean, appearing to have been recently swept. In point of fact, that was exactly what had happened.

Nguyen Thai Hoc was the street where the outdoor market was located. Each morning before dawn, farmers and fishermen and all sorts of other merchants would set up stalls or tables along the street and hawk their produce and wares. Without any refrigeration and little money for ice, the tropical sun, by noon, would make it impossible to keep perishables, therefore the market would close about noon and be swept down. While it was in operation though, business was brisk. Because of the lack of dependable electricity and

91

refrigeration, marketing was a daily task. It also provided a convenient time to pick up the latest news and gossip a bit.

Continuing through the city, Minh pointed out all of the local attractions. Monuments to fallen heroes, shrines and temples, the theater and hotel and so much more. I was overwhelmed by the sights, sounds and smells. This small city on the sea was a cornucopia for the senses.

Most of the buildings were low and of brick or masonry. Some had thatched sides or roofs, but these were on the outskirts. The theater and restaurant and several buildings in the center of town showed the influence of the French. Multi-storied, with overhanging balconies lined with red brick, these attractive buildings were made even more imposing by the contrast with the surrounding streets with their traditional Asian homes.

Leaving the city, with its many tree-lined broad streets and narrow connecting lanes and alleys, the lambretta wheezed up a small hill and sputtered to a stop. The driver wanted to be paid in advance before proceeding farther. He had been stiffed by too many Americans lately, especially when there were no policemen nearby.

I gladly paid him what he asked but before I could hand over the money, Minh took it and kept back half. She argued a bit with the driver and stepped out, as if to walk. He flashed a toothy grin, took half the money and we were off.

He was robbing us, Minh explained. Never, ever give anyone over here what they ask for because they have already doubled the price and then some. Mildly chagrined, I agreed that I knew better. I just hated to haggle over prices. Minh laughed. In our country that is a way of life, she explained. You will just have to get used to it.

The road to the beach was rough, but well-traveled. It was lined with palm trees and fringed by small farms. Paddy dikes divided the land much as stone walls did in New England. Farmers and water buffalo were scattered in the fields and a few small food stands sprouted in the shade of some tall elm-like trees.

Minh directed the driver to take the right fork where the road divided. This was the road down to the back beach which was off-limits to American army personnel. Since I was with Minh, I didn't worry too much about the off-limits signs posted so conspicuously all along the road. Until we met an M.P. jeep!

Looking back we saw the jeep turn around. I just knew we were about to be busted. The jeep roared up the road and pulled up close behind us. Suddenly it scooted by and turned in by a small, squat building hidden behind some dense palms. As we drove by, Minh and I recognized one of the military police officers. He had spent a lot of time at the 36th getting penicillin shots for a nasty case of carnal flu.

M.P.'s were in big trouble if they contracted venereal diseases so they usually made friends with someone in a medical unit and connived to get their shots off the record.

Feeling secure once more, I smiled inwardly at the foibles of mankind. That squat, little house was a bar notorious for spreading the malady that the M.P.'s seemed bent on re-acquiring.

The lambretta stopped at the beach and we made for the southern-most expanse of sand. Beyond this was a rocky expanse which was uncovered at low tide. There were a number of people poking among the mossy rocks and filling buckets and baskets with snails and crabs. Minh showed me how to find these small delicacies and soon we had helped a toddler fill her tiny basket.

On a hill above the beach sat a Buddhist temple, and beside it a grove of banana trees. Minh approached a man in the grove and he offered a bunch of the dwarf green fruit to her and her American friend. We accepted two small bananas and continued along the hilly path to an overlook with a magnificent view of the water.

The South China Sea spread out before us in a breathtaking vista. A morning storm had left a few scattered thunderheads and these had now turned white and billowy. They rose thousands of feet into the air like gigantic, convoluted minarets on a faraway mosque. The contrast with the flat, azure sea was spectacular. Sitting on the hill, gazing at the panorama before them, neither medic nor Mama-san could utter a word. Finally, with great reluctance, and in a strange, contemplative silence, we left this island of calm and beauty in the troubled countryside. There was so much more to see and so little time.

As we walked along, our hands touched and fingers entwined. The sidelong glances at one another became longer and longer as the day wore on.

This can't be happening to me, Minh thought nervously. I won't let it happen. This can only end in sorrow and I don't need any more of that.

And yet, she couldn't bring herself to let go of my hand.

"Please show me the front beach, Minh," I asked, breaking into her reverie. "I've heard so much about it from the cooks and signal men and the other medical staff who have been here for months. One of the guys said that you can surf here in the windy season."

"I don't know surf," Minh replied, "but I would love to show you the beach."

Finding another lambretta took forever since few Americans spent much time or money in this area. By the time we reached the front beach it was supper time. And what a contrast from "bai truoc", the back beach!

A small club, with an open-air stage featuring Vietnamese bands singing rock and roll, was bordered by a large patio cluttered with tables and chairs. A kitchen inside the club supplied steaks and hamburgers to go with the cold beer and soda. Youngsters hovered around the relaxing G.I.'s offering shoe shines, fruits or their services as errand boys. Other locals peeled and sliced fruit, juicy mangoes and pineapples for a very reasonable price. Not many G.I.'s were availing themselves of the fresh fruit, preferring instead beer and steaks as they ogled the raven-haired young beauties prancing about in the sea and on the sand.

Australian lifeguards, with their peculiar, heavy rescue craft nearby, were perched on spotting towers. The sea was nearly calm, with waves less than a foot high lapping quietly on the sand. The Aussies looked bored.

With darkness only an hour away, we turned inland. In the distance we could see the last rays of the setting sun reflecting off the red, tiled roofs of the grand old French villas.

"It's been a great day, Minh," I said huskily, brushing a wisp of hair out of her eyes. "I really want to do this again sometime."

"Me too," she responded eagerly. "Maybe next Sunday?"

She rode back to the main gate of the base with me and said good-night there. No one on the base knew where she lived, and she wanted to keep it that way, at least for now. But an eerie feeling sent a cold shiver up her spine. What was happening to her? This quiet G.I. was provoking feelings that she had kept suppressed for such a long time. Somehow she had to take control of these disturbing thoughts. Tomorrow, she thought wickedly. Tonight she just wanted to enjoy these warm feelings!

Chapter Twelve

Reality came slowly for me, but when it arrived it hit squarely between the eyes. Flying dust-offs had been dangerous and fear had ridden every flight with me. But it was more than fear. There was a kind of exhilaration mixed with the anxiety. An exhilaration born of living on the edge. It was not unlike the sensations described by men who challenge death rock climbing, car racing or in similar pursuits.

At first, when I watched tracers arcing up towards the chopper or heard the impact of a bullet, my stomach churned and I broke into a cold sweat, knowing that there was no way to duck, no place to hide from the danger beneath. Gradually the stark fear subsided and was replaced by a dull realization that I had survived these trips before and could survive them again. This acceptance carried over to the nightly incoming rockets.

It became a macabre game to sit on the hootch roof and watch incoming rounds hit. Only a near miss would send us scrambling to the bunker. There was never a feeling of invulnerability, only acceptance. Besides, with only one or two major exceptions, there were only a handful of nights when the number of rockets exceeded two or three.

The medical training provided at Fort Sam Houston had succeeded in producing capable technicians who were able to respond to difficult conditions and carry out our mission effectively. It was unfortunate that there had been no psychological preparation for the horrors that would inevitably have to be faced. Perhaps no training could adequately prepare anyone for such grim realities.

The 36th Evac. had seen two consecutive days of light casualties and began scheduling some elective surgery. Hernias, hemorrhoids and cysts were taken care of in the morning and a few lucky Vietnamese were treated in the afternoon. A young girl with a severe cleft lip and palate was one of the fortunate recipients of surgical care during this lull. She had been spotted by an off-duty doctor and her parents had agreed to send her to the 36th for treatment. I scrubbed in on the case and was surprised to see an extra sterile tray set up with a book on it. The surgeon had never attempted this procedure before and would try it by the numbers. The operation was an unqualified success, but I was amused by the grease pencil lines sketched on the girl's face to guide the probing scalpel. Well, everyone has to start somewhere, I thought.

This war, as all wars before, provided a training ground for trauma surgery and new techniques. Experimental burn lotions with previously unproven antibacterial properties were given a thorough testing and proved their worth. More bizarre techniques were tried as last resorts in some limited circumstances. I assisted when a dog was sacrificed, shaved and the skin removed to form huge patches of cover for a woman severely burned by napalm. Since she had no skin remaining for donor patches of her own, the dog skin represented her only hope for survival. It failed.

An elderly Vietnamese farmer was brought in with advanced cancer of the esophagus. A portion of his small intestine was resected and grafted into place to substitute for the diseased tissue. The man lived for several weeks but ultimately succumbed to the dread disease. The jokes about the odors of his burping lived on, however.

After an afternoon of elective surgery, I was on my way back to the hootch for a catnap when I heard an approaching chopper. Waiting at the helipad with a sinking feeling that the day was not yet over, I soon found my fears coming true. The Medevac chopper held two badly burned sailors and was followed by an ambulance with four more. Two rockets had been fired at a U.S. Navy vessel in the harbor and both had found their marks. The ensuing fires had seriously injured the six seamen.

In pre-op, I began the difficult task of removing the burned clothing from one of the men. To my horror, large pieces of charred skin and flesh came away with the cloth. The sailor had been given morphine but it wasn't even touching the excruciating pain. He opened his seared eyelids and pleaded for water. Although fluid replacement was critical, it couldn't be given by mouth since surgery was imminent.

I soaked a cloth and held it to the sailor's lips to help relieve the overpowering thirst. The action of sucking was too painful for his scorched lips, however, and reluctantly I withdrew the sopping cloth. With no time to waste, we wheeled the sailor into the O.R. and put him under. Simultaneously, a cut-down was performed to find a vein which would accept an I.V., a chore which proved very difficult due to the extensive damage and collapsed veins.

With only two surgeons on base at the time and almost an hour necessary to get any additional help, I was pressed into service to help debride the wounds. As we began the operation a nurse entered the room and called a surgeon. The other sailors were in serious condition and if one doctor could break out to work in the other room there might be a chance to save two men instead of one. The decision was made instantly and Dr. Joe and Specialist Mike were on their own.

Debriding consisted of removing as much of the dead tissue as possible. The odor of burned flesh was nauseating. We poured a peppermint-scented liquid on our face masks to block it out. The work was gruesome and intimidating, with third degree burns covering most of his body. Despite our best efforts the procedure was going to take too long. The surgeon called for an experimental new burn lotion. We smeared the preparation over the brutalized form and hurried to post-op. By the time we were ready for the next patient our relief had arrived and taken over.

Wearily, I made my way to the recovery area behind the curtains. I was drawn to the young sailor and sat down near his bed. As I watched the tortured chest rising and falling, fighting for each breath, and listened to the wheezing from seared lungs, I knew that our efforts had not been good enough. I fell asleep in the chair and woke up an hour later to silence. The wheezing had stopped. The boy's agony was ended.

Sleep would not come easily that night. The awful reality of what was happening around me had finally become personal. In a few short moments I had formed a bond with the sailor, and his suffering and death could not be held at a professional arms' distance. I was not prepared for the powerful conflicting emotions that surged within me. I realized that a professional detachment was needed to maintain effectiveness, but could I ever again achieve that insulation? Would I feel like this after every operation?

That night, Minh stopped by the hootch on her way home. She saw the torment in my eyes and the bottle in my hand. She asked me to walk her to the main gate. All the way out she listened patiently as I tried to describe what had taken place that day. She recognized the pain and frustration, but also heard the beginning of self-doubt. She knew how crippling that emotion could be and finally broke in to reassure me that my efforts were making a difference, regardless of how it seemed. I was not to be consoled that night, however, and she left with a heavy heart, determined to stop in again in the morning.

I was still sleeping at dawn when she arrived at the base so she passed through the hootch without waking me. She had made up her mind to invite this "different" G.I. to supper at her house, breaking her long-held rule of insulation from the soldiers.

Minh had spoken to her father about the baby-faced medic and he had recognized something more than curiosity in his daughter's voice. She wasn't yet ready to admit to herself that she cared for this G.I. as more than a friend. She saw me almost everyday and we would contrive to eat lunch together whenever possible. The other housemaids were teasing her and calling me "Papa-san number 11", after my hootch number. She dared not think too far ahead where this relationship might lead. Her greatest concern at the moment was just to be there when I needed her. Her years of living with this cruel war had provided her with a great inner strength which now must be directed outward to help a man who needed her support.

Shortly after Minh had come by, I was awakened by the C.Q., the soldier on duty as Charge of Quarters. The emergency room had called looking for all available O.R. technicians. A nearby village had been attacked by a Vietcong force and a large number of casualties were expected.

All day and into the night the five operating tables were constantly busy. Men, women and children had been senselessly maimed and killed. It was the worst assault on a small village in that area since the Tet offensive in February. By late afternoon the entire staff was exhausted.

The intense concentration required during an operation was physically and mentally draining. Efficiency diminished as fatigue set in and mistakes in judgment were apt to occur. Beyond fatigue, a numbness took over and the work became automatic, as if performed by a robot.

I was at this stage when the last casualty was lifted onto the table. The little boy was about six years old and he was in very bad shape. After two hours of intensive work the worst of the damage had been repaired but more surgery would be needed when he was stronger and able to bear it. He would live, but his life would never be the same, for he had lost an arm and a leg.

The evening sun was becoming obscured by dark clouds and a fine mist was settling the red dust outside the side door of the operating room. I stood there in a daze, staring at the dirt path leading to the incinerator. Body parts were treated with respect. If they were mutilated and removed they were cremated. I numbly focused my eyes on the dust at my feet. The plastic bag had broken open and its contents lay on the ground. I reached down and picked up the mangled leg and the tiny hand. For several of the longest moments of my life I just stood there, holding the sacred limbs which had been so traumatically taken from the child. Over and over my lips formed the silent question, "Why God, why?"

But there was no answer.

And then, in a great primal burst, a piercing wail erupted from deep within my breast. I screamed the question with all of the force of my being.

And still there came no reply.

A corpsman appeared, gently took the limbs, and hurried away as I sat down, my body wracked with waves of great, heaving sobs. I was beyond contemplating words like "man's inhumanity to man." This massacre of innocents had found substance in my hands but my mind refused to comprehend the facts.

I awoke in the morning and was told that I had "freaked out" and had been given a very substantial sedative. As reason slowly returned, I was sure of two things; I would continue to work my tail off to help the helpless victims of this madness, and I would never go to church again!

Through all of the dark days I had relied on faith in God. Now I was shaken. I could no longer sit and consider why these terrible acts were occurring. How could any God allow such carnage, such atrocities to be inflicted on His people? There were probably some good theological answers but I was beyond searching my memory for them. Had God ever held the broken pieces of a little boy in his hands and heard the cries of so many dying innocents? Not on such a physical plane, I bet.

Finally, a reluctant acceptance of the situation brought a strange calm to this angry young medic. My days were filled with surgery, my nights with Minh. As we spent more time together I began to heal. My Vietnamese slowly improved, as did Minh's English. We talked of our families and backgrounds, delighting in learning of all our shared interests.

As we walked downtown in Minh's neighborhood we discovered that neither of us could pass a beggar without offering something spontaneously. Usually there was no money so we would fish in our pockets for an orange or other fruit from the mess hall. I became an instant hit with the children and most of the other people we encountered on the streets. I delighted in trying out my halting Vietnamese and the vendors and passersby delighted in listening and correcting me.

It was marvelous, I thought, how well you can get along with people if you make an effort to understand them and respect them as equals. Not everyone, of course, was delighted to see an American accompanying a native daughter as we explored the city. Insults and cigarette butts were thrown at us and occasionally we would be spit upon, usually by gangs of young thugs who hated the Americans for their treatment of the local population. But even many of these people could be turned around when confronted in their own tongue, chided for their disrespect of a man who had no wife or girlfriend in America, and who had come here to help them. My poor phrasing was always accompanied by a wide grin and that often seemed to make the difference.

Our courtship was of the whirlwind variety, and the obstacles in our path were formidable. Peer pressure among the Americans dictated that Vietnamese women and girls were good for a "short time" but that any kind of serious relationship was out of the question. Many of the residents in hootch number 9 where Minh worked threatened her with losing her job if she continued to see the G.I. in hootch number 11. The G.I. in number 11, namely me, was threatened in more physical ways. In addition to the bodily danger, I was told that a transfer to a much less desirable location far out in the "boonies" could be arranged.

But true love, it seems, always manages to find a way to persist.

In this case, we made it well known that among Minh's many friends and acquaintances downtown were some of the nastier gang leaders. The gangs, called cowboys, had well deserved reputations for mugging, robbing and occasionally killing G.I.'s as they were in the city enjoying some free time.

In order to reinforce her counterthreat, Minh waited outside the main gate with a couple of rough-looking characters and pointed to some of the boys from hootch 9 as they left camp. These good old boys got the message and quickly passed it on. The serious harassment stopped at once. I was glad at the turn of events but concerned about Minh's vehemence and ability to muster a hit squad.

"Minhoi," I asked one evening, "would those men really have done whatever you asked?"

She smiled cryptically and changed the subject. She never did answer the question.

Base regulations prohibited leaving the camp without a pass from the commanding officer. Passes were generally easy to obtain, but expired at 11:00 P.M., curfew time. When I learned that the top sergeant had a girlfriend and a house downtown, I became friends with "Top" and soon was able to pick up an occasional overnight pass.

One night Minh invited me for supper, promising that if I could stay late, I would be able to meet her father. I couldn't get a pass for the night so I checked the roster to see who had C.Q. duty. Part of the duty, which rotated among the enlisted men, was bed check. As luck would have it, a fellow medic would have the duty that night. I looked him up, gave him a small incentive to count me present, and caught a lambretta for town.

There was no trouble finding the house and I was soon experiencing the delights of Vietnamese cooking. Make that the qualified delights. The American palate requires a breaking-in period for much traditional Vietnamese cooking, particularly the special shrimp and fish sauces that are a staple in so much of the cooking. The "nuoc mam" fish sauce, so highly favored by the French, could be accommodated rather quickly, but "mam ca" and "mam tom", the fish and shrimp pastes, could only be tolerated by rare individuals, possibly those who had suffered taste bud injuries early in life.

Late that evening Suu arrived and the two of us became instant friends. We had heard much about each other from our mutual acquaintance and she was thrilled to act as interpreter, despite her lack of English skills. The evening passed all too quickly and soon it was bedtime. Suu was asleep in a jiffy, while Minh and I sat and talked in the dark. With my heart overflowing, I asked Minh if she would marry me and come to live in America. Her two children would be mine and I would love and care for them as my own.

"I will," she answered solemnly and without hesitation. "I am so tired of war and how I am treated here. And I love you. Will we have children?"

"I hope so," I gasped, still in shock from her answer. "If we do they will be half and half, and most likely have to put up with prejudice and hostility. I know we can handle it, but I sure hate to think of the kids going through that."

"Minhoi," she replied calmly, "our children will be beautiful. Their spirits will allow them to withstand any such problems they might face. After all, they will be **our** children and together, we can overcome any challenge."

I didn't understand every word but grasped the full meaning of what she had said. My heart was full.

The next day we applied at the city registrar's office for a marriage permit, and two days later were married. We realized that to reveal our union would be an invitation for renewed trouble on base and so decided to keep it secret for the time being.

Business remained brisk at the 36th. Atrocities piled one upon another and I was unable to get away to see my bride for weeks.

Most of the men stationed at the hospital and in support services were able to obtain passes and travel to the city or beach whenever they were off duty. Only the surgical personnel were restricted, since there were not enough of us to cover the active work and handle the various levels of standby. As a result, tensions began to mount in the unit.

First call meant a restriction to the company area and no alcohol. There was never a working public address system, so first call really meant that you were expected to be within shouting distance of your hootch. Second call was less restrictive, but still compelled a short rein on activities. It was expected that a medic on second call would check in at the orderly room at least once every three hours.

The upshot of these restrictions was a case of good old fashioned cabin fever. The surgical technicians were forced to spend both their work time and off duty time together. With sleep at a premium, conflicts were bound to arise within the confines of the hootch. Sleep versus the radio or tape player, country music versus Motown and card games versus studying grew into disputes far out of proportion to their importance.

One night the jangled nerves and short tempers boiled over and spilled into a fist fight. A bloody nose or black eye could have been tolerated and forgotten in the unit, but sprained fingers meant that a man was unable to scrub in on an operation.

Major Mahoney went on the warpath. The brawlers, who were both skilled and highly motivated technicians, were given a disciplinary hearing and received Article 15 punishments. These were only one step below a court martial. Because their skills were so badly needed and they were in critical jobs in a combat zone, they were fortunate indeed that their penalties were not more severe. As it was, they each lost a month's salary, were reduced one grade in rank and restricted to base for two months.

The Article 15 proceeding got everyone's attention, with Major Mahoney taking particular note. Realizing that the fight was merely a symptom of the real problem, she moved swiftly to defuse the tensions in the surgical unit. She changed shift hours, increased the working hours of her nurse-officers and finagled more free time and passes for the operating room technicians. The changes were galvanic.

Hootch life became bearable and working relationships in the O.R. improved dramatically. Once again, jokes began to fly over the operating tables, reducing stress and increasing stamina. The addition of a portable radio added quiet background music between cases as the rooms were scrubbed down. The officer corps of doctors and nurses slowly started to fraternize more and more with the enlisted technicians, without whom they could not have functioned. The 36th Evacuation Hospital Unit was becoming a close-knit team at last. And we would need that closeness in the trials ahead.

For two solid weeks there was no time for elective surgery. A steady stream of civilian casualties kept the team busy from dawn to dark everyday. Most of the fighting occurred at night and the wounded were unable to call for assistance until the following day.

As a result, many of the cases were almost hopeless by the time they reached the hospital. During this period, my confidence and skills continued to improve.

There were no difficult calls to make in triage, so I found time to improve my concentration and speed at the table. I learned to anticipate the surgeons' needs while working with each of them. They all worked at different speeds and each had his own way of approaching various procedures. Unfortunately, there was only one good vascular man who could handle the difficult heart cases and only a single orthopedist, and given the nature of so many of the wounds, the demand for their talents far exceeded the time they had available. All too often the best man for the job was unavailable and the second string just couldn't measure up. This situation was probably true stateside as well, but back in the world, most surgery could be postponed or a specialist brought in from elsewhere. There was nothing that could be done to alleviate the problem here, and so it had to be taken philosophically. That was easier said than done.

One rotund little doctor with droopy jowls and a nervous habit of rapidly blinking his eyes had been a gynecologist in civilian life. He was not happy at being drafted and made sure that everyone around him knew it. I thought I was cursed, as I drew this particular doctor so often.

Once, on a very calm day in the O.R., with no patients backed up and no prospect of wounded arriving, I was assisting Dr. Jowls with a routine gunshot wound to the abdomen. Routine, because a single trauma such as this was much preferred over the multiple shrapnel wounds which so often caused hidden damage which was hard to detect. As this wound was being repaired, we encountered a large tapeworm, not an unusual find among Vietnamese patients. The doctor scowled and made a derogatory remark about the victim's dietary habits, and began to close the incision.

"Hold it, Doc," I ventured. "You forgot to remove the tapeworm."

"I didn't forget anything, Specialist," he rejoined testily. "These Gooks all have worms. It's not worth the effort, besides, if you take out this one, he'll have another in a few weeks. Pass me another tie."

"O.K. Doc, but it's hospital policy to remove tapeworms whenever time permits. Anyhow, it will only take two minutes and save this guy a lot of problems later on. Besides, your surgery will have a better chance of being successful if the worm is removed and not sapping this man's strength."

"Hall," Jowls spat, "you're on report."

"What in hell for?" I challenged.

"Insubordination, for starters, and then whatever else I can think of. You techs think you know it all after one operation. I've got more knowledge in my little finger than you will ever have."

With that, he sutured the incision and left the room. As I cleaned up and wiped the table down with alcohol the anesthetist walked over and punched me on the shoulder.

"Old Jowls is in his usual nasty mood today," he laughed. "Don't worry about all that bluster. I'll make sure no report is filed on you. Actually, I'm planning on filing on him. I wouldn't work with him for awhile, though."

"Thanks, Doc," I replied with a sigh of resignation. "If you ever need a favor, just holler."

When Sam, the gas man hollered a month later, I couldn't help.

During the same hectic two weeks a new surgeon arrived at the 36th. He was replacing a terrific general surgeon who had been very popular, as well as a tireless worker. On this new surgeon's first day in surgery a child was brought in who had been playing behind her home and stepped on a booby trap. The mine had been homemade and fortunately had little explosive power, nevertheless, there were multiple fragment injuries of the lower extremities. All were routine debridements, with no broken bones and little serious tissue or nerve damage.

As the new surgeon worked he began to sweat profusely, and twice dropped clamps on the floor. He joked once about his obstetric practice in New Jersey and then became deadly serious. As he applied a scalpel to lengthen a puncture wound below the knee, he suddenly twitched and the knife sliced into the popliteal artery, just behind the knee. A geyser of blood spurted into the air and spattered his face, which had been far too close to the wound anyway. He backed away from the table blanching, declaring that he couldn't handle this.

As he walked out of the O.R. the gas man yelled at him to return immediately. Beyond hearing at that point, the flustered doctor never looked back.

I had been the only assistant at the table and no one else was in the room except the circulating technician who was there to adjust lights, count sponges and assist in other non-sterile ways. I sponged the accidental incision but the blood was pumping so forcefully that I couldn't locate the ends of the severed artery. I took a handful of gauze sponges and pressed them against the wound as tightly as possible. No way could I handle this problem alone. The circulating tech would have to help. I shouted at the medic to put on a pair of sterile gloves and move in.

With a small retractor in one hand and a Kelly clamp in the other, I had my new assistant suction the spurting blood. The flow momentarily stopped and I found one end of the artery and gently squeezed the serrated clamp onto it.

Damn, I thought, it would be the distal end towards the foot. I knew I had to find and clamp the proximal end quickly. I strained to remember how crucial the popliteal artery was to survival, how much blood would be lost and what the effect would be. The unspoken question was answered by the anesthetist who drawled that the little girl's blood pressure was dropping alarmingly. And she was a very little girl.

I called for more suction and frantically searched the wound for the source of the pumping fluid. Suddenly I remembered that the major vessels are under a great deal of tension and tend to retract like rubber bands when they are severed. I dug my fingers deeply into the dark muscle tissue and there it was, the elusive vessel, pumping the little girl's life from her still body. I affixed another clamp and the flow stopped.

There was no time to relax and congratulate myself. I knew there was no way I could perform the delicate anastomosis, sewing the artery back together. The circulator hurried out and soon returned with the first call surgeon. Ten minutes later the vessel was repaired and beginning to clot around the sutures. The remaining lacerations were cleaned and the girl was taken to post-op.

I helped the circulating technician clean the room and prepare for the next operation, and then joined the surgeon and gas man for a cup of coffee. My thoughts were with the new surgeon who had panicked. I had been here long enough to lose all false illusions about the infallibility of doctors, but this incident had shaken me. I began to reflect on my own mortality and the old ghosts of fear of failure that I thought had been banished from my mind. Instant decisions that could mean life or death for a fellow human were part of the everyday life over here, and not just in the medical realm. The old cold sweats started to wash over me and I hastily left to see how the girl was doing. It wouldn't pay to dwell on these thoughts any longer.

The girl made a full recovery and became one of my favorites during her time on a recovery ward. I would always remember her soft doe-eyes and ready smile. The surgeon who had fled the O.R. left the 36th the same day. We never heard of him again.

One more incident occurred in that fateful two weeks that forever blighted my lofty respect for the practitioners of medicine. A Vietnamese soldier was brought in for treatment of a gunshot wound to the chest. As he waited in the pre-op hallway he was X-rayed, blood-typed and an I.V. of Ringer's lactate was started. One of the best chest men was on call and examined the terrified soldier. He ordered that the man be taken to O.R. and prepped for surgery. He would be in shortly when the casualty was stabilized.

Fifteen minutes later the anesthetist sent for the surgeon. The nurse returned and said to go ahead with the anesthesia, the doctor would be right in. The wounded recruit was put under right away and the wound prepped. Ten minutes later there was still no sign of the surgeon.

The normally quiet gas man roared at the nurse. If the surgeon didn't make an appearance within five minutes, the patient would have to be awakened and his survival would be threatened.

A minute later the nurse slipped into the room, chagrined. Meekly, she explained that the doctor was having a cup of coffee with a fellow chest specialist from another hospital who had just arrived for a visit. He had haughtily told her to have everyone hold their horses, he would be there soon enough. Besides, the patient wasn't "one of ours."

A few minutes later the procrastinating physician entered the room with a flourish. Before he could gown and glove, the soldier died. He checked the fixed pupils and stilled pulse and started out of the room. The nurse, so angry and upset that she couldn't speak, motioned the surgeon to come back. Would he try heart massage, or a heparin injection or anything?

The cutter with the golden fingers had a heart of lead. There was no sense wasting time and drugs and blood on a hopeless case, he told her. A hopeless non-American case. He exited the room, on his way to have another coffee, no doubt.

The nurse, the gas man and I looked at one another in amazement. Our shock at this callous action rendered us speechless. Perhaps the unfortunate young man would not have survived surgery. But not to exercise that option was unfathomable. More than that, it was immoral and criminal.

The surgical report signed by the doctor stated that the patient had died of irreparable damage to the heart by trauma. The chief surgeon told the three assistants and the gas man that there would be no attachments to the surgical report. Our concerns were irrelevant and unsupported. Any pursuit of the matter would be considered insubordinate and mutinous.

Sam, the gas man, gave me some good advice that dark day. It was highly spiced by some of the most unprintable language I had ever heard in an operating room, but it boiled down to changing what needed change and walking away from a truly hopeless cause and marshaling your strength for the next battle. There was much more advice exchanged that night among Sam, Mary the nurse and me. In fact, as the bottle of Dewar's finest emptied, the room filled with invectives and dire threats that needed to be expelled, but realistically had to remain unfulfilled.

For all of the bad taste left in our mouths after that dark morning's affair, we recognized that such incidents were as rare as a day without wounded. Almost all of the doctors and nurses were making heroic efforts to save lives under conditions which they had never even imagined, and even the villain of the day had never shown such behavior before, nor would he again. It was only tragic that when one of them had a bad day, it could mean a far worse day for a patient.

Chapter Thirteen

For two weeks Minh had seen little of her husband. She was aware of the increased casualty load and understood that he couldn't get away, but that understanding did little to help her disposition. They had trysted for brief moments on the rare evenings when both of them had finished work at the same time but the passion that accompanied their love was building beyond any capability to hold it in check.

And then, a miracle.

Another technician was transferred to the surgical unit, and by coincidence the casualty load diminished. On the first available night after work, I secured an overnight pass from Top and headed for the city. My bride was waiting with a hot meal and even hotter breath.

In the morning, Minh asked if I would like a child. Startled, I replied of course. She didn't say another word, just smiled contentedly with a hint of a secret at the corners of her lips.

I couldn't get a pass for the next night but ached to see my wife. I decided on a bold plan that would be repeated many times during the following months. Stuffing clothing and a pillow under the blanket, I borrowed a small stuffed monkey from a friend and arranged a sheet around it so that the stuffed toy resembled the back of my head.

Not too flattering but good enough to fool the C.Q.. Since I wasn't on call, I only had to worry about an attack on the base and the resultant red alert. I was technically A.W.O.L. and taking a whale of a chance .... but l'amour, toujours l'amour.

Minh's father had come for a visit and prepared a meal for his new son-in-law. Minh explained that her Dad had pulled out all the stops. This was going to be our wedding feast, and all I had to do was try a little of everything, burp occasionally and say "ngon lam" often.

Sounds easy, I thought. Wonder what "ngon lam" means.

The first course was a spicy soup with bean thread noodles and tiny pieces of pork and sundry spices. It was delicious, prompting a regular chorus of "ngon lams" and the obligatory burps. "Ngon lam", it seems, meant delicious.

The soup was followed by steaming bowls of rice with a mixture of vegetables resembling beet greens and okra. With a little vinegar and soy sauce added, it was savory indeed. The meat course was unlike anything I had tried before. I had prided myself in trying all types of wild game and even critters that weren't usually considered game. Opossum, muskrat, beaver, and woodchuck had graced my table in the past, but never had I seen the likes of what Suu was now offering.

The fare was long and round and most certainly some kind of giant eel. Smoked eel was quite popular along the St. Lawrence River and the Great Lakes so I was eager to try this variety. This eel, however, hadn't been smoked and wasn't exactly an eel. It was a python that Suu had bargained for at the market. It was considered a special delicacy as the big snakes were becoming rare near the villages and cities due to the food shortages caused by the war. Even song birds were eagerly trapped to supplement the meager portions of meat that were becoming rare on the table. The big snake was delicious!

The final course that night featured two kinds of meat which Suu had procured strictly for his son-in-law. The water buffalo was a bit gamey in flavor but not at all tough. The dog was delectable!

Minh was furious with her father for serving dog and told him so. That's for the North Vietnamese, she complained. She was afraid of giving her husband the wrong impression. Mortified, she tried to explain that only the northerners who came down in 1955 ate dog anymore. Her father was just having his little joke.

I nodded my understanding, burped loudly and said, "ngon lam."

Suu roared his approval and collapsed in laughter.

Humiliated now, Minh chased us out of the house and sullenly cleaned up. I had been about to tell my blushing bride that I understood, but was curious about how many northerners were in town since there were so many farmers coming to market each day with fat puppies in bamboo baskets over their shoulders. One look at her face convinced me that this was not the time for a frivolous remark.

Suu and I sat down outside on the porch and talked, neither understanding what the other said, and neither caring. We communicated using gestures, pantomiming the hot day and cool evening, the good meal and an embarrassed Minh. Eventually Suu threw in a phrase in French and I pounced on it. My high school and college French returned far better than I dared expect and suddenly we could really understand one another. A bit later Minh joined us and shortly, half the neighborhood was squatting around the front porch chatting amiably with the newly-weds. It was another memory I would cherish for the rest of my life.

Suu left for Binh Phuoc in the morning to visit the rest of his family. He took a letter and some money for Thu and Tri and promised to bring them up for a visit upon his return. This could prove to be a dangerous move should the Vietcong return, since they were known for using children to force parents into providing assistance, but Minh was willing to take the chance. She missed her children and wanted me to meet them.

For the next few weeks there were few casualties and I slipped away frequently to spend the night with Minh. On one special Sunday she convinced me to go to the large Catholic church in the city. She had never been inside and was curious to see some of the strange rites that she had heard about. I hesitated, uncomfortable about entering after not attending Mass for so long, but Minh's persistence wore me down.

The church was simply furnished but looked very much like any Catholic church I had ever been in back in the world. The ornately carved altar faced the congregation and statues of Jesus and the Virgin Mary flanked a small side altar. The only difference which was readily apparent was the seating arrangement. Men and boys sat on one side of the center aisle, women and girls on the other. When responses to the priest's songs and chants were sung, the congregation alternated, with the sweet, soft voices of the women answered by the rich tenor offerings of the men. The result was a breathtaking experience.

Tonal in nature, the Vietnamese language uses words with several different meanings, depending on how they are pronounced. The result is a lilting, sing-song dialect. When sung, especially with the alternating voices in church, the effects are hypnotic.

True to her nature, Minh went against the grain and sat in the back beside her husband, drawing icy stares of disapproval.

When the Mass ended we had intended to leave quickly, but as we went outside we were stopped by one of the parishioners.

"You are the first American I have ever seen in our church," he said. "Not only that, you even joined in the singing. I was only sorry that you did not take communion with us. Even so, I would like you both to come to my home for some tea and a little food. I would like to ask you about America."

As Minh translated, I was preoccupied. Something had happened in the church. It may have been the realization that here were people who had been at war for over a thousand years, suffered unbelievable hardships, and even now were in the throes of a deadly conflict, but still attended Mass, prayed to God and maintained a spirit of hope. As I struggled with these churning thoughts and emotions I became aware of Minh tugging at my arm. I smiled and apologized, but remained distracted.

Before we could leave with our host-to-be, dozens of church-goers crowded around, asking questions and beaming with open, smiling faces. When Minh explained that she was a Buddhist and I was her Catholic husband, the people pressed even closer. Most of the Americans that they encountered were certainly not interested in marrying a Vietnamese girl and were more apt to be seen on the bar streets than in church.

As Minh tried to translate for me, I felt a wave of sorrow and guilt wash over me. I was worse than the drunks and abusers of these people. Many of them had likely never known God, and as bad as their actions might be, they were more blameless than one who had known God's word and then rejected it. Once again, Minh had provided the impetus for me to regain some sanity. What a very precious jewel I had found.

We followed the old man to his home for some tea. He lived in a tiny shack on stilts over a foul smelling marsh. The shack was one of hundreds jammed together on the outskirts of the city. They were constructed of old wood scraps, bamboo, palm fronds and anything else that could be used to keep out the wind and rain. Most of the people who lived here were refugees from the north. Some had come from Danang and the Central Highlands, others from North Vietnam, but they all had two things in common -- no money and a

113

hope of escaping the communists.

The only land available for building was the marshy area which flooded each spring. Stilt houses solved this problem, but created many others. The lack of sanitary facilities and good drinking water kept any number of nasty diseases around. With no money for doctors or medicine, most of the children had open sores and showed signs of malnutrition. Scattered here and there were racks of drying fish. Some were salted, most were not. In the air there was a constant drone from dozens of kinds of flies. In the country, garbage and human waste could be spread on the fields for fertilizer. Here, everything was thrown beneath the houses.

As I followed Minh and our host into his shack, I considered the contrast with the neat streets and homes in most of Vung Tau. I had thought that those streets spoke of the poverty of this war-torn country, but this was almost beyond comprehension. Inside the one-room house there was little in the way of furnishings. There was a small three-legged table with two broken chairs on one side of the room and four rolled-up sleeping mats in the corner. A small screened cabinet to deter the voracious roaches and rats completed the inventory of furniture.

The gracious old gentleman brought out a warm can of Coca-Cola for his guests to share. Unwilling to take his last can, we refused, and quickly wished we hadn't. Our host produced two plastic cups and poured water into each, offering a drink. We knew better than to drink the water, but after refusing the Coke had little choice without seriously offending the man. As we nervously sipped our drinks the old man started a tiny one-burner kerosene stove and prepared a spare meal of rice and greens. He apologized for being out of any kind of sauce to season the food. When his back was turned, both of us managed to pour our water into a crack in the floor.

As we ate he explained that his wife and two daughters had been killed by bombs while walking to the nearby village where his sister lived. His two teen-age sons had been conscripted into the army and he had fled south to Vung Tau to live with a cousin. He hadn't been able to find his cousin but a kindly man had invited him to move in here with his small family. He was treated as an uncle to the couple's small son and did not have to search for work. He related that his pride would not allow him to live there without providing

114

something, and so he went to the river twice a week to gather reeds from which he wove baskets for sale at the market. His adopted family happened to be away today, he told us, or they would have been overjoyed to share a meal and some conversation with two young people so obviously in love.

After a couple of hours of talk the old man noticeably tired. We said our good-byes and thanked him for the warm hospitality. As we made our way back to town we both began to speak at once.

"Minhoi," I asked quietly, "is everyone here so open and generous? He had literally nothing, but he shared it with us without hesitation. I'm so humbled."

"Well, most people will share with a stranger just as he did," Minh responded. "We are all so used to being poor that it makes no difference who comes to call. It would be disrespectful to turn someone away."

"But he sought us out and invited us without our coming to his door or asking for anything."

"Well, I guess he was lonely and wanted to meet an American."

"Well yourself," I continued. "I don't know if I will ever understand this country and the people here. Last week a little boy was killed when he tried to put a bomb in a bar where a group of G.I.'s were dancing. Today, a dirt-poor old man invites us in to share the last bit of food he has in the house. And every night you tell me not to talk too loudly because the walls have ears, but then we walk downtown hand in hand and talk with everyone we meet. I just don't get it!"

Minh smiled and kept silent. This American she had married kept pointing out so many paradoxes in her country and even she couldn't understand some of them. What a world! Maybe as we lived longer together and our understanding of each other's language improved, some of these larger truths would make sense. She was sure of one thing -- we would live together longer, and we would be happy -- if only we could get more time together now!

A week after meeting the old man from Binh Dinh, I hatched a little plot with a fellow medic. We would round up some outdated medicine and supplies and take them down to the stilt town for distribution. It was well known that penicillin sometimes became outdated and unusable. Officially it was destined for the incinerator, but usually found its way to the black market where a certain nurse and her boyfriend sold it for thousands of dollars.

The army maintained that most black market supplies ultimately wound up in enemy hands. Bob and I had no such designs, but realized that if we were caught in our humanitarian endeavor, the penalty would be the same -- a court martial and Long Binh Stockade, or worse.

Be that as it may, we collected the goods along with a generous supply of fruit and foodstuffs from the mess hall and borrowed one of the cracker box ambulances. Flashing a good facsimile of a pass at the main gate, we nervously drove down the road to the city.

Leaving the far side of the city we bounced onto the rutted dirt road leading to stilt-town, as it was called. Rounding the first bend we nearly collided with two jeeps that were parked in the middle of the narrow road. Standing beside the jeeps were six M.P.'s. They were not smiling.

I knew that once the back door of the ambulance was opened, another door would close on us. I kept the engine running and hoped that my brain would do likewise. I didn't recognize any of the M.P.'s so the clandestine shot angle was out.

What next? O.K., it would have to be the emergency run gambit. Without giving the military policemen a chance to speak, I brusquely asked them to remove the vehicles and let us pass. We had a pick-up to make at stilt-town. It wasn't life or death but we wanted to get back before dark and go drinking.

No reaction. Then a scowl, as a beefy hand was thrust into the cab.

"Are you reaching for my driver's license or a ten spot?" I queried, as little beads of sweat began their tell-tale excursion down my forehead, around my nose and into the corners of my mouth.

So, I thought, this is what prison tastes like. Salty!

"You're some joker, Doc," growled the first M.P.. "Don't you recognize me? You gave me a shot last month and some good advice. Geez, Doc, I thought you guys were supposed to be smart."

"Oh Yeah," laughed a very sweaty medic. "I didn't recognize you with your pants on."

It was an old joke but it broke the tension. As we were about to continue on I asked why the road block.

"Oh, there was some V.C. activity here last night and the road isn't secure yet. But you go ahead. Medical personnel are exceptions."

Out of the frying pan, I thought. Bob and I didn't speak until we reached the village safely. We were barely on the outskirts of the city, but might as well have been deep in the jungle. The V.C. were everywhere and often seemed to strike on a whim. Medical personnel were certainly not exceptions to them.

We tried to unload quickly but were soon engulfed by women and crying babies who needed to see a "bacsi", or doctor. The ambulance did have a few drawbacks. We opened a mini-clinic and soon were giving shots and dressing sores. A number of older people sounded like they had tuberculosis or some other deadly malady.

Just before dark we finished up the simple treatments and gave the rest of the supplies to the old man, sure that he would make good use of them. Tears glistened in his eyes as he thanked the medics over and over.

Thank you, grandfather, I thought. You have given me far more than I have given to you. God be with you.

The roadblock was gone as we approached the city. In the distance there were muffled shots and a loud explosion. Driving recklessly now, as darkness fell, we sped through the city and noted with alarm that the streets were deserted.

"This doesn't look good, Bob."

"Any bright ideas, Doc?"

"You bet. We had better "di-di mau" back to the base. That claxon sure sounds like they're under a red alert. And if they are, the gates will be sealed, even to an ambulance."

And sealed they were.

There was no hope of entering via the main gate. We had just two choices -- go back to town and hole up and probably face a court martial, or try to find another way in.

We had heard that there were many gates in the perimeter fence which enclosed the airfield and hospital, but neither of us had had any occasion to use them. We followed an overgrown track around the west side of the airfield until we spotted a light. It was a search light mounted on a truck. It was also behind the perimeter fence, where two guards were casting a suspicious eye towards us. We followed the track up to the gate and hailed the guards.

"What the Hell are you boys doing out there?" they responded.

"Don't you know we've been on a red alert since six o'clock? You'd better get your butts back to the main gate with your casualties on the double."

"Well, we're trying, but we got twisted around a bit. Can you let us in here so we can get to the hospital a little quicker?"

"Sorry, fellows. We couldn't even if we wanted to. The gate is locked and we don't have a key. You'd better head for the main gate. Oh, by the way, don't go off that track. There are mines planted outside the second row of barbed wire."

We turned the ambulance around and headed along its backtrack. As we turned onto the dirt road leading back to town, an old Papa-san appeared driving a pony cart. Two very worried medics hailed the horse-drawn taxi.

"Hey Papa-san, is there any way to get onto the base without going all the way around to the main gate?"

"Hey yourself, G.I., take that road," he said, pointing to the east.

We scrambled back into our very conspicuous vehicle and drove east as fast as we could. The road was rough but there was no grass growing in it. A good sign, perhaps, that it was well used? We drove half a mile and noticed a narrow track leading from the road to the perimeter fence. At the end of the track was a gate. An open gate, with no guards in sight.

We looked at each other in astonishment. Could we be so lucky, or was it a trap? It was impossible to believe that an unguarded gate would be left open. An explosion and bright light from the airfield made up our minds. With hearts pounding and fists clenched tightly, we accelerated along the grassy track and through the gate. We continued at breakneck speed until we hit a good dirt road. The hospital soon came into view and we wheeled into the helipad area. We were never challenged.

I turned to Bob and, giddy with emotion, informed him that I had just set a new record for the Guiness Book -- the most Hail Mary's ever said by one person in ten minutes!

As we stepped into the hootch a nurse came trotting down the company street in her green scrub suit.

Oh oh, I thought, there must be trouble. As I watched, she ducked into the bomb shelter on the side of the hootch. Curious, Bob and I followed. In the sand-bagged bunker a party was in progress. Half a dozen rockets had hit the base since six o'clock but there had been no casualties. It was still party time. The wandering medics joined the party and were soon well on our way to unwinding from the long night.

The next day Bob reported the open gate, being careful not to reveal the circumstances of how it was discovered. Top said he would check it out with the airfield security people and that was the end of it. From then on, the gate was locked and guarded, but I always wondered how the driver of that cart had known about the gate.

The red alert was called off at noon the following day, but nerves remained on edge for a week. A large oil tank had been hit and the thick black smoke it spewed into the air for a week was a constant reminder of the accuracy of the mortar crew. During that week all civilian employees went through another security check. All passed. Following the check, the post barber was caught with a bomb in his bag. Every man who had felt the barber's razor at this throat while being shaved took a deep breath.

The combination of the barber's arrest and the recent alert triggered a most unfortunate incident. A recently-arrived cook was pulling guard duty one evening when he spotted a young Vietnamese man running along the company street. As the man approached the gate the sentry shouted for him to halt. Not hearing or not understanding, the man continued to run. The cook fired a burst from his M-14 automatic rifle and a slug tore through the man's chest. He was taken to the O.R. and prepped immediately.

I was the circulating technician and was asked by the surgeon to take some slides of the operation for his files. Pictures in the O.R. were usually prohibited but it was not rare for a doctor to make such a request. In this case the series of pictures would help to record a new procedure for the surgeon.

In the course of the operation the full story of the shooting emerged. The civilian was a fourteen year old boy who worked at the mess hall. He had worked late and was hurrying to get to the main gate before dark. He spoke no English and would not have understood a shout to "halt".

The cook had forgotten the words, "dung lai" which were printed on a card he had received when he arrived in-country. A few basic phrases which could save a man's life were on the card, but men seldom bothered to learn them.

Young Nguyen Van Cao lost the use of this right arm because he had been in a hurry, and because he hadn't learned any English, and because a scared young cook hadn't learned any Vietnamese, and because ......

From the tragic to the sublime -- my emotions whipsawed back and forth on a daily basis -- and sometimes hourly. Shortly after the shooting, I was on my way downtown again to see Minh. She was my only link to sanity in these trying days. Our night was filled with passion, shutting out the insane world around us. I knew I would never make the eleven o'clock curfew at the main gate and forgot that I didn't have an overnight pass. All in all, a very costly lapse in memory.

With a seven-thirty deadline for a special surgical case, I arose at five-thirty and found a cyclo driver. When I reached the base I headed straight for the hootch to change. Bob met me at the door with a grim face. The C.Q. had marked three men absent without leave last night, and I was one of them.

With a sinking heart I made for the orderly room. Top wasn't there, but the new company commander was. The captain had been transferred and his replacement was a first lieutenant in the 101st Airborne, a Screaming Eagle who had been grounded. He was an unhappy trooper and was about to spread the grief around.

I said good morning and made a lame excuse for coming by so early. The flightless eagle hadn't yet read the night log. I left the room and headed for the latrine. From there I could watch the orderly room without being observed.

In a few minutes the lieutenant left the building, heading for the mess hall. I scurried back to the orderly room and caught the day clerk just as he was bringing the duty roster and night report to the commander's office.

The clerk had been in the company almost a year and was just counting the days until he rotated back to the world. I had seen him carrying his short stick with the days marked off and spent some time talking with him. Could he be counted on?

There was only one way to find out.

The direct approach worked and soon the altered night report, sans one relieved medic's name, was on the lieutenant's desk.

Details, I chuckled to myself, as I walked to the showers. I had learned long ago that paying attention to the slightest details made the difference in coming home with a big buck or eating track soup. Details here could mean the difference between a sentence at the infamous Long Binh Prison and a happy reunion with my wife. I would have to be much more careful in the future.

Chapter Fourteen

War continued to chew up the countryside and the strife-weary inhabitants trying to make a living there. Everyday, as Minh traveled to the army base, she saw the effects of the growing flood of refugees. More and more of her countrymen were fleeing the escalating bombing in the north and moving to the more secure coastal zone.

Vung Tau, the peaceful seaside resort, was becoming a city overrun with refugees. With no homes or jobs, these displaced persons strained the already limited facilities and threatened to destroy the very fabric of peace which they were seeking. Competition for the most menial of jobs suddenly erupted into violent confrontations as the new arrivals vied with long-time residents for a few "dong", just enough money to buy a day's food. Thievery and muggings, while not commonplace, increased in frequency. Young girls were encouraged by their desperate families to seek work in the tawdry bars and massage parlors, establishments that sprang up as more American G.I.'s arrived.

An even more tangible consequence of the increased fighting was the steadily growing number of beggars on the streets. Increasingly, their numbers included disabled veterans and maimed civilians. There was a small government office on Le Loi street which served as a veteran's outreach center. For block after block along this street there were literally dozens of double amputees pushing their legless bodies along on modified skateboards. Young men with no arms were guiding blind ex-soldiers down the street.

Minh would see in one day more suffering kinsmen than she would have encountered in five years back in the Delta. As she rode to the base she prayed each day that the Americans would soon prevail and help her poor country to end the war. She came to believe that only through a Supreme Being's intervention would her country's travails come to a halt. She was also well aware that her neighbors, and indeed, all of the townsfolk, were eager to see the Americans win and then leave the country.

As much as these allies were needed and respected for their fighting abilities and material aid, they were also feared and despised. They provided so much military and medical assistance and then turned around and made whores of the young women and shabbily treated the rest of the populace. She had never read "The Ugly American", but it could have been written about their presence in Vietnam.

Her people were generally demure and respectful of privacy and politeness. The Americans were loud, overbearing and boorish. They were also, for the most part, prejudiced against the smaller, yellow-skinned inhabitants of this land.

Not a day went by when cans and stones and other missiles were not hurled at pedestrians and shopkeepers by G.I.'s passing in trucks and jeeps. Livestock was shot with callous disregard and atrocities were perpetrated by these fine young men who were here to help repel the communist threat. Minh knew that not all of these tall, young soldiers acted in such a manner, but sometimes it was difficult to separate the wheat from the chaff. Black, White or Hispanic -- there was no single racial group which could be singled out for a greater contribution to these actions.

In sorting out her thoughts, she gained a little insight into the problem American soldiers had distinguishing Vietcong from peaceful villager. She could understand the terrible stress the allies must feel when the enemy looked identical to friendly forces and civilians. Small wonder that mistakes were made.

Every day brought new stories of outrageous behavior to spur the gossip of the women as they worked at the laundry. Minh knew that most of the stories were true, and that there were other actions which never came to light that might be more heinous than those being discussed. Nevertheless, she felt somehow obligated to defend the Americans who were here risking their lives for purposes which many of them found nebulous, at best. She spent many an hour sharing her views with her co-workers, and not finding much support. The "big picture" of American help was so easily overshadowed by the many incidents of local mistreatment that were continually in front of them.

One day, as she was assisting with bandaging on a ward filled with newly arrived Vietnamese casualties, she overheard a conversation that sent chills up her spine. A man was describing the massacre of an entire village. The story was horrible, and became unbelievable when the man stated that the village had been systematically slaughtered by Americans!

Minh refused to believe it. This had to be more propaganda spread by the V.C. to discredit the allies. As she listened further she felt herself becoming ill - more from the realization that the story might be true than from the gory details. That night she somberly told me what she had heard.

I was quiet for a long time, and then confided that I had heard the same story a few days earlier from a G.I. who had recently transferred to the base. He didn't have the full details but the gist was the same.

Neither of us could fully comprehend the savagery of such an action. We argued over the state of mind that could induce such a horrendous crime. Surely thousands, or tens of thousands of soldiers had been under stress and seen their buddies crippled and killed, and been powerless to do anything about it. But they didn't abandon all shreds of human decency and morality to massacre women, children and infants. And of course it was virtually impossible to tell the enemy, the Viet Cong, from peace-loving farmers and merchants, but when there are no weapons being fired and no resistance -- what possible justification could there be for such murderous actions? The fact that such incidents had occurred in other wars in other times did nothing to justify them now.

Much later, the story of the massacre at My Lai would become public. Americans and Vietnamese and citizens of the world would be shocked and saddened. One could imagine the French saying, "C'est la Guerre!" and hear the echoes of "War is Hell."

If only the writers of history books and the makers of movies could somehow convey the real import of those fine, too-distant phrases, I thought. If only politicians and generals could really feel the lifeblood draining from the victims of these "Little Hells." And of course, if only madmen and power-hungry dictators could forego their evil ambitions so that just men the world over would not be forced to make the decisions to go to war to stop them!

We talked long and often of these things and of peace and life beyond war. We always came to the same conclusion -- the only hope for peace was through prayer. A thousand years of fighting in this little corner of the world had resolved nothing!

In an infrequent lull on a rainy Sunday, the medic and the Mama-san made a dash for sanity. We met at the market square and walked to the theater. Minh wanted to show off the pride of the town. The local opera company was staging one of her favorite plays and two nationally known stars from the Saigon National Opera Company were singing the leads.

I once attended a touring opera performance in Syracuse and had been to some concerts by well known American opera singers in the diminutive Boathouse Summer Theater in Schroon Lake, but this would be a very different cultural event.

There were no black ties and evening dresses in evidence as we entered the theater. Baggy trousers and lightweight, short-sleeved shirts were the norm. In the lobby we bought a program, fan and two sticks of sugar cane. The program and sugar cane were nice to have, but the fan was essential. The heat and humidity in the crowded theater was outrageous.

The theater seated well over a thousand patrons and was packed to the aisles. The double-tiered balconies were festooned with posters of the opera stars and every seat was taken. The orchestra consisted of a dozen musicians with several kinds of guitars, drums and clarinet-like woodwinds.

Minh spotted two vacant seats on the lower level halfway to the stage. As we made our way through the crowd, I noticed that I was the only Caucasian in the theater. I was becoming accustomed to that distinction in some parts of the city, but jammed in the center of this crowd with the nearest exit hundreds of tightly-packed bodies away, I felt uneasy, even a bit claustrophobic.

The lights were still up and the orchestra was playing a sprightly overture as I looked around. I felt like a minnow in a school of hungry bass. It seemed that every eye in the place was on me. Noticing my discomfort, Minh tried to put me at ease. She spoke rapidly to the people beside her and a dozen voices burst into laughter. I didn't understand a word, but figured that it must have been dirty to evoke such a raucous response.

Soon the lights dimmed and the opera commenced. One of the most beautiful woman I had ever seen crossed the stage, and in a

125

voice which matched her beauty, began the opening aria. The stage was soon filled with heavily made-up actors wearing ornate costumes signifying the roles they were playing. Backdrop scenery was minimal but the costumes and dancing created the illusion of a fully decorated set.

As Minh explained the story I became captivated by the music. The lead voices were magnificent. Their range and ability to sustain tones through long, involved vibratos were worthy of their star billing.

As the lights came up for the first intermission, a shower of fine shavings rained down on Minh's head. Turning around, I received the same. Looking up, we spied two young men tearing apart cigarettes and spraying them down from the edge of the balcony. Ignoring this purposeful shower, I settled in to eat my sweet "mia", sugar cane, as inconspicuously as possible. I was sure that with this many people in the theater, some were certain to be V.C., and I wanted no trouble.

Once more the shower of tobacco began to fall on us, but this time Minh had had enough. She stood up in the middle of the crowd, and shaking her fist, shouted a stream of curses in a most conspicuous voice. I recognized enough of the words to bring a good old fashioned blush to my cheeks. I half expected to see the culprits leap from the balcony with flashing daggers. Instead, the men nearest Minh echoed her words and added a few of their own. There was a scattering of applause and laughter and the balcony creeps sat down and weren't heard from again.

As marvelous as the opera was, I found it hard to concentrate for the remainder of the performance. After the final curtain and encores, I was anxious to get to the street and grab a breath of fresh air. My hopes were dashed when Minh collared me and began slicing her way forward towards the stage.

Oh Lord, I thought, what now?

A few minutes later I was being introduced to the leader of the orchestra, an old friend of Minh's. He took us backstage to meet some of the local cast. As we chatted, out came Kim Mai. Minh boldly said hello and introduced her husband, the idiot standing behind her with his mouth open, drooling. The star shook my hand and Minh laughingly told her that I would never wash that hand again. I understood the remark, of course, and promptly blushed again.

What a bothersome habit, I thought.

Kim Mai graciously spoke with us for a few more minutes before she left for the dressing room. On our way out, Minh explained that this star in Vietnam was the equivalent of Elvis Presley or Connie Francis in the United States.

I had never been impressed with movie stars or celebrities but realized what a thrill this had been for Minh. As I learned later, she had never been impressed by celebrities either, but had overcome her natural reticence to give me the chance to see stars. More and more we began to realize just how much we had in common.

A week after the opera, Suu came to town with Minh's children. I met them on their first night in town and fell in love with them. Tri was very reserved around this strange man with the hairy legs, but Thu took to me right away.

Minh and Suu were delighted. There was enough money now to find a good sitter and Minh made up her mind that she would not be separated from the children again. In the morning there would be time to put the word out that she was looking for a good, responsible baby-sitter and would pay well.

As Minh sat there with her husband and her father, watching the children play on the floor, her contentment was marred by a sudden chill, evoking a shudder. A black thought of danger swept through her mind and departed as quickly as it had appeared. She had felt this way in the past and the feeling had never betrayed her. Bad news was on the way!

Minh had foretold her Aunt's torture and a close friend's death with uncanny accuracy. Now she was faced with this unbidden prescience again, but this time there was no hint of the nature of the trouble, or who it would befall.

As I left for the base to make the eleven o'clock curfew, Minh felt her face flush and her hair stand up straight. Oh no, she thought, please don't let it be him.

The streets were really not safe for a lone G.I. at night but thus far I had not had a problem finding a ride back to base. On lucky evenings I had caught a deuce and a half army truck returning with other soldiers and saved cyclo fare or a long walk along the lonely dirt road.

Tonight, Minh accompanied me to the main street where the

trucks made their runs. She was scared and didn't want to let me out of her sight. She waited until an empty lambretta appeared and hailed it for me. As I disappeared into the darkness, she whispered a prayer to Buddha to be with me. Walking back to the house, she felt the sense of foreboding return.

In the morning, upon reaching the base, Minh rushed to my hootch. Oh God, she prayed, let him be alright. Barging in, letting the screen door slam behind her, she awakened half a dozen cranky sleepers. Ignoring their mumbled threats she hurried to the far end of the hootch and looked into the upper bunk where her husband slept.

It was empty!

The blanket was drawn tight and it appeared that no one had slept there during the night. A lump rose in her throat and she thought that she would scream. Before a sound could escape her, the door opened and in walked her husband, still dripping from the shower. Relieved, and angry and upset, she punched me on the shoulder.

"Don't ever do that again," she said, and then walked out the door.

I sure won't, I thought. I wonder what I'm not supposed to do.

Minh returned home that night to find her father talking with a potential sitter. The woman seemed competent and intelligent and was hired on the spot. Suu had taken a job near Baria and would be leaving the next day. Minh was sad to see him go. Her Dad had always been her hero and she was in such good spirits when he was around. Well, at least her children were here now, and she could finally provide for them. The next step was to start on the paperwork necessary to leave Vietnam with her medic.

On the first day at work with her children ensconced with the sitter, Minh felt a sense of uneasiness. She tried to pass it off as a natural worry about her childrens care, but she knew deep down that this was something else. Something menacing.

The malaise remained with her all day. It didn't help that I was busy in surgery and couldn't get free even to say hi. She left work a little early and stopped to buy a sandwich just outside the main gate. After one bite she gagged and started to vomit. The black vision was in her mind again. She hurriedly found a cyclo and urged the driver to get her home with all haste. She had seen her children in the black thoughts and panicked.

The cyclo screeched to a halt outside the alley leading to her house. Minh threw some money to the driver and raced along the narrow lane. Before reaching the house she heard someone call her name.

There, beside a pool of dirty water, were her precious little darlings, soaking wet and covered with mud from head to toe. The sitter was scolding them for disobeying, while the children laughed and got dirtier. Relieved, Minh grabbed them in her arms, bade good night to the sitter and started for the house. Approaching the door, she was startled to see a man leaning against the door frame. He smiled at her and she recognized him right away. He had been in the woods in Baria the night she had been taken by the Vietcong. What could he be doing here in the daylight?

Her unspoken question was answered immediately.

"You have been difficult to locate," the man declared, flashing a sardonic smile.

Minh's heart sank and her blood ran cold. This was what she had been warned of. She had nearly forgotten that long ago promise that they would search her out when the time was right.

"We know that you are now a trusted employee and will have no trouble getting information for us. Do you have anything to say?"

Minh thought quickly. If she refused to help, her children were in terrible jeopardy, but if she agreed, and didn't follow through, both she and the children would be in mortal peril. With a smile, she asked the man into the house. Over a cup of tea she promised to help, though she didn't know what a lowly housemaid could learn for them.

The man quietly explained that she should keep track of the number of wounded and the numbers of medical personnel that transferred in and out. Nothing complicated, he related. Just a few basic facts that would be added to many others that more people were gathering for him.

Minh agreed to do as she was told and asked how long before the information was needed. She was told that he would return in two weeks. As the man made to leave, he picked Tri up and playfully swung him between his legs. When he put him down, his hands lingered for a moment on Tri's little neck.

The meaning was clear.

And then the soft-spoken intruder was gone, into the night. Minh collapsed weakly onto the bed.

The next day was Sunday. We had planned to take the children to the beach if I could change a call shift with someone. Minh debated whether she should tell of the visit by the Vietcong. In her heart she knew that she could never help the communists in even the slightest way, but she had to play along with them for the time being. She thought of feeding them false information, but decided that if they really had other sources of intelligence and detected her deception, the consequences would be dire. Her head was dizzy with the enormity of the predicament.

The sound of feet shuffling on the concrete porch brought Minh to instant alert. It was only me, sitting on the bench and removing my shoes. I came in and unloaded a sack full of goodies from the base exchange. My smile vanished as Minh filled me in on the night visitor and his request. Would we never be free of these threats to our future, we wondered?

Walking to the main road, we discussed what alternatives lay before us. Nothing seemed viable. Hailing a lambretta, we rode to the beach in silence, each trying to think of an answer to the dilemma.

At the beach, Minh made her decision. The children would have to go back to her mother's for awhile and she would have to move again. This time she would be extra cautious going to and from work. It was just possible that her information was of such little consequence that they would not make much of an effort to search for her again. She hoped they didn't know about me, but that seemed unrealistic.

The danger and nagging sense of hopelessness was beginning to spread out like a spider web, threatening to ensnare the people she loved the most. She was well aware that her best recourse was to quit her job and move back to the Delta, but her safety mattered little if she couldn't be with her husband.

With Lieng's help, Minh arranged for two days off to take her children down to her mother's home. She didn't elaborate on the problems she was facing, but told them that the children were in danger if they stayed in Vung Tau. She would be back to visit as often as she could. Maybe in a few months the situation would change. Her mother and sisters understood and happily accepted the little ones back. Returning to Vung Tau, Minh descended into a deep funk.

The following day at work, she stopped by to talk with Lieng. Her friend had met an American who worked in the supply tent and was seriously thinking of marrying him. When she heard Minh's story of the second visit by the V.C., she knew that her friends days at the 36th were numbered. There was little doubt that the Vietcong would find her again when they wished to. Lieng's fiancee had some connections with private American engineering companies who might be able to find a job for her. In the meantime, Minh would have to find a new place to live.

It was too dangerous to ask too many people to help find an apartment or house since it was impossible to tell who might be under the influence of the Vietcong. After two days of judicious searching, she found a small, two room apartment. It was located in a crowded refugee-packed district a short distance from the main road leading to the base. Its most attractive feature was a stout masonry wall separating the rooms from the rest of the squat building. The back door could be reached through a narrow alley, offering a bit of extra privacy. As Minh looked around at the spare furnishings and barred window, she nodded in satisfaction. This would do for the time being. This would have to do!

For the next week I tried to convince Minh to leave the 36th Evac. and take a job with Pacific Architects and Engineers. I knew that it would mean we would see precious little of each other, but her safety was impossibly compromised if she remained working at the hospital. Though I tried my best, the water buffalo-stubbornness was more than I could shake.

Minh had made up her mind to stay with the hospital regardless of the consequences. She honestly believed that by keeping her eyes open and varying her routes home each day she could elude the V.C. in their search for her. On the surface she maintained a brave front, but deep in her heart she was afraid that all her bravado and care would count for nothing when the Vietcong really wanted to find her.

So be it, she thought. If I must be apart from my children for awhile, at least I can remain near my husband. Nothing can keep us apart. Nothing!

Chapter Fifteen

The temperature hit 95 degrees by 11:00 A.M. on the first day of December. The heat wave was unusual for this date in Vung Tau, but not unheard of. As the surgical team left the operating room and crossed the compound to the mess hall, the topic of conversation was the oppressive heat and humidity which had been holding the hospital captive for over a week. The only air conditioning on the base was in the O.R., and it seemed to break down once a day. The wards were much worse off, cooled by fans which only stirred the heat and redirected it.

The patients were hardest hit by the sweltering weather. Bed sores and heat rashes raced out of control, further complicating their recovery. Nurses and aides worked through row after row of cots, changing dressings and dispensing medications. This chore soon went beyond drudgery. Because the dressings and wounds were so quickly contaminated by perspiration, they required more frequent changing, and this was a task dreaded by patient and nurse alike.

Dressings and bandages adhered snugly to caked blood and healing flesh. The process of re-dressing wounds, which were so often massive in extent, caused excruciating pain. Even the most battle-hardened warrior came to dread the daily routine. Watching a tough young man cry and hearing him scream had a profound effect on the nursing staff. Most of them had been ready to deal with the physical wounds, but few were prepared for the debilitating effects of treating a seemingly endless procession of trauma cases. Trauma which had been inflicted by the intentional efforts of fellow human beings. Any break from the trauma cases was most welcome.

In the mess hall that day, Captain Ibach was the center of attention. "We are going to have an opportunity today," he announced excitedly, "to perform an operation which most surgeons only dream of. This afternoon we will receive Siamese Twins.

132

They are about a year old and require separation to afford them any chance of survival. Let's all pray that we don't get a load of casualties today. This will be an historic moment in the annals of the U.S. Medical Corps."

Word of the unusual operation spread like wildfire. All of the off-duty surgical staff gathered at the hospital in hopes of glimpsing the hapless twins. I was chosen as a circulating technician for the procedure. The excitement which had been building reached a crescendo when the chopper settled on the helipad and the twins came into view. Rumors of how and where they were joined had been flying all day. As the little pair was lifted from their cradle, one of the nurses exclaimed that they must have a shared liver since they appeared jaundiced. When it was pointed out to her that the yellow cast to their faces was a pretty natural hue, since they were Vietnamese, her face took on a much redder color.

In the operating room, Captain Ibach was assisted by two surgeons and two scrub nurses. Three circulating technicians were on hand to provide equipment and supplies, and attend to any unforeseen needs that might arise. Before the procedure started one of the surgeons handed a 35 mm camera to me and asked if I could take pictures of the operation. The Leica was unfamiliar to me but a few minutes of instruction gave me enough of the basics to proceed.

Finally, the twins were rolled in and lifted to the table. The little brother and sister were groggy from the pre-medication but still alert enough to smile and gurgle, completely captivating their audience.

The children were joined at the chest and abdomen, sharing a common liver, spleen and other organs. The surgeons were faced with a difficult decision. Since the organs could not be divided, the twin receiving them would have a chance for survival. The other would not.

The children's parents had already made the hardest decision, to separate the twins at all costs. Now it was up to the doctors to evaluate the strongest child and carry out the procedure. The surgical staff had been making life and death calls for months, but this was a different situation. This was the difference between pre-meditation and a spur of the moment choice. This was agony.

At last it was decided to give both organs to the boy, who was larger and stronger. The actual operation was far from routine but

133

remarkably uncomplicated. Throughout the procedure I snapped shot after shot. When the operation was over there were two pictures remaining on the roll of 36 exposures. I used them as the twins were placed in separate cradles for the first time in their short lives.

The mood in the room after the successful operation was subdued. Everyone was aware that only one of the twins could live. It was in this atmosphere that I re-wound the film and opened the back of the camera.

It was empty!

The once in a lifetime pictures would never materialize. The surgeon was livid. He began a vicious tirade, directed against the unlucky photographer. It is likely that blows would have resulted but for the hasty intervention of Captain Ibach, who wisely pointed out the obvious. I had been unfamiliar with the touch of the camera and could not have been able to feel the lack of film. The doctor should have checked to be sure it was loaded. Fortunately for all concerned, a nurse had also been taking slides and her camera had been loaded. After apologies all around, the team left for post-op where the twins would be resting.

During the night the little girl died. Her brother would recover and be transferred to a hospital in Saigon. None of the surgical team would ever hear of him again.

By mid-December I was wondering if there would ever be a routine to settle into. Elective surgery and fresh casualties continued at a frightening pace. Rocket attacks at night were no longer predictable. Sometimes three or four days would pass without a mortar or rocket round slamming in, and then there would be attacks for five nights in a row. The time of day when a round might explode also changed. While the night brought two to four shells, the daytime attacks were almost always limited to one or two rounds. Multiple shots were too easy to trace and return fire could be directed with deadly accuracy. Still, the V.C. were able to direct fire into the base almost at will, providing that their attacks were brief.

Under constant pressure, the men in hootch 11 were beginning to form friendships at last. Sharing the common workload and facing the same daily tensions finally created a bond among us. More than any other factor though, was the arrival of the new commanding officer. His background with the 101st Airborne and his general dislike for many of the un-military attitudes and activities of the medical personnel produced a mutual animosity. He became the common enemy that so often brings men together.

The captain rode his new charges hard. He assigned the medical personnel to numerous extraneous duties. When we were off-duty in the hospital he put us on details filling and replacing sandbags. We were given shifts on guard duty and at the motor pool. Technicians' normal duties included scrubbing down the floors, walls and equipment in the operating rooms, pre-op and post-op wards, and maintaining a super clean working environment, so physical labor was not new to us. What was new was the rigid discipline and make-work jobs that had previously been handled by other support troops with less training.

The new Captain was sending a message. An odious one.

A week before Christmas, a surgical technician came off a grueling twelve hour shift in the O.R. and was ordered to report for guard duty. He was to rotate on a twelve hour shift, with four hours on and four off. Sometime, in the early hours of the morning, he fell asleep. When the officer of the guard came by with a replacement he found the sleeping sentry. He was arrested and brought to the orderly room. Shortly thereafter, a very angry Captain appeared. He stormed around the room, promising court martial proceedings and firing squads. The surgical specialist was properly intimidated. Placed under guard, he was to be taken to Long Binh stockade the following day to await trial.

Early the next morning the entire camp had heard about the incident. Sam the gas man, and the head nurse were in the orderly room long before the Captain arrived.

"What in Hell do you think you're doing with one of my people?" thundered Major Mahoney. "This man was exhausted when he came off twelve hours of surgery. How could he be put on guard duty after pulling a full shift working for me? You have a whole camp to pull guards from and you insist on stealing my men just to prove some silly little point. This time you've gone too far."

The Captain never replied. Instead, he reached for an army manual and began thumbing through the pages. Sam became furious and knocked the book to the floor.

"You're a ridiculous caricature of a soldier," he shouted angrily. "I'm putting in a call to the 44th Medical Brigade headquarters in

Long Binh. When I'm through with you you'll wish that you had stayed wherever you came from."

Again, the Captain remained silent. He glared at the intruders in his office and suddenly left the room. Surprised, Sam and Major Mahoney left for the operating theater where they would make their calls to headquarters. Within an hour they had secured the release of the specialist and received a promise of a visit from a representative of the Judge Advocate Generals office, the legal arm of the army.

Unbelievably, the military lawyer arrived the next day and set up an immediate hearing. Despite the serious nature of the charge, the whole affair ended at the preliminary hearing. The soldier was exonerated and the Captain was ordered to revise his guard duty procedures. Medical personnel could still be used on guard duty, but only if no other men were available, and if they received time off after an active shift. The Captain accepted the decision like a good soldier, but he harbored a bitter resentment for Major Mahoney and her staff.

Overnight passes were completely eliminated and all passes for hospital staff became nearly impossible to obtain. Any paperwork for medical staff which had to be processed by the Captain's office was subject to prolonged delays and often lost.

The Captain's actions were a declaration of war. The medical specialists banded together to fight the martinet. We became a tightly-knit unit, working together in the O.R. and off duty, and became expert at covering for one another whenever it was necessary. In retrospect, the Captain was probably the best thing that could have happened to bring us together.

The restrictions on passes made it difficult for Minh and I to spend time together. We stole time for lunch on occasion and for short periods after work. When any of the medical techs. had C.Q. duty I would slip out of the camp and spend the night in the city with Minh, being careful to return in the hectic early morning traffic when guard shifts were changing. My desire to be with my wife increased daily, especially when I learned we were going to have a baby.

The joy and excitement of impending fatherhood was soon tempered by the realization that a mountain of paperwork lay ahead. I had learned that our Vietnamese civil marriage was not recognized by the army and that miles of red tape lay between us and any successful emigration to America. In the orderly room, I was told that there were no forms on hand for an application for marriage. Come back after Christmas and try again!

A minor delay, I thought optimistically, as I looked forward to the approaching holiday.

Christmas at the 36th was a paradox. The wards were decorated with handmade drawings of snowmen and angels. Pictures of Santa Claus and Christmas trees adorned the walls and tape recorders played carols and holiday tunes. The Red Cross provided special packages of personal products, while the nurses bought fruit at the local market and distributed the fresh bounty to homesick G.I.'s. In hootch 11, a palm frond was stuck in a jar of water and decorated with popcorn and candy.

The operating rooms had no special decorations.

At 2:00 A.M. on Christmas Eve, I was on first call. The only case was an injured G.I. who had gotten drunk and wrecked a jeep. He had a broken leg which required two hours of surgery to repair. He had, of course, vomited during the procedure, which did nothing to improve the dispositions of the surgical team. Such complications were common enough, but who wanted to put up with them on Christmas Eve?

At 6:00 A.M. I went off duty and met Minh as she came in for work. We shared a simple breakfast of a hard roll and tea, and talked of our plans for Christmas Day. Both of us were off duty for the holiday and had decided to celebrate by visiting some of the local attractions. Minh was particularly eager to show me some of the beautiful temples and shrines. Our hearts were light as we separated for the day -- she to her work at hootch 9 and I to my bunk for some rest.

I arose for lunch and stopped to check the orderly room bulletin board. My friend Doug had been scheduled for guard duty tonight but had taken ill. There in his place was my name.

Great, I thought, now I'll be beat tomorrow when Minh and I finally get some free time together in the daylight. Angry, and feeling just a little sorry for myself, I headed for the beer tent. Maybe a quick one will perk me up, I lied.

At six o'clock I reported for the stint on guard duty. I would start on the ten to two shift downtown at the officers' villa where the doctors and nurses lived. I had pulled that duty before during daylight hours. How much different could it be at night?

A six foot fence topped with barbed wire surrounded the villa. The only entrance to the compound was through a gate which opened onto a busy street near the west end of the city. There was a guard post at the gate with a tin roof and four open sides from the waist up. Not much protection if a sapper drove by with a bomb or some kid rode by on a bike and tossed a grenade!

During the day the guard was expected to stop all civilians who desired entry and check their I.D. cards and bags. Several cleaning ladies and maintenance men worked at the villa and delivery men were frequently coming and going. Most of the workers were non-plussed by the entry security checks, but many were indignant when their bags were searched as they left. Theft was not uncommon but the honest employees hated being treated like common criminals. As a result, some of the men on guard duty rarely checked bags, even bags with entering civilians. It was a mystery why a bomb had never been planted at the villa. Of course the officers were never aware of how cursory the security checks often were, and no doubt slept more comfortably in their ignorance.

At ten P.M. I began my shift at the villa. Motorbikes and cyclos were still active, but traffic was starting to thin out as the eleven o'clock curfew neared. Just before midnight a lone motorbike came putting down the street. The only light was at the guard shack so the progress of the bike had to be gauged by sound. The engine noise changed as it approached the entrance to the villa.

He's slowing down, I thought. This could be trouble. There aren't supposed to be any civilians here after dark.

The M-14 in my hands automatically came up as the rider neared. Before I knew what was happening the motor died and the bike coasted into the thin circle of light and came to a halt almost against the guard hut. The man dismounted and found himself staring into the muzzle of an automatic rifle.

"Lam nhia?" demanded the nervous sentry. What do you want here?

"Hut thuoc," answered the man. I would like a smoke.

"Khong phai, di-di mau," I responded harshly, keeping my weapon leveled on the man's chest. Nothing doing, move out now.

"Ong noi tieng Viet hay lam," the man rejoined. "Xin Ong cau

138

thuoc, khong?" You speak our language well. Could I please have a cigarette?

"Toi khong hut, mau-mau di." I don't smoke. Now beat it right away.

The man looked calmly at the rifle aimed at his heart and smiled. His hand went to his pocket and I clicked off the safety, tightening my finger on the trigger.

This was it.

Still smiling, the man slowly withdrew a fistful of money from his pocket and offered to exchange it for M.P.C.'s, military script.

Without moving a muscle I stared the man down. Either he was the coolest bomber in the country, or the dumbest conman. For a very long minute we simply stared at one another.

When the man realized that there would be no sale, he hopped on the motorbike, still smiling, and sped off into the night. When the engine noise had faded away I slipped the safety back on and breathed a long sigh of relief. That had been too hairy. I had actually come a whisker away from dropping the man in his tracks. The uncertainty of the situation had brought back all the old training lessons. When in doubt, shoot first and save your ass. And that was a direct quote from every training sergeant I had ever had. I knew now that if the necessity arose, I could fire my weapon and take a life. I had just been a heartbeat away from doing so.

Half an hour after the luckiest cyclist in Vung Tau had departed, a truck rumbled from the villa and stopped at the gate. The driver was Sam the gas man.

"Mike, we've been called to the O.R.. Some kind of attack with plenty of wounded. What are you doing on guard duty? We're going to need all the help we can get."

"You'd better check in with the officer of the guard to release me," I answered. "Good Luck!"

At one-thirty a jeep bounced down the street and slid to a stop at the gate.

"Specialist Hall, you're being relieved. They need you at the hospital right away."

"Okey Doke," I answered. "Do you know what's going on?"

"I'm not sure," responded the driver, "but I think a bunch of civilians got blown up somewhere."

I briefed my replacement on the earlier encounter with the civilian and jumped into the jeep. "Let's make tracks, this doesn't sound too good."

In a hurry, I cleared my weapon and rushed into the operating theater with the M-14 slung on my shoulder, a practice which was frowned upon, to say the least.

No one noticed.

The pre-op area was like a scene from Dante's Inferno. Children were lying everywhere, screaming and crying. Mixed in the bloody throng were a handful of adults, also screaming and wailing. These were not cries of anxiety for their wounded children, but the agonizing screams of unbearable pain.

The Vietcong had thrown white phosphorus grenades into a Christmas Eve church service. Dozens of worshipers were horribly wounded by the shrapnel and burning chemical. White phosphorus, when splattered on flesh, continues to burn its way into and through the body. Only by dousing the wounds with copper sulfate can the reaction be neutralized. And the supply of copper sulfate was far too small to adequately treat everyone.

I scrubbed in and immediately went to a table. The O.R. was adjacent to our pre-op hallway and the sounds of screaming children filled my ears. As I began prepping the unconscious child on the table I looked into the surgeon's eyes. They were filled with tears.

The little girl on the table could not have been more than four years old. Her tiny body had been almost completely burned. We would make a heroic effort to save her but her odds were one in a million of surviving. Before the debriding was finished she died.

I lifted her into my arms and carried her from the room. All eyes were on me as I gave the lifeless little form to another technician and returned to prepare the table for another victim. I could feel the eyes burning into my back as I left pre-op, and the renewed wails of anguish were more than I could bear. Tears welled in my eyes as I spread a new sheet on the operating table.

Oh God, how could they do this to You on Your birthday?

And then the table was occupied and waiting for the skilled hands of the surgical team to begin anew. But it took little skill to remove the charred flesh and shrapnel from these grotesque wounds. This was meatball surgery, if ever there was any.

By 5:00 A.M. we had worked on twelve cases in this room; the other O.R. had completed eight. And still the screaming in pre-op op continued.

There was a total of five tablés in the two rooms, but only four anesthesiologists. Sam moved two tables end to end, and using two sets of equipment, passed gas to two patients at a time. It was a risky arrangement, but it probably saved a life.

The next victim was an old woman who had been burned on the face and throat, where the fiery chemical had eaten into the trachea and larynx. She tried to scream but the only sound that came out was a terrifying high-pitched gurgle. As she fought to breathe, the searing pain overcame her. She thrashed about on the table, throwing off the oxygen mask and nearly toppling Sam from his stool. He checked his little patient on the other table and then turned his attention to the old woman.

Before he could regain control, she writhed off the table, landing on the floor.

"For God's sake, get her back on the table, Mike," Sam yelled. "We have to get oxygen to her."

I picked her up and felt for a carotid pulse, but there was no response.

"Sam, she's had it. There's no pulse or respiration. Should I try to revive her?"

"No," he murmured sadly. "We have too many others waiting that might have a chance if we can get to them quickly enough. Take her out and bring in another. We have no choice."

I looked into Sam's eyes and remembered the long-ago promise to repay his kindness, but there was no earthly way to remove the pain from those eyes. I prayed that God would give us the strength and skill to help these poor children in this terrible hour of trial.

I wrapped the woman in a sheet and wheeled her out. This time, no one noticed. Too many gurneys had gone in and out for one more to make a difference. The screaming and moaning had diminished but only because there were fewer casualties remaining. We were out of copper sulfate and a nurse was trying to make do with some of the experimental burn cream. It didn't help much.

I cradled a baby in my arms and brought her into the operating room. She had been burned on the head and chest, but only superficially. There would be terrible scarring but she should survive. As Sam put her under the anesthesia she gave a great sigh and stopped breathing. Making sure that his other patient was stable,

141

he turned his full efforts to the baby. Her wounds didn't indicate a problem with her lungs, so there had to be something else. He began resuscitation, but to no avail. She died quickly and quietly. No one would ever know for certain why.

By 9:00 A.M. on Christmas morning, the last casualty had been treated. The operating rooms were empty, but there would be ghosts lingering for weeks. The cries of the innocents would remain with the surgical and nursing staffs for the rest of our lives. Twenty-seven beautiful souls had been frantically and lovingly treated in the operating rooms since midnight. By the end of the week, only ten of them would remain alive, all horribly scarred.

The abominable conflagration in that little church had devastated the lives of so many families, and etched forever the true horrors of war on the hearts of the medics who worked that night. Would any of us ever be able to celebrate Christmas again without thinking of the children and that long and tragic night?

"Merry Christmas, Sam."

"Merry Christmas, Mike."

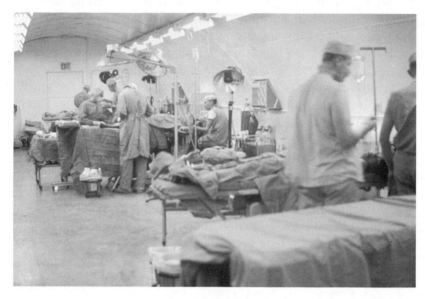

O.R. # 1, 36th Evac

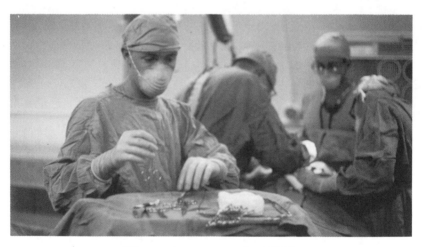

The author at work, 1968

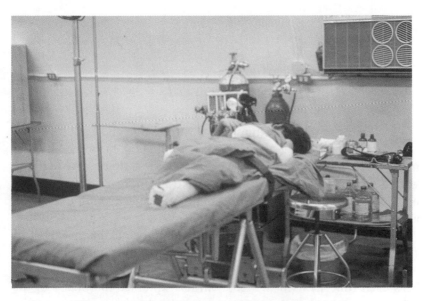

Nguyen Thi Mai, my med-cap interpreter

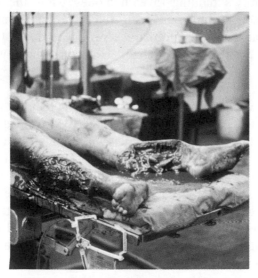

"Franklin"

Chapter Sixteen

A week after the Christmas that wasn't, Minh and I got away for a Sunday together. We attended Mass at the church in the city and turned even more heads than we had the first time. We left the service early this time in order to make the most of this rare day together. For the first time, I brought my camera along to capture our mini-vacation for posterity.

Walking down a street known for its notorious bars, I tried to snap a few pictures of the girls lolling about in the doorways. They were apparently camera-shy as they ducked inside or covered their faces each time I raised the lens. Minh explained that many of the girls were not hardened prostitutes, just simple girls who were often doing their family's bidding to earn money while the Americans were still in their country. Having lived through famine, Minh understood what hunger could drive a person to do, but she could never find it in her heart to moralize. Unless you have walked in a person's shoes, she reasoned, how could you know what was in their heart?

By evening we had visited all the shrines and temples within easy access of the city, and a few that were not. We decided to splurge with a meal at the best restaurant in town. For about ten dollars, American, we feasted on seafood and beef, chicken and rice, vegetables without number and fancy cakes for dessert.

The owner stopped by our table to inquire after the meal. He spoke fluent English, French, Mandarin Chinese and Vietnamese and regaled us with his stories of life in San Francisco and Paris. He was only waiting for the war to end, when he was sure Vung Tau would return to its former glory as a resort city. He lived well now, but hoped to live opulently in the future. Wasn't that the American dream, he queried laughingly.

After dinner, we walked silently for awhile, lost in similar thoughts. Somehow it seemed obscene for one to live so well when so many people all around were suffering and dying. Would there ever be peace and real, lasting happiness in this country, and for ourselves? As we walked we were approached by a succession of beggars. None were refused.

In order to break the melancholic mood we were slipping into, I suggested we go to the cinema. Minh readily agreed. We hailed a horse-drawn cab and clopped down the street.

The cinema was located near the center of town on Le Loi Street. It was a wide boulevard compared to most of the streets in the city, but this evening there was little traffic, other than a few bicycles and pedi-cabs.

We arrived at the theater in the middle of the show. The movie was Chinese, with Vietnamese sub-titles. I was thoroughly lost whenever the action ceased and dialogue took over. The audience seemed bored as well, for when the film ended prematurely with a break they began cheering for the second feature to begin.

The second film was French, with both Vietnamese and English sub-titles. Both were unnecessary, however, since the movie was an ancient Tarzan film with far more action than words.

Minh was ecstatic. She had seen this movie years ago at the French army camp. As a matter of fact, she had watched it dozens of times. Movies had been such a rare treat that many children had memorized them word for word.

As Minh watched the screen, I watched her. She was positively glowing. I thought my heart would burst with the love that I felt for her and our growing child. She caught me looking and blushed.

After the show, we stopped at an outdoor stall for a snack. Minh carefully ordered steaming hot dishes. When pressed for an explanation she replied that American stomachs often did not take kindly to the delicacies served up by many of the street vendors. Gratefully, I spooned down the pepper soup and made a mental note never to eat any uncooked food when venturing downtown. The next day I fell ill. Not just ill, but violently stomach-heaving, loose bowel ill. My stomach and intestines were constantly on fire and stubbornly rejected any hint of food. For days I just wanted to curl up and die.

Minh came to see me in the hospital everyday, but I was so sick I could barely talk. I lost twenty pounds from a hundred and fifty pound frame that could ill afford to lose weight. When I was finally released for duty I felt like a butterfly in the wind.

It was almost a month before I regained my strength and weight. That illness would haunt me for the rest of my life with a recurring chronic colitis that had an eerie habit of appearing for a few days each month. It could be controlled with medicines, but it made me very aware of the need to carry toilet paper whenever I worked in the woods.

Naturally, purple hearts weren't awarded for such debilitating trauma, but reprimands were. Eating or drinking anything off base on the local economy had been off limits for all medical personnel since the arrival of the first troops, but the order had generally been ignored. With care, a person could do just fine, but one slip and he might well find himself in the hospital, or worse.

After the bout with dysentery, I was summoned to the orderly room to explain how I thought I might have acquired it. Knowing that the Captain was aware of my interest in a local girl, I decided not to bluff. I explained about the dinner and the fact that I had married the "local girl," who was even more local than the Captain realized. She worked here on the base.

The Captain was furious. He ranted and raved for half an hour about the dangers of fraternizing and the mission of the troops in Vietnam. He concluded by promising to have me transferred to Tay Ninh or Pleiku for the rest of my tour of duty.

I was set to play my ace, Minh's downtown cowboy connections, when I realized I had been trumped. The Captain was straight. He never left the base. There was no way to get to him.

At a loss for words, I left the orderly room and headed for the beer tent. I had a lot of thinking to do. Entering the tent I spied a familiar face ... my old friend Bill, from dust-off days. We had shared danger and boredom together, and would be friends for life, however long that might be. I explained my problem, and Bill laughed.

"You think you have troubles," he chuckled. "You should see the wart I have on my back. It's as big as a quarter. And wouldn't you know it, there's a big ugly hair that keeps growing out of it. Every time I pull it out, the damn thing grows right back. The girls downtown love it but I just want to be rid of it. And you think you have problems!"

I couldn't help but laugh. Bill was a clown who could probably have cheered up Job. He was also getting short, with only a couple of months left in country.

"I'll tell you what. If you cut out this stinking wart I'll come back over here and fly you and your wife back to the world. And that's a promise!"

I agreed, and soon we were drinking and talking and forgetting. I hadn't spent much time here in the beer tent, but it was certainly a homey place to be today. Without Minh, I was sure that I would have spent most off duty hours drinking with buddies. Alcohol eased so many pains.

When Bill left, I stayed for a final beer. As I was about to leave I felt an arm slide around my neck. It dropped into a strangle hold and began to tighten. I tried to see which of my drunken friend it was, but the arm tightened and began to cut off my wind. Gasping, I chopped an elbow back into a well-padded mid-section. With a last hard squeeze, the arm suddenly relaxed and dropped away.

Sergeant Bluefeather was very, very drunk.

He stood toe to toe with me and hissed into my face, "If you do anything to hurt Mama-san number 9 I'll personally kill you. She's the best damn Mama-san on this base and I won't let anybody do her dirt. Have you got that?"

"You bet, Blue," answered a very shaken specialist. "You probably won't believe this, but I love that woman. When I go back to the world, she goes with me."

"I've heard that one a lot, white boy. But this black man is telling you that if anything happens to that Mama-san you're going back in a body bag."

"Blue, you're a big guy, and your arm is bigger than my leg, but I'm telling you the truth. That lady is going to have my child and go back home with me."

Big mistake!

Bluefeather hadn't known about the baby. His brawny arm snaked out and circled my neck for a second time. It might have been the last time if it weren't for a couple of burly brothers who pulled Blue off this choking, half-dead medic.

Stan, the cast man, had played football with the Chicago Bears before he was drafted. He and his friend pulled me off the floor and splashed a beer in my face. Sputtering and gulping for breath, I

146

managed a weak thank you.

Stan was a friend and he realized how close a call he had just interrupted. When Blue sobered up he would have to impart a little wisdom to him concerning Mike and Minh. Sergeant Bluefeather was not a man to go back on his word.

I woke up in the morning with a head the size of a rain barrel. As a matter of fact, that's the first place I stuck it. I tried to remember the previous night's highlights. Deciding that there hadn't been any, I began to recall the lowlights. There were plenty of them. Bluefeather's beer breath and iron-armed strangle hold took top billing as bad news, until I remembered the Captain's promise. This was going to be some day!

The first order of business was to figure out a way to bypass the Captain and start the marriage paperwork, all the while avoiding the black man with the Indian name and arms of steel.

Nothing to it, I thought. Maybe a trip to the beer tent would help. That thought sobered me instantly. Perhaps some mess hall coffee would do the trick.

As luck would have it, Doug was just coming off a shift in the O.R. and joined me for a hot cup or two. He had some outstanding news. The Captain was being transferred today. Apparently all the complaints submitted by the doctors and Major Mahoney had hit paydirt.

Oh Lord, I prayed, if only he leaves without signing my transfer papers.

Minutes later, Stan walked into the mess hall and grinning, sauntered over and grabbed me in a headlock.

"Man, you are the sorriest dude I have ever seen. First, you try to get yourself killed, then you let it out that you've gone and knocked up some Mama-san. Man, you are worse than sorry. I don't know why I even let you near my cast room."

"Stan, my good man, the Mama-san is my wife, and she's not knocked up, she's having our child. I would sure appreciate it if you would so inform our friend Blue. I do believe that the man means business."

"Mike, you sorry medical dude, I know that old Blue means what he says. I'll talk to him for you but you're going to owe me, big time!"

"I'll cover that debt, Stan. Anyhow, Doug just told me that old

147

Captain Chicken Hawk is flying the coop. Transferred. Have you heard who his replacement is, 'cause that's a man I want to meet?"

"No man, I hadn't even heard we were losing the fine Captain, but no one could be as bad as that dude. You stay cool and I'll go fix it up with your buddy Blue."

Doug and I finished our coffee and trekked back to the hootch.

"Mike," he asked, "do you honestly think that they're going to let you take Minh back with you? I think you're whistling in the wind for all the good it will do. These guys really get off on rules and red tape. They don't want anybody marrying anybody. I'm not trying to throw a wet blanket on your plans, but I just hope you know what you're getting into."

"Thanks, Doug, but I'm going to win this one. Minh and I have some mighty powerful help. He can help us overcome any red tape or prejudice or any other darn thing that stands in our way."

"Hey, that's great Mike. I didn't know you knew Westmoreland."

"Right, Doug. No, I mean the Big Guy upstairs. Come on, give me a break. You love reading all those books about Kit Carson and the mountain men. Well, I'm a mountain man myself, and between Minh and God and I, there's nothing we can't accomplish."

"O.K., mountain man, but if you need help, just call on old Jim Bridger here, and I'll cover your back, just like in the old days."

Much later, as I thought about this bold talk, I knew that there was no choice but to back it up with bold action. I had matured over the last months and gained a mountain of confidence. The task ahead would truly be formidable, but I felt certain that with God's help Minh and I would ultimately prevail. And now to the matter at hand.

I waited until the Captain left the orderly room and then boldly entered the lair of our foe. The specialist on duty repeated that no marriage applications had come in yet. Try again in a few weeks. Recognizing a stone wall when I faced one, I thanked the clerk and then played the ace once more.

"I want to see you type out a requisition for those forms right now, Buddy-Boy, and I'll mail it myself. If you have a problem with that, I can arrange a little reception for you the next time you go downtown. Do I make myself clear?"

The startled clerk nodded his head and began typing. A few

minutes later I dropped the request into the mail slot. I wasn't proud of resorting to threats, but I would use any means available to me to cut through the bureaucratic maze of red tape. With a wry grin, I recalled the adage, "God helps those who help themselves," and wondered how many felons had considered that phrase to justify their actions.

That night, Minh listened as her husband related the happenings of the day to her. She was thoughtful as I chuckled about the frightened clerk.

Have I created a monster, she mused? What will this crazy American do next, kidnap a general and demand a marriage paper as ransom? She wanted to tell him to slow down, be careful. One wrong step could jeopardize everything that they were working for. In the end, she decided to hold her counsel. This determined young man whom she loved had plenty of commom sense. He wouldn't step over the line and destroy their hopes for the future. Now if only he didn't have to leave to meet the curfew. She sighed deeply and longed for the day when they would have a home of their own and her husband would be with her every night.

For the next few weeks there was a lull in the fighting in the sector served by the 36th Evac., with a corresponding reduction in casualties. A notable exception was a patrol that encountered a V.C. ambush just north of Baria. One soldier was seriously wounded in the head and medevaced to the 24th Evav. in Saigon which specialized in head trauma. The other casualty came to Vung Tau.

I was just beginning my shift when the radio in the emergency room crackled. One litter, one ambulatory coming in with an e.t.a. of twenty minutes. The litter case was multiple fragment wounds with a possible traumatic amputation of both feet. The radioman called the villa for an extra surgeon and nurse. That call saved the man's life.

I had a table set up by the time the luckless G.I. was wheeled in to O.R. number one. He appeared to be no more than seventeen years old. His face was ashen from the loss of blood, the deathly pale hue that so often meant no hope of survival. His clothing had been cut away in pre-op and when he was lifted onto the table and the un-sterile sheet removed, the circulating nurse gasped in disbelief. Both of the young man's arms and legs were horribly mangled, only the tourniquets keeping him from bleeding to death.

149

As bad as the wounds to his extremities were, the soldier had a more immediate life-threatening problem. A sucking chest wound was nearly collapsing his lungs. From the numerous lacerations and puncture wounds to the abdomen, it appeared that he had come in close frontal contact with a Claymore mine or some similar deadly device.

By some miracle, the hospital's best chest cutter, Doc DeAngelis, was on duty. He immediately opened the chest and located the damage. While he began to repair the torn arteries, the second surgeon started debriding the injured feet.

DeAngelis ordered me to roll stockinette around the limbs to constrict the peripheral vessels. The hemorrhaging slowed noticeably, but there was still major arterial bleeding. More blood was ordered, until there were five units attached simultaneously. With all of that, the man began slipping away.

The entire team picked up the pace and worked furiously against the clock. And then, as if in answer to our prayers, Doc Kelly, the orthopedist, walked in. He had been checking on his patients in the bone ward and by sheer luck had heard of this case. He scrubbed in at once and began to evaluate the mutilated hands.

For five hours the team of seven labored to save the boy. Finally, our efforts were completed. The aortic arch and one lung had been repaired and would heal without complications. Dozens of minor shrapnel wounds had been debrided and dressed. But the satisfaction of denying death its victim was muted. Both hands had been amputated. The nerve and vessel damage had been irreparable.

One foot had been blown off and was only attached by shreds of skin. That too was removed. And to complete the violence wreaked against the unfortunate young soldier, we removed his right leg just below the knee.

The task of saving this life had been nothing short of Herculean. Had he arrived with other casualties, he would never have survived, since the doctors would have been spread out among the other cases. Coming in alone saved his life.

Following the operation, a nurse wrapped the severed limbs in a sheet and started for the graves registration tent where the incinerator was located. She stopped at the O.R. door and began to tremble. I moved quickly to the door, put my arm around her and took her burden. Our eyes met and I saw in her tears my own face, just a few short months ago. I murmured a few words which neither of us believed and delivered the body parts to graves registration.

Walking back to help scrub down the O.R., I held my hand straight out before me. It was steady. Was I becoming inured to such terrible devastation? Were my feelings mummified?

No, I was sure that wasn't true, but how could I explain the calm that surrounded me in the midst of such overwhelming tragedy? My heart ached for that young man, but something was missing now. Some depth of feeling, some sense of revulsion or pathos had departed. Throughout the clean up chores I pondered this change which had crept upon me so gradually, so insidiously. Would I ever be able to feel true sorrow, or grief again?

Only time would tell.

For the next two weeks the soldier remained at the 36th. When he was strong enough he would be shipped to Japan for a recuperation period before going home. Home to an uncertain future in a V.A. Hospital, or as a perpetual burden to his family.

During the two weeks at the 36th, I stopped by regularly to talk with Franklin. Most patients were called "Buddy" or "Pal," but I had to use Franklin's name. The boy had gotten to me. At first he wouldn't acknowledge anyone, but gradually he opened up and would ask for more medication to ease the pain. It was a week before he would discuss his injuries. He didn't know what had hit him and was unable to remember anything about the ambush. He was, however, well aware of his present condition and was suffering with great anxiety.

He was actually twenty-one years old and married, with two small children. He had worked in an auto plant in Detroit while his wife stayed home with the babies. She had a high school education, but no real job skills or training. The more he thought about his family, the more depressed he became.

One day he asked me to give him some pills or a shot which would let him die. At least that way, his wife would get some insurance.

I was at a loss for words. I went to the base Chaplain for advice. While there I asked about a Catholic wedding ceremony for Minh and I. The Chaplain was sympathetic, but firm. He repeated the army list of rules for civilian marriages and directed me to the company commander.

151

Even the Chaplain was a real bureaucrat, I thought as I walked away. On the way back to the orthopedic ward, I recalled one of my favorite poems, "Mending Wall," by Robert Frost. I had the feeling that I had just been stonewalled again, and couldn't see how "good fences make good neighbors."

At the ward, my arrival drew a smile from the embittered amputee.

Hey, this is great, I thought, until I heard the reason for the smile.

"Did you bring the stuff?" I was asked.

"The only stuff I brought this time is some good news," I answered with a false smile. "You'll be eligible for a good pension that will bring in much more money in the long run than a death benefit. I know you don't care about that right now, but if you take some time to think it over, it would be worth considering."

The instant I spoke I knew that the words sounded hollow. Franklin's face lost all expression. Closing his eyes signified that our little chat was over. It was the only control Franklin still maintained in his life. I had done my best, but couldn't fool myself into believing that I had made a difference. I never saw Franklin again.

Shortly after Franklin's departure for Tokyo, I got a day off in the middle of the week. Though Minh was working all day, I decided to go down to her house to get some rest and read a book. Lying on the bed, watching the procession of ants across the ceiling and down the wall, I was unable to concentrate on reading. Instead, my mind began to wander along back roads, totally out of control.

It was hard to get the quadruple amputee out of my mind. I had assisted with dozens of amputations since arriving here, but none had affected me more. My thoughts drifted back to the film that had been shown at Fort Sam Houston. President Johnson, in a twangy, whining drawl, began the introduction with, "Why Vietnam?". The explanation had been carefully constructed to appeal to the young men targeted for action in Southeast Asia. America was the kindly Uncle who was intervening to save a poor relative from the onslaught of communism.

I still believed the President, but wondered if the costs would be worth the effort. I was troubled by the reports and evidence of atrocities perpetrated by both sides, and the mounting testimony that

152

this kind of war was impossible to win under the current restrictions. My early misgivings would be justified much later when I studied the volumes of history written about the constraints put on the military during the war. My convictions about the need for this war would also waver once all the evidence was in.

To break away from these troubling thoughts, I used a trick I had learned while spending many hours in a dentist chair as a youngster. I would mentally transport myself to a more comfortable location, or a memory of good times past. Grandma would have called it "woolgathering", while Mr. Caramia, my former history teacher, would have said I was daydreaming.

Leaving this sultry setting now, I found myself in the North Woods on a crisp October day. The trees were wearing their fall coat of many colors and the smell of fallen leaves permeated my eager nostrils. I saw myself quietly following the spoor of a hulking black bear.

The bear had destroyed my tent and I was out to slay the big bruin. It was feeding on freshly fallen beechnuts, leaving an easy trail to follow. The overturned leaves were still moist and dark where they had been pawed out of the way. The bear's sharp nose was busy locating the sweet nuts and failed to warn him of his pursuer until it was too late. A well aimed shot from the old Winchester sent the behemoth to his knees.

The bear scrambled to his feet and charged downhill, directly at the determined hunter.

At fifty yards, he veered to the right, offering another shot. Again the rifle cracked, and he was mortally hit, and again he regained his feet. He crashed onward, putting a huge boulder between himself and the hunter. Emerging from behind the granite crag, he roared his anger and pain.

At thirty feet I fired again. The bear slumped to the ground. As I approached the downed animal, it rose on its forelegs and snarled defiantly. Backing off, I administered the coup de grace and leaned weakly against a nearby maple tree.

Exhilaration, relief and a sense of accomplishment swirled within me. The bear was huge, and certainly dominant in this environment. But this hunter had entered the domain of the forest monarch and bested him. Another day, the bear might have won. And then the wave of sadness that always accompanied a kill swept over me. I had been a participant in a timeless encounter. The satisfaction of completing a successful hunt was tempered by the awe I felt as a man privileged to be a part of this natural experience. And now, much work awaited me.

A knock on the door roused me from my reverie, but the memories of that hunt would linger for hours. As I answered the door, the strong scent of the bear and sweet smell of decaying leaves sent a chill up my spine. I could almost taste the salty sweat trickling into the corners of my mouth as I packed out the bear meat, one heavy load at a time. With a sense of foreboding, I hoped that some of the memories from my tour of duty here would not invade the future with such realism.

Before I could reach the door it swung open and in walked Suu with Tot and her two grandchildren. Thu ran to me and gave me a big hug. Tri hung back, as usual. Suu explained that they had come for a brief visit. Next week they would have to return to the Delta.

Tot regarded her son-in-law with a curious eye. He wasn't as big as she imagined most Americans, but at least he wasn't terribly ugly!

Minh returned from work that night and entered a house filled with the delicious aroma of her father's cooking. What a terrific surprise! She held her children closely, but they seemed aloof. Their mothers absence was taking its toll. Minh sadly noted their distant smiles, nearly breaking down and crying when she thought of all the time she had missed with them.

Soon, she hoped, very soon we will be together for all time.

The evening passed swiftly. I tried to tell Tot how happy I was to meet her, but my inflections really butchered the beautiful sing-song language, and I actually told her that she smelled badly. Suu was beside himself with laughter.

"Vui," Minh patiently explained. "Say vui, not tui."

Tot's sense of humor was not as well developed as her husband's, and she busied herself cleaning dishes rather than listen to any more abuse, deserved or otherwise.

I spent nearly every night of the next week at Minh's house. I had learned enough words to communicate with Suu quite well, but still had great difficulty understanding Vietnamese when it was spoken. Suu and I did much better speaking in French. Suu was quite fluent, while I did remarkably well remembering my five years of studying the language. I tried to draw Suu out to learn of his exploits in the war, but the older man refused to discuss the subject. He repeated Minh's admonition that the walls have ears.

I knew that I was speaking with a very courageous man, a true hero in his country, and was all the more frustrated that he was unable to talk about it. When the week had ended, parting was a sad occasion. There was still the ever-present worry that the V.C. would return, so there was no question of the children remaining.

Only a few months more, I prayed. Our family will be ready for America.

Back at the base I was finally able to catch the new commanding officer alone. I explained that we were already married but needed to complete the army paperwork in order to bring our family back home with us. The C.O., a first lieutenant named Gene, was only twenty-three years old. This was his first command and he wanted to do everything by the book, but this case seemed special to him.

"Specialist Hall," he began, "I am required to interview you and provide counseling on the inadvisability of marrying a Vietnamese civilian. It would seem that you have already done that, and under the circumstances, any counseling I could do would be after the fact. Therefore, I will approve your application. You will also need a letter from the Chaplain stating that he has interviewed you and provided counsel as well. Then there are a number of forms to fill out for your wife, including a police background check, medical exam, consular approvals and a half dozen more. Do you still want to proceed?"

"That's affirmative, sir. Can you get the necessary papers for me?"

"They should all be available right here, Hall. I'm surprised that you don't already have this much done."

"Well sir, the papers haven't been made available to me. I've been trying for some time now, but the answer has always been the same, the papers are on order."

"Well Hall, you seem committed to this course of action so I'll get right on it. If there's anything else I can do, just stop in."

I left the orderly room with wings on my feet. I had to tell Minh that our luck had finally changed. This could be the break we were waiting for. I found her at the hootch and repeated the good news. If we could get through the next few months we would be on our way.

Chapter Seventeen

March of 1969 was a bad month. I was caught downtown one night during a rocket attack, unable to reach the base. When the red alert was lifted and I returned to the hospital, the First Sergeant was waiting. Without a pass I had no acceptable excuse. An administrative hearing was convened and I was hit with an Article 15. The penalty was the loss of a months pay and a one month restriction to base. Both were painful, but I realized that a court martial would have been far worse.

The commanding officer promised the court martial if the same offense was committed in the future. He made no mention of the marriage application, or the status of the forms which were still "on order". The stone wall continued.

The casualty load during March continued unabated. Vietcong activity was steadily growing, but seemed centered well south of Vung Tau. I began to spend more time in C.M.S., central material supply, than in the operating room. The C.M.S. crew was whacky, no doubt about it. Most of them had spent several months in surgery and had been rotated to central supply to finish out their tours. I fit right in.

During one particularly off-beat week, we put a can opener in a hemorrhoid instrument set, tin shears for an eye operation and a dead cockroach in a laparotomy pack! The oddball tools and the bug were all properly sterilized, harmless and afforded the surgeons a laugh. Unfortunately, one prudish nurse made a stink about the roach and the shenanigans were ended. Well....almost ended.

The Surgeon General's office was preparing to inspect the 36th as part of a major inspection tour in the country. When they arrived at Vung Tau the operating technicians made sure that there was an appropriate welcome. In the autoclave room was a giant three foot by ten foot sign proclaiming, "Vietnam, the Edsel of American

Foreign Policy."

In the number two autoclave, nestled side by side, were two steaming lobsters, their aroma wafting throughout the room. As the inspection team neared the room, a nurse broke from the group for a pre-inspection snoop. A passing glance and cursory sniff told her all she needed to know. The inspection team bypassed the C.M.S. Quonset.

Somehow I missed the crackdown on central supply following the inspection. Probably because I was involved with the good-bye party for "Tricky Dick." He was a good friend from the signal corps company next door. He was also the clown prince of jokes. There wasn't a medic in hootch eleven who hadn't been the butt of one or more of his jokes. From short-sheeted bunks to shaving cream in boots, he had done it all.

One of the joke-meister's master strokes had been replacing the duty roster with one which he had concocted. Scheduling had been mixed up for days after that move. I well remembered the morning I had returned from Minhs and found an official-looking message to report to the C.O. to explain being A.W.O.L. again. Tricky Dick had intercepted me just as I was entering the orderly room.

Oh, to get revenge!

At the party that night, I made sure that good old Dick never had an empty hand. Not relying entirely on the booze, one of the medics had come up with a reasonable facsimile of knock-out drops. The pharmacist's assistant had given his assurance that they were harmless. By two a.m. Dick was in the arms of Morpheus.

By three a.m. he was in the arms of myself, Jim and Stan the cast man.

And by three-thirty a.m. he was on a bunk, encased in plaster from his waist to his toes.

Terrible luck that, passing out on the roof of the hootch and rolling off! His broken legs would be fine, eventually. Too bad that after a year in Vietnam, he and his wife would be separated by a plaster cast for another six months!

A wild scream split the air just after dawn. Hootch eleven awoke with a start. Dick was yelling and swearing and peeing at the same time. At least the yelling and swearing didn't further aggravate his troubles.

"A fine mess you'll be in when you meet your wife at the

airport," I purred. "We tried to catch you last night but you were over the edge before anyone could get near you. It's just lucky you didn't crack your head open. Ah, you're a fortunate one!"

"Sure, sure, I broke my legs," Dick scoffed. "Now someone get me out of this thing before I miss my plane."

Right on cue, in walked Stan with a nurse.

"Hey there, Man. How are you feeling this morning?" Stan asked with great concern. "Lieutenant Stroker here helped me with the cast last night. How does he look to you, Lieutenant?"

"Well, except for his God-awful color and breath, he should pull through. Specialist, you gave us quite a scare last night. Your right tibia was protruding right through the skin. A real nasty break."

That was the extra touch of realism that really set the hook. Dick was convinced that he and his young wife would have a very Platonic, and very frustrating reunion. As we carried on with appropriately long faces, the C.Q. rushed into the hootch. "Fresh wounded, Guys, they need everybody tout de suite. Let's di-di mau."

"Don't worry, Dick," someone shouted. "We'll send for a litter to take you to the airfield. Ta-ta."

By noon the casualties had been treated and the operating rooms scrubbed and re-set. As I headed for the mess hall I suddenly remembered Dick.

Oh Man, I thought, is that guy going to be steamed!

Running to the hootch, I saw Jim, who filled me in on the rest of the story. It seemed that everyone forgot Dick in the rush to take care of the legitimate casualties. He had screamed his head off for hours before someone came by. He managed to convince them that he was not a patient out for a little illegal R. and R., and that he really did have a very important plane to catch.

As he was wheeled out of the hootch he caught sight of Stan the cast man. Stan broke the news to him that it was all a joke. Dick didn't laugh. He pleaded with the burly ex-tackle to remove the cast, but Stan was needed at the hospital. He sent Dick to the cast room and told him to ask someone there to use the electric cast cutter.

In the cast room, the technician on duty refused to touch the plaster without a doctor's order. Dick apparently went slightly berserk, wielding the miniature buzz saw himself. Fortunately, the cast technician gave in and freed him from the plaster prison. "Tricky Dick" was never heard from again.

As the weeks of restriction dragged by, I became restless. When volunteers were sought for a Medcap mission I was first in line. Maybe second.

Medcaps were short hops into the country to set up clinics in villages for one-time treatment of civilians. They were part of the effort to win the hearts and minds of the Vietnamese. The trip today was to a small fishing village called Binh Da.

Doctor Paul was one of the most dedicated surgeons that I had met at the 36th Evac.. His free time was devoted to helping anyone in need in any way possible. He frequently stopped by the Vietnamese hospital, Le Loi, and assisted in whatever way he could. He had only two weeks left on his tour, but continued to volunteer for Medcaps, which always held an element of danger.

Paul was a most un-military individual. He insisted that everyone call him by his first name with no prefixes of any kind. That suited my civilian mentality just fine. As we finished loading supplies onto the Huey which would ferry us to the town, the nurse who was to assist us twisted her ankle. Unable to walk, she was carried to a jeep and taken to the villa. There were no volunteers to replace her, so the mission went out short-handed.

Flying over the flat coastal plain, I was again struck by the number of bomb craters. The entire landscape was pock-marked with the handiwork of the giant B-52's. For mile after mile so much of the land area was taken up by the craters. And yet, farmers continued to plant among them, though their yield must surely have been severely reduced. I marveled at the resilience of these people. After a thousand years of war, resilience was all they had left.

Farther to the west, stretching for miles, was a forest. As the chopper drew nearer, the woods took on a grotesque appearance. Herbicides had recently denuded a huge block of trees. They stood silently in rows, gaunt and red, looking like so many twisted scarecrows in a field where nothing grows.

What an ecological disaster, I thought out loud.

"What a human disaster," Paul rejoined. "Those chemicals will be in the soil and water for years. Think of the effects on the people eating plants grown here, or drinking that polluted water. Can you imagine the birth defects that will result?"

We fell silent for the remainder of the flight. Soon, the village was in sight, and after circling twice to check out the landing zone, the pilot side-slipped the Huey through the heavy air to a muddy paddy dike just outside the line of huts.

"Sorry, Doc. You'll have to walk from here. I can't see anything solid to land on close in."

Paul was a veteran of many Medcaps and swung into action immediately. With the pilot's help, we unloaded the boxes of supplies and a small, portable examining table. We were met by dozens of laughing children, eager to help carry something to the town. In minutes, the supplies were stacked in a neat pile outside the largest house.

"This must be the mayor's house," Paul grinned. "We'll have to have his permission before we go to work. We've been here before but situations are volatile out here and there may have been some changes since our last visit. We can't very well announce these trips ahead of time because that would be a gold-plated invitation for Charlie to stop by. I don't really mind treating a V.C., can't tell them apart anyway, but I sure don't want to get blown up out here or risk the lives of these poor devils."

"Paul, I think the head man is on his way," I offered. "That fellow over there looks pompous enough to be a chief, or mayor or whatever he's called. With that unctious smile he's probably already calculating what he can swindle out of us today. I guess that goes with the territory, though. Politicians are the same the world over."

The mayor turned out to be a real peach. He was a fisherman who had earned the respect of his neighbors by defying the Vietcong's insistence that the village shelter and feed them on a long term basis. He had lost his three sons in the war, and felt that he had nothing further to lose. He was a marked man now, and he knew it. Still, he continued to fish and settle local disputes as they arose.

He greeted the medical team with a wide grin, revealing a mouth full of dark, betel-stained teeth. He spoke no English, relying on the services of a girl who had learned enough pidgin English to communicate with the Americans. She was a beautiful young woman of fifteen or sixteen. Her name was Nguyen Thi Mai.

Paul knew only a word or two of Vietnamese, and joked about his tin ear for music and languages. That left the communications to

Mai and myself. Our first efforts were clumsy, but soon we were laughing at each others attempts at translating and all barriers fell away.

The mayor offered his humble home as a work area but Paul preferred the better lighting in the street. We found a bamboo screen to furnish a bit of privacy and keep down the dust, and soon the clinic was in operation.

Boils and festering sores were the most frequent and obvious complaints. More insidious were the coughs and sallow faces that revealed tuberculosis and emphysema. Cholera, plague, malaria and general malnutrition could all be found here if complete diagnostic tests were run. These were impossible on a limited Medcap, so only the most obvious diseases and ailments were treated specifically. Inoculations for many of the deadly diseases were provided, and antibiotics were dispensed as needed.

Before we left, Paul and I brought out boxes of tooth brushes and played a game of soccer with the children. The winning team got to hand out the brushes. The soccer ball was in sad shape and I made a note to get a new one out here if we ever returned. We left several boxes of bandages and anti-bacterial creams with the mayor and wished him long life and happiness. Only the latter was a real possibility.

While we had been vaccinating and cleaning up infections, I learned that Mai was an orphan. She supported herself and her younger brother by weaving sleeping mats and baskets from reeds and splits of bamboo.

As I sat in the chopper on my newly-purchased mat, I couldn't get her face out of my mind. She was so beautiful, yet there was a strange shadow over her countenance; a look of long-suffering resignation that surely didn't belong on one so young. Paul guessed my thoughts.

"These people have suffered with war since they were born," he counseled. "And their parents and grandparents before them have never known peace. Don't grieve over them, they're used to this life and have adapted to it far better than we have. Pray for peace, if you must, and help them in whatever way you can. You and I will never return to this village again or likely meet any of these people, but part of us will be here with them, and part of them will be with us. That probably doesn't make much sense but that's how I feel.

Lord knows, I'm no Doctor Schweitzer, but if I can do something to help someone once in awhile, I guess that's my Karma. Capiche?"

"Anh biet, Paul. I understand."

The short flight back to the base was uneventful. Paul joined me at the hootch for a cold beer and caught the next jeep for the villa.

It had been a long day but I felt better than I had in weeks. For once there had been no man-made trauma to repair, no bodies ripped asunder by the results of political ambitions. If all Medcaps were that safe and rewarding, I might just volunteer again. That night I slept the sweet, dreamless sleep of the just.

At breakfast the next morning the powdered eggs were gooier than usual, but I attacked them with a new ferocity. I was still euphoric, recalling the successful Medcap of the previous day. As I was finishing my coffee I heard a chopper settling on the pad next to the E.R.. I was on second call and most likely wouldn't be needed, but decided to wander over and see what was happening.

The Medevac had three wounded civilians that Le Loi couldn't handle. A village to the north had been attacked at dawn and Le Loi Hospital was overflowing. I entered the emergency room adjacent to pre-op to see how I could help. My heart leapt to my throat as I recognized the first victim.

It was Mai.

A grenade had exploded at point blank range, ripping her to pieces. There was little hope that she would survive. I ran to the O.R. and began to scrub, my face set in a fierce scowl. I was determined that Death would not win today.

Mai was first on the table.

Drs. Obrist and McCall were good. In seconds they determined that nothing had penetrated the pleural cavity. While their little patient's blood was being typed and I.V.'s set up, they began clamping off torn blood vessels. The damage was massive.

I called for another instrument pack for amputations. A nurse scrubbed in to help and the four of us worked swiftly. Before the surgeons could ask for suction or an instrument, it was in their hands. Stick-ties and hemostats literally flew from hand to hand. As her blood pressure dropped, the gas man urged us to hurry. The replacement fluids were having a hard time covering lost ground.

Jagged edges of bone were trimmed smoothly and skin flaps were temporarily sewn in place. Getting her stabilized was our first priority. The wounds could be re-opened later for a permanent job of stump reductions. Time was the enemy now.

As the last bleeders were finally tied off, Mai's courageous little heart suddenly stopped beating. Later, I was told that I shouted "No" so sharply that Obrist almost had a heart attack himself. I was unaware of the outburst.

The circulating technician rapidly prepared electric paddles while Doctor McCall slapped electrolyte paste on the unmoving chest. The paddles were quickly positioned and Mai's limp body heaved upward as the surge of electricity entered her chest between the paddles. Instantly her heart jumped to life, renewing its vital function. The nurse choked back a sob as the anesthetist stuck his thumb up. She would make it.

As we cleaned the room, Linda, the nurse, asked me why I had been so hyper during the operation, literally yelling when one of the technicians took a picture of the procedure. I explained about the Medcap and the help Mai had been. Without thinking, Linda related that the attack had probably been triggered by our visit. The V.C. had made the clinic an object lesson for any other village that cooperated with the Americans.

I hadn't thought of that. Linda's statement was almost certainly the truth. I reeled with the awful realization of what had happened. Mai was fighting for her life in post-op with a missing foot, a mangled hand and a leg removed at mid-thigh, all because some foolish, do-gooder Americans had meddled in her world where they didn't belong. All of Paul's high-minded words meant nothing in the face of this.

After the Christmas massacre of the innocents, I had wanted to get in a plane and bomb the hell out of the savages who had inflicted such ravagement. Now that same feeling throbbed inside my head.

Oh God, how I want revenge.

Linda looked at me quizzically. The unspoken words were written on my face for her to read.

"Don't even consider doing anything stupid," she advised. "You aren't the only one with a corner on the revenge market. We've all had that urge at some time over here, but it just doesn't do anything constructive. Some kind of vengeance might give you a quick fix, but you would pay for it for the rest of your life."

"I know that, Linda, but this isn't war. It's .... I don't know what. There's nothing to describe what's happening here. There aren't any words that can really convey my feelings."

"Mike, you've seen those t-shirts that guys are taking home. They say "When I die I'll go to Heaven 'cause I've spent my time in Hell, Vietnam!" Well, that pretty well sums it up for me, too. And don't tell me that a woman can't get as angry as a man. I hate this bloody war so much that sometimes I want to drop a bomb on the whole damn country just to stop it. But if I did, the fighting would only move next door into Cambodia or some other place. So what's the use? Suck it up and hang in there. We'll cliché our way back to the world."

With a hug, and tears of anger running down her face, Linda left the O.R.. I knew she was headed for her bottle of Scotch. Everyone had his or her own way of coping.

I set my jaw and finished replacing supplies in the O.R., the urge for vengeance still seething within me.

Chapter Eighteen

At the conclusion of my month of base confinement, I laid careful plans for visiting Minh downtown. I spoke with the First Sergeant, who was in charge of setting up C.Q. rosters. Together we worked out a mutually beneficial arrangement. I would turn over my P.X. ration card each month to the sergeant, and in return, the sergeant would inspect the nightly reports and be sure that my name didn't appear on them. It wasn't foolproof, but it wasn't bad. If only I could be as lucky dealing with the commanding officer.

Since the Article 15, the Lieutenant wanted nothing to do with me. The necessary papers still weren't available and I realized that they probably would never be there. I would have to make an end run.

With the departure of Tricky Dick, I knew no one at the 39th Signal Corps, where there might be another source of applications. The only other possibility was to go to the sprawling base at Long Binh where all of the administrative records were handled. There, I could play it by ear and finagle a way to get the papers. But how to get to Long Binh?

A notice posted on the company bulletin board provided the solution. A soldier-of-the-month competition was held regularly. The winner was sent to Long Binh to represent the unit in a Brigade-wide competition. The reward for winning was a big atta-boy, a two day pass to Long Binh (whoopee), and a reputation as a nerd, or brown-noser.

No sweat, I thought. My reputation as a malcontent gone native was already well established and I really didn't care much about that anyway. I inquired around the camp until I found a man who had been in a previous contest. I learned the type of questions asked and boned up before the next oral exam, which was coming up in a week. It seemed that most of the questions concerned the chain of command, from the president on down, and the rest were taken from the headlines in "Pacific Stars and Stripes," the army newspaper.

The next step was to convince Major Mahoney that she should put me up as the 36th's representative. She had a hearty laugh at the request, but I worked a bit of Irish charm on her and a week later was competing against four other soldiers for the "honor" of going to Long Binh. Fortunately, all of the others had been selected at random by their units and none really wanted to be there. As a result, no sooner than I could say William Westmoreland (Who is the field commander of the Armed Forces in Vietnam?), and Vida Blue (Who is the American League most valuable player for 1969?), I was on my way to Long Binh, and not to the stockade!

While her husband was in Long Binh, Minh stopped at his hootch early each morning to touch his bed. It kept him closer to her and she needed that closeness now more than ever. She was continually ridiculed and criticized by some of her co-workers and neighbors. How foolish she was, to think that an American would keep his promise to take her home with him. If she did go, it would be as a servant for his family, or worse yet, for his wife in America. Minh suffered a constant barrage of abuse for her stupidity in getting involved with a G.I.. At the very least, she was told, you could have picked an officer. They make much more money.

Minh paid little heed to their prattling, but she realized that she was taking a lot on faith. She was pretty sure that she knew her husband well, but countless stories were making the rounds about Vietnamese women who had gone to America only to be discarded or enslaved. And then there were all of the local girls who had been given commitments by their G.I. lovers, and then been forsaken, many of whom had borne children with these "butterfly" Americans. The evidence of these broken unions could be seen everywhere, their half Anglo faces giving away their secrets.

One Mama-san in another hootch had lived with three different Americans in the last six years, bearing three children by them. She was an exceptional case, but nonetheless tragic.

Exceptionally stupid, thought Minh. For her own case she would have to trust in her judgment and intuition. After all, he had married her hadn't he? He was in Long Binh to get their paperwork wasn't he? Lately though, there seemed to be more questions than answers. "Troi oi," she thought, between the gossipy women and this baby kicking me, I'm starting to come unglued. I wish that man would hurry up and get back here.

Meanwhile, at the 44th Medical Brigade headquarters in Long Binh, I was making out just fine. I came in second in the contest, which suited my purposes as well as I could expect. Finding a friendly clerk to come up with the proper applications took more time than I had planned, but eventually I prevailed. I still needed all of the signatures and investigations, but finally, the long-awaited first step had been taken.

As I made my way through the swirling red dust in the compound, I heard someone call my name. I didn't need any bad news just now so I kept on walking, pretending not to hear.

Suddenly, a hand gripped my shoulder. I spun around, and there in front of me stood a grinning red-headed apparition with a half-empty bottle of bourbon in his hand. Willy Smith, from Fort Sam Houston and Lakeland, Florida stuck out his free hand and offered a drink with the other.

"Mike, you old rattlesnake, whatinell are you doing here? I heard you were dead. Shot down on a dust-off or something."

"Sorry, Willy, but you got some bad information. I'm still alive and kicking. Mostly kicking. What are you doing here? I heard you were at the hospital in Cu Chi."

"And so I am, my good fellow. I came down here on a supply run. Cu Chi has been real hairy lately, so I grabbed this opportunity like a monkey grabs a banana. Let's find the beer tent. Someone might get nervous if they see me outside with this bottle."

Willy had half an hour before his convoy was to leave, and two old friends made up for lost time in a hurry. The facilities at Cu Chi were primitive compared to what I worked with. Willy described the mortar attacks and damage to the hospital with no more emotion than he would have expressed if he had been talking about yesterdays baseball scores.

It was all a matter of conditioning, I thought. Both of us had rotated to Vietnam in the same week. I had drawn relatively good duty, while my friend was stuck in a rough situation. Willy had aged a hundred years. His ready smile had been replaced by a cynical grimace and a pessimistic outlook on life. He was up for a short in-country R. and R. and promised to look me up in Vung Tau.

167

As I watched Willy stagger down the dusty street toward the waiting supply trucks, whiskey bottle dangling limply from his hand, I said a little prayer for both of them; the fun-loving, water-skiing kid from Lakeland that I had known at Fort Sam, and the rheumy, alcoholic old-young man I had just hugged good-bye. "Damn this war," I cried out loud. No one heard.

The next morning I was bumped from my flight by our new nurse's luggage and a load of fresh fruit for the mess hall. I knew that I'd been lucky to get a chopper manifest, so I wasn't too disappointed. A few hours later I climbed into the tail of a C-130 cargo plane and shared the ride with a load of replacement troops, bound for the Mekong Delta by way of Vung Tau.

They were green and scared, I thought. I could see hundreds of silent questions behind the faces, some still covered with peach fuzz. But just then, I didn't have any answers. At twenty-five, two months short of twenty-six, I felt old and tired. These boys would have to find their own answers.

Arriving back at the 36th near supper time, I went to hootch nine to find my wife and share some dinner with her. I was told that she had gone home sick earlier in the day. With a knot creeping into my stomach, I showered, checked the duty roster and headed downtown with the precious papers. Ducking through the alley I met the family from an adjoining apartment.

"Chao Ong," they said in unison.

"Chao Ong, va Ba, manhoi?" I replied. "I'm fine, and you?" The family went on their way, laughing and talking about the young G.I. who lived next door for a few hours at a time. They respected him for his attempt to learn their language, and also for the fresh oranges and bandages he brought from time to time.

In the house I found Minh lying down, snoring like a buzz saw. I left the papers on the table and went outside to visit with some more neighbors. I enjoyed talking with them, but also felt that if they became friends, Minh would have some ready help should the need ever arise. The specter of V.C. kidnappers was never far from my mind.

As I chatted with the grandfather, I looked about and was struck by the similarity of children in America and in Vietnam. The little girls were jumping rope and playing a form of hopscotch, just like the kids back home. The boys were making toy boats to sail in the

168

gutter and chasing lizards in the back yard. I tried to imagine the war being fought in Schroon Lake and Syracuse and throughout the United States. A chill went up my spine as I imagined my sisters and parents being bombed and maimed. No wonder it was so hard to write letters home. Everything here was so negative, and the only positive part of my life, Minh and the expected baby, were obviously unwelcome subjects for my parents.

A shout of "Hey Minhoi," interrupted my musings. Minh had awakened and was waving the papers at me.

Together we went down the list of requirements that would need to be fulfilled. Most of them seemed straight-forward, but that could be deceiving. Minh took the forms which needed Vietnamese approval and I put the rest in my shirt. It was dark now, and I had to start for the base. I was on first call at midnight.

Minh was feeling fine now, just a little indigestion from the pickles and ice cream, or whatever crazy foods she had eaten. She walked her husband out to the main road, as usual, and gave him an extra hug and kiss. She was getting that black foreboding again. She forced herself to smile, and with a last caution to be careful, she waited until he was swallowed up by the darkness.

Choosing not to ride for the time being, I decided to walk for awhile. I crossed over a well-used footpath to the next dirt road and slowed down to enjoy the perfumed air. The evening was muggy, but the flowers emitting that heavy scent were worth the walk. As I approached the intersection with the main road to the base I heard a disturbance up ahead. In the darkness it was impossible to tell what was happening. Cautiously, I eased into the tree line beside the road and moved closer.

Rounding the bend in the road I looked upon a terrible scene. Illuminated by the lanterns of a horse-drawn cab, five black soldiers were grabbing the reins of the little horse and trying to tip the cab over. The driver, a wizened little man with a white goatee, was feebly snapping a small buggy whip over their heads. The men appeared drunk or high, and were chanting, "Come on down, Uncle Ho."

While I watched from the safety of the trees, the whip cut one of the attackers on the check. With a vicious lunge, the soldiers snatched the diminutive Ho Chi Minh look-alike from the buggy and brutally stomped and beat him. There was a sickening crunch as his head was kicked over and over.

All of a sudden, a shout from up the road announced the arrival of two Vietnamese Rangers. They belonged to the most elite fighting unit in the country and were battle-tested. They sized up the situation at a glance and pulled grenades from their vests.

The black soldiers began to run but they were too late. The concussion and shrapnel ripped into the fleeing muggers and sent them sprawling. As the lights of a truck approached, the rangers disappeared into the trees. As luck would have it the truck was from the 36th Evac.. The driver and a passenger loaded the wounded G.I.'s into the back of the deuce and a half and sped up the road with horn blowing and lights flashing.

Emerging from the trees, I knew that I couldn't have done anything to help the old man. Without a sidearm, I would have ended up face down with him. And had I revealed my presence to the truck driver I would have had a tough time explaining what I was doing on the road at that hour.

A quick examination of the ill-fated driver confirmed what my ears had already diagnosed. The old man's skull was split and there was no life left in him.

I made for the main road with all haste. Catching a ride with the first passing lambretta, I raced to the O.R. and changed into scrub greens. I was ready when the first of the murderers hit the table. Most of their wounds were superficial, but there were some very deep punctures to the buttocks. As we worked, I related the story of the attack to the doctor and anesthetist. They were flabbergasted. They assured me that a full report of the incident would reach the commanding officer.

Pretty late, I thought. It's too bad the rangers hadn't come along five minutes sooner.

All of the attackers survived without complications. I thought of filching a pass from the orderly room to cover the trip to town but decided against taking a chance on revealing my clandestine visit. Instead, I asked the doctors to file their report based on an anonymous witness. I also asked them to keep me abreast of the investigation.

By the time the commanding officer contacted the Vung Tau police, the horse, carriage and body had disappeared. No one reported a missing person and the police learned nothing in their inquiries.

I soon learned from the doctors that the Lieutenant believed their testimony, but without a body or any other evidence, it was the word of the witness against the statements of the five men. They claimed that they were attacked by unknown assailants in the woods. The blood and signs of a grenade attack at the site could support either story. Even if I were to testify, there would be no chance of a conviction, the doctors told me, and if the body turned up, the men would claim that he was just a passer-by who go caught in the action. It looked like another stone wall.

"Doc," I said with a determined look in my eye, "is it possible to contact the commanding officer of those men and make him aware of the circumstances surrounding their actions?"

"I've already seen to that, Mike, but without a conviction, these heroes are going to receive purple hearts instead of a long stretch in prison where they belong. Do you think the two rangers might come forward?"

"Doubtful, sir. With relations between our armies as tenuous as they are, I can't see those two men taking a chance on military justice, American or Vietnamese. Can you?"

"I guess not. Well, it looks like that's all we can do. It stinks, but those are the facts."

"Doc, just one more thing," I continued. "Can you tell me what unit those men are from? I'm just curious."

"That's no problem. Just don't do anything foolish."

"No sir. I would never."

With what passed for a smile, the Doc gave me the information the next day. I sought out a friend who worked with the cook's unit and asked a favor.

"They're bad dudes, Mike," my friend confided fearfully. "Don't even mess with them or you'll wake up some morning, dead."

"No problem," I replied, "You just get a message to them. Tell them that if they ever leave this base again during the rest of their tour, they're dead men. They've been identified by a Papa-san in camp who will be watching them. No truck, or jeep or vehicle of any kind will be able to get them downtown and back to base safely. Those rangers mean business. They would blow up a whole truck load of G.I.s just to get at those scum. You make sure they understand that. Got it?"

"Oh man, I've got it. Is that really true?"

"Would you bet your life on it being a lie?"

"Not me. I'll see that they get the word."

"While you're at it, you might also tell them that they had better sleep with one eye open, because some night their hootch may accidentally blow up. They might be safer if they transferred to a high-risk field unit. Tell them that, too."

Without waiting for a reply, I turned on my heel and left. I couldn't bring them to trial, but I could insure them of a very uneasy time for the remainder of their tours. It wasn't much, but it was something.

Showering that morning, I reflected on my actions. They certainly weren't in keeping with my Christian upbringing, but even Jesus had driven the money-changers from the Temple with a lash. The more I thought about it, the more I approved of what I had done. After all, I hadn't really set the men up for any physical harm, as much as they deserved it. Ah well, I would have to leave their final punishment up to God, and take my own chances with the Supreme Judge for my actions. One thing was for sure, those five wouldn't threaten the lives of any more innocent people for a while.

Chapter Nineteen

The case load in surgery diminished shortly after the incident with the driver of the horse cab, and I was rotated into C.M.S. on a permanent basis. The work was boring and I soon found out why the crew there pulled so many nutty stunts. Cleaning instruments and packing them into surgical packs designed for specific operations was a necessary function, but quite unexciting after working in surgery. The only real excitement here was incurring the wrath of the head nurse when a dyak was omitted from a pack.

Dyaks were small round cylinders containing a chemical which changed color when sufficient heat in the autoclave reached the interior of the pack where the dyaks were placed. An un-turned dyak meant an unsterile pack or a defective dyak. Unsterility was always assumed. With a limited amount of instruments, an unsterile pack could create a significant delay which might jeopardize a life.

I never argued over the importance of C.M.S., only the lack of action. I had been up to my neck in surgery since entering the country and now I was going through a kind of withdrawal. If I hadn't already become involved with my life's vocation in wildlife biology, I was sure that I would have gone on to medical school and studied to become a surgeon.

Shifts were more regular these days, and as the time for the baby's birth drew near, I managed to spend more time with Minh. The commanding officer was not happy that I had procured the forms on my own, but agreed to sign them when they were complete. The chaplain never seemed to be available for a meeting, but everything else fell into place.

By the end of May, Minh began having problems carrying the baby. A doctor at the 36th examined her and advised her to stop working immediately. She was due in mid-June. Though we needed the money, she was only too happy to heed the doctor's advice. A

173

long rest was definitely in order.

At five p.m. on the thirteenth of June, Minh felt the first of many labor pains. I was with her at the house, and at her bidding, ran to the street to find a taxi.

There was nothing in sight. No cyclos, no horse cabs, no trucks.

Coming back to the house, I found Minh in the throes of another contraction. There was no time to lose. I had assisted with a few deliveries but preferred that a doctor take care of this particular patient.

With no other transportation in sight, I prevailed upon a neighbor to take us to the 36th on his Honda motorcycle. Somehow we made room for three and a half people on the bike and roared off to the base.

The road was incredibly bumpy, forcing us to slow down to avoid the worst of the ruts and holes. By the time we reached the main gate at the base Minh was in great distress. Our neighbor couldn't enter the gate since he didn't have an I.D. card issued by the army. I thanked him for the ride and hurriedly begged a ride to the hospital with the M.P.'s. They were obliging and dropped this imminently expecting couple at the O.R. door.

Minh waited in pre-op while I located help. The duty nurse was new and didn't know either of us. She suggested that I take my pregnant wife downtown to Le Loi. I patiently explained that both she and I worked here and that Doctor Obrist had promised to deliver the baby.

The nurse noisily arose with a disgusted sigh and suggested that I call the villa to rouse the good doctor. At that point Minh walked into the room. Her water had just broken, she began to explain, when the nurse literally shouted her down.

"This hospital is for Americans and wounded civilians. You will have to leave."

Once more I tried to explain the situation, but the nurse haughtily cut me off.

"If you don't leave right now she's going to drop that baby right on my clean floor."

Sometime between clean and floor I lost my cool. I grabbed the startled prig by her starched collar and was about to shake some sense into her when a doctor came on the scene. He was on me in a flash and pulled me away from the disheveled nurse. Before the fuming surgeon could say a word, I pointed to Minh. The doctor's practiced look took in the wet clothes and judged her time was close at hand. I rapidly laid out the problem and asked him for help.

The surgeon was new to the unit, and since I had been working at central supply for the past two months, we hadn't met. The nurse, sensing an ally, demanded a court martial and M.P.'s, but the doctor held her off.

"Specialist Hall," he exclaimed, "you could be in big trouble for grabbing that officer, but the most important thing right now is your wife. I haven't delivered a baby in fifteen years, since my intern days. I just can't take the responsibility. You'd better get her down to Le Loi."

"Sir," I shouted, "It doesn't appear that there will be time for that. I'd like permission to take her in the O.R. and deliver the baby myself. I will take the full responsibility."

At that, the nurse couldn't hold back any longer. "Specialist whatever your name is, native women here have been giving birth in the paddy fields for centuries without the help of American doctors. Take her to Le Loi for her own people to help."

"Nurse Bitch, or whatever your name is," I exploded, "for centuries the infant mortality rate at birth over here has been among the highest in the world. Le Loi is a pest hole, completely unfit to handle newborn infants. I will tell you one thing -- if any harm comes to this woman or this baby -- there is no place in this country where you can hide from me. And that's no threat -- it's a promise. Come on Minhoi, we're out of here!"

Hustling down the corridor to the door, I shouted back. "If I could call an air strike in on this place, I'd do it right now, in a second. You're a disgusting excuse for a human being!"

Outside the hospital we spied the ambulance. I swung open the double doors in back and out popped two very surprised, and very high, G.I.'s. They had been smoking marijuana in what they thought was a safe place. Minh climbed on a litter in the back and tried not to breathe too deeply. In the meantime, I started up the old cracker box and pointed its nose towards town. With the pedal to the floor we raced out the main gate and barreled down the rutted road once more. The M.P.'s declined to follow, probably surmising that an emergency was in progress. How right they would have been!

Sliding to an abrupt halt outside Le Loi, I rushed to the back of the ambulance to get Minh. She was in such pain that walking was impossible. For a brief moment I thought that everything would happen right there. And then the pain subsided momentarily and Minh climbed down.

I held her hand as we walked the few steps to the hospital door. I pulled the handle and met resistance. The door was locked.

Oh my God, I thought. They're closed for the night. I forgot all about that quaint custom.

An old man passing by on the street confirmed my worst fears. If it was an emergency, he told us, we might try the Korean Army Hospital across town.

Fighting panic, I helped my suffering wife into the seat beside me and floored the accelerator. The old ambulance shot out into the lane. At breakneck speed we made our way through the narrow streets, Minh guiding us until the next contraction drove all thoughts of directions from her head. It took all of her considerable will power not to push the baby out. She knew that there were only minutes left, if that.

We screeched to a halt at the next intersection. I rolled down the window and asked directions but no one could understand my frantic attempts to communicate. Finally, a youngster hopped in with us and pointed the way. It was only another two blocks.

Bumping up over the curb, I guided our gallant old conveyance over the dirt compound directly to the front door. No time to look for an emergency entrance. For the third time that evening we tried a hospital for help with the child.

And the third time was a charm!

A perky little nurse with a permanent smile led us to an operating room and helped Minh onto a table. She found a pair of stirrups and attached them to one end. She spoke only Korean, but by gesture she let us know that she was going for a doctor.

I breathed a sigh of relief.

Minh pushed.

The time had arrived.

Washing my hands, I quickly opened the delivery pack which the nurse had pointed out. I spread a sterile drape beneath Minh's legs and drew some warm water in the basin. Holding my panting wife's hand, I felt the final push begin. Her fingernails gave me the first clue, as they dug into my flesh.

Seconds later the baby's head appeared. I cradled it and waited for the shoulders. When they didn't follow, I gently assisted the delivery until the entire body was out. Suctioning the mouth and nose, I was rewarded by a healthy squall. Our son was announcing his arrival to the world. Clamping the umbilicus, I tied it off near the child's navel and snipped it free. Minh tried to prop herself up to watch and give some free advice, but the effort was too great. She had to trust her husband to take care of them.

After sponging the baby with warm water and wrapping him in a clean cloth, I brought him to his mother. She held him to her breast and kissed his tiny head. "Troi oi, Minhoi," she murmured, "our son. Chung minh cau con trai. Con dep lam."

"I know," I answered huskily. "We have a very handsome son. He has your eyes and my cheeks. My hair too, worse luck."

At that point, the doctor swept into the room.

"Well, well," he exclaimed with a big grin. "It seems that I'm just in time to sign the papers and collect my fee. You two have a most beautiful son. He looks just like my son when he was born. Tell me, did he cry in English or Vietnamese? And what is his name?"

"He is Ngoc," Minh answered firmly, "but what will we call him in English, Minhoi?"

"He is Michael Jr. .... we will call him Michael," answered a beaming husband.

Looking around the room, I noticed that four more nurses had come in while the doctor had been speaking with us. The young nurses were fascinated by the child. They took turns holding him and giggling about what a beautiful baby he was. At least that was my best interpretation of their Korean. The doctor and nurses ushered our little family into a small room where we were welcome to spend the night. As they talked, I explained how we had happened to come to the hospital. The doctor was furious.

"Incompetent bureaucrats are one thing," he raged, "but such blatant prejudice and disregard for human life is unbelievable. How could they deny you in the very hospital where you both work? It stretches the imagination."

"Doctor, I want to thank you for your kindness," Minh offered. "We don't have much money, but we will pay you whatever the charge may be."

The doctor dismissed her comment with a wave of his hand. "There is no fee, young lady. How much could I charge for signing a piece of paper?"

I grinned wryly, thinking of how much it was costing us to get our marriage certificate signed. But for now, there were more important issues at hand. When the nurses and doctor had gone I lay down beside my wife and son and held them close.

That night there were two nurses outside the door to help Minh and the baby. At daylight, a tray of food appeared in the room. The doctor returned about ten a.m. and examined mother and child. Pronouncing them healthy and lucky, he released them with the proviso that Minh bring the child to him for his shots and all of his health care needs. The nurses were overjoyed when Minh agreed. We all shook hands and I went outside to find a ride home.

A smiling nurse was waiting by the old ambulance with a box of baby lotion and other sundries. I just shook my head. I had completely forgotten that I had the ambulance down here. Returning it later on could prove interesting.

Chapter Twenty

Striking an officer, stealing an ambulance and A.W.O.L.; the charges didn't lose any of their significance as I rolled them over in my mind. My wife and son were safely ensconced at home now, and it was time to return to the base and face up to my actions. A neighbor was staying with Minh for a couple of days so I would not be needed for a while. Well, what was the worst they could do? After all, I had been Soldier-of-the-Month!

I drove through the main gate without receiving a second glance. That was a good sign, at least. As the old cracker box lumbered down the muddy road to the hospital, I rehearsed a defense. Temporary insanity? In my own mind I could justify everything and then some, but in my military mind, oh the doubts. Swinging in beside the helipad, I cut the engine. Taking a deep breath, I opened the door and started for the emergency room. I hadn't gone ten paces when the E.R. door opened and Doug stepped out. Catching sight of his wayward ami, he broke into a wide grin and gave out a ringing war whoop.

"Hey old mountain man, you have got the best timing of anybody I know. Some prune-faced, fat-rumped nurse has been to the C.O. trying to get you in front of a firing squad. But Major Mahoney lit into her like a roman candle. When she heard what happened she threatened to kick that nurse's can all the way to Hanoi. As it is, she may end up transferring her to the boonies. Anyhow, Major M. stuck her neck out ten miles for you and promised the old man that you'd be back tonight. You really owe that lady."

"Doug, old hoss, when we get back to the world I'm going to take you out and buy you the biggest steak you have ever seen. Is Mahoney on duty now?"

"I don't know, but that new Doc is. The one who wouldn't deliver the baby. Hey, how is Minh? Did she have the baby?"

"Oh yeah, she sure did. We have a healthy son and Minh is doing just fine, no thanks to this outfit."

"Whoa back there, pardner. Don't blame the whole outfit for one stupid nurse. Doc Obrist and Sam the gas man were ready to chew some nails when they found out about Minh. The whole gang here was ready to help if they had known. It's just too darn bad that the new nurse and doctor were the ones on duty last night. That screwed up everything."

"Thanks for the vote of confidence, old pal, but what about the ambulance? Has anybody said anything?"

"Not a word so far. You know, I don't think it was even missed."

"I've got to see the Major now, but when I get back I'll have to tell you about the stooges in the back of the ambulance. I think Minh inhaled enough pot to get her through her labor. It's a long story."

In the emergency room I was told that Dr. Newman was in post-op with an accident victim. Seems that some cowboy tried to play matador with a water buffalo and was gored in the abdomen. I shook my head and strode purposefully to post-op. Dr. Newman was just adjusting a Penrose drain when I walked in. He straightened up and took my hand, pumping it vigorously.

"I want to apologize for the nurse's remarks last night. You and your wife were under a lot of stress and she nearly sent you over the brink with her callous handling of the situation. Please tell me, how is your wife?"

"My wife and son are doing fine. I delivered the baby myself at the Korean hospital. By the way, if we can ever do anything to help them out, please make an effort to do so. They went out of their way with kindness to us."

"I'll remember that," replied the doctor. "In the meantime, you had better see Major Mahoney. She's a tough woman but she's fair and takes care of her own. She must like you because she really gave the Lieutenant what for. I think she's over at C.M.S. right now."

"Thanks for your help, Doc, and don't forget about the Koreans."

"I won't," he answered, "and good luck to you and your wife and son."

At C.M.S., Major Mahoney shook her fist in my face. "You

boob," she shouted, "don't you know any better than to take a swing at an officer?"

Before I could contradict her, she continued. "Haven't you heard of turning on your heel and just walking away? Enlisted men have been shot for less than what you did. What have you got to say for yourself? No, I don't even want to hear it. You've probably been rehearsing it all day and it will all be so much blarney anyway. Well, what the Hell! I haven't been lied to yet today, as far as I know. Let's get a cup of joe and you can tell me all about the baby. I presume you had enough sense to do that right."

Over the coffee I filled her in, leaving nothing out. When I was through I had to add one more thing. "Major, you once pulled me in to the O.R. off second call when I was half drunk. You read the riot act to me and made me sweat through ten hours of surgery under those hot lights. I was sicker than a dog all night but I concentrated on doing a flawless job. And I did it! You complimented me in the morning for sticking with it, and apologized because you thought that I had been on first call, when drinking is off limits. And one more thing, even though it's permissible, I never had so much as a beer on second call after that. In point of fact, I've been heavy into Coca-Cola for the past two months."

"Hall, I knew you'd spread the blarney if I gave you the chance. Now tell me again how an English name like Hall makes you Irish."

"Well Ma'am, me mother was a Sullivan, and as I told you before, I used to say that if me sainted mother hadn't married me father, me name would be Sullivan. But as my good cousin, Johnny Sullivan, pointed out, if me mother hadn't married me father, me name would be "bastard". So there!"

"Ah Michael me lad," she brogued, "you do have the blarney, and more's the pity. But from now on you may call me Colonel Mahoney. The promotion came through this week. Now go get cleaned up. You smell like you've just delivered a baby."

"Yes Ma'am, I mean Colonel," I grinned.

And with steps as light as my heart, I headed for the showers. I would have need of these light moments in the weeks to come.

The interview with the commanding officer was brief. There would be no formal charges filed in light of Colonel Mahoney's statements on my behalf and the corroboration from Doctor Newman. For his part, the Lieutenant would be happy enough to be rid of this troublesome medic in another two months.

The medic felt likewise. As for the marriage forms, it seemed that I had been given the wrong forms in Long Binh. The new requirements were much stricter and included a six month waiting period between the first filing and a final action on the petition. I couldn't believe my ears. I had come so far, only to collide with the mother of all stone walls. There must be a way to cut through the red tape.

The young commanding officer answered in a voice that was genuinely sincere. "Mike, if there were any way that I could expedite this process for you I would do it. I was working as an accountant when I was drafted and after officers training school I was shipped directly over here. I'm no hard case and I know you're no foul-up. I know about your trips downtown at night, but I understand why you have done what you have done. If you weren't married I probably wouldn't have looked the other way."

I considered this last statement. So Top hadn't kept his part of the bargain, eh. That was good to know.

"Anyway," the Lieutenant continued, "I can try to push the application through as a prior submission before the new regulations take effect. It's a long shot but worth a try. Meanwhile, please try to stay out of trouble." I tried to answer but was cut off before I could begin.

"I know, I know. None of this was your fault. I'm sure you really feel that way, but regardless of fault, if something else goes wrong, a certain nurse will be going over my head and cause more trouble than you and I and Colonel Mahoney together can handle. Do you get my drift?"

I hadn't yet read the hot new paperback circulating around the camp, but if I had I would have recognized the character of "Hot Lips Hoolihan" right away. I assured the Lieutenant that there would be no more trouble and dismissed myself. I fervently hoped that I could maintain my equilibrium for the next couple of months. The news about the application had been a heavy blow. Perhaps I had taken a Polyannic view of the process. I should have known that army procedures aren't that simple.

A day later, still in a quandary, I was able to contact the Judge Advocate General's office in Long Binh. A legal aide began to stonewall me until I dropped Colonel Mahoney's name. The name meant nothing to the assistant attorney, but the rank and my fast and loose use of her authority brought quick results. A lawyer picked up the phone and listened dutifully as I explained the problem.

"Specialist Hall," he finally said, "your rights in this case are clearly defined. The U.S. Army cannot recognize your marriage to a Vietnamese National since they require you to follow their procedures before such a marriage can take place. If, however, you have the Vietnamese document confirming your legal, civil marriage, you can apply to the American Counsel at the Embassy in Saigon for a birth certificate for your child. You could then take your child with you when you leave the country, but since you are still in the military, and they have not recognized your marriage, there is no way your wife can accompany you. I'm sorry but there is no latitude here for making an exception."

I questioned the attorney for several minutes, but learned nothing that would help. I never realized that the lawyer was misinformed and passed on some very inaccurate information. I could have presented my wife to both the American Embassy and the Vietnamese visa office with our marriage certificate and the Korean doctor's affidavit of the birth, and obtained an exit visa for Minh and an American passport for little Mike. Actually, Ngoc was technically an American citizen by dint of his father's nationality. Unfortunately, I was still a tyro when it came to bureaucratic maneuverings. I took the lawyer's advice at face value and hung up the phone in utter dejection.

At the end of the work day I tried another angle. Relying on whatever deposits remained in my bank of good will with Colonel Mahoney, I called the villa and asked to speak with her. I was thunderstruck to hear that she was being transferred the next day and couldn't come to the phone. I tried invoking a medical emergency as the reason for the call. The detached voice at the villa replied that there was no way the Colonel, with emphasis on the work Colonel, could respond to anything at this time. Disconsolately, I replaced the receiver and shuffled out of the orderly room.

Passing by the beer tent, the siren song of laughter and music beckoned. I briefly considered drowning my sorrows, but the picture of a wife and son waiting at home was a stronger call. I picked up a pass and cadged a ride with a pair of M.P.'s. As they let me off, one of the men asked if I still worked at the 36th. I nodded affirmatively, and the soldier-policeman asked if he could make an unofficial appointment the following day to treat his case of carnal flu. Wearily, I agreed and named a time and place.

"Thanks, Doc," he chirped. "I won't forget it."

"Yes you will," I replied softly, as the jeep drove off. "You guys always forget the consequences of your "short-times".

Crossing the street into the alley, I couldn't help but smile, recalling Willy's brief in-country R. and R. visit to Vung Tau. I hadn't been familiar with the bars downtown, though I had heard some of the ones to avoid. I had joined my old friend for a couple of drinks, but when the baby-sans strolled over to beguile us with their obvious charms and wheedle a few Vung Tau teas, I wished my pal luck and struck out for Minh's.

My welcome had been less than warm until I convinced her that I was totally innocent of anything other than buying an over-priced drink in order to leave without a gang of cowboys following me out. The two hours I had spent lying on the floor beside our bed while convincing her of the truth were not soon forgotten, nor were the gestures she made with a cleaver should I ever go beyond merely buying a drink. But the smile came from recalling Willy's letter three weeks later. He had caught a nasty case of V.D. from that episode and blamed me for taking him to an "unclean" bar.

My thoughts turned somber again as I entered the house. Minh was nursing the baby and the sheer domesticity of the scene brought a lump to my throat. As I kissed her hello she sensed my mood. With Ngoc in my lap, I slowly outlined the problem we were facing. Minh didn't interrupt as I finished the explanation of the forces arrayed against us. When I was through, she pulled me close, whispering that regardless of what happened in the future, she would continue to love me and do whatever it might take to be together. With the little one beside us, we lay down in each other's arms and slept.

At ten o'clock I left for the base. And as she did every night that I left, Minh prayed that I would be safe from the prowling cowboys and Vietcong. On this night she added a special prayer that if we were separated, it would be for only a short time.

Deep in her heart, Minh was strong in her conviction that our love would carry us through the coming hard times. She was only too aware of her friends' cautions however, and knew for a certainty that once they heard that her husband was returning to America alone, there would be non-stop "I told you so's". Knowing what lay ahead though, and enduring it, were two different things. She would again need every bit of courage and endurance epitomized by her buffalo namesake to weather the most difficult storm of her life.

In August, a week before her husband had orders to ship out, Minh's family risked another visit. They were totally captivated by little Ngoc. He was a happy baby and showed signs of becoming a delightful little boy. Even Tot dropped her usual reserve to fondle and play with her grandson. Suu, of course, was proudest of all. He bragged about his son-in-law and new grandson to his closest friends, though he dared not spread the word too widely.

While everyone was fussing over her son, Minh was assiduously putting together a support system for the future. She arranged with Lieng for mail communications, using her friend's husband's address. It would be surer and far more rapid than the mail system in Vietnam. Lieng too, hoped to go to America someday in the future with her American husband. She helped Minh with all the preparations for the approaching separation. Together they stockpiled a few supplies from the P.X..

Thu watched her little brothers while Minh and Lieng made sure that all was in readiness. Lieng provided Minh with vitally needed support, but privately, she was unsure of the future. She had seen too many women send their Americans home, never to hear from them again. She hoped that Mike would be different.

Finally, like the last day of summer warmth, the eve of my departure sadly arrived. Suu cooked a special dinner while Minh and I clung to each other and to the children. Though the meal was delicious, no one had an appetite. Lieng stopped by to say good-bye and soon left in tears. As the neighbors dropped in one by one, the full import of what was about to happen rushed over us. When darkness fell, we pulled a curtain around the bed and laid down to say good-bye, neither knowing if we would ever see the other again. The uncertainties of living with this war made so many promises turn to dust, and both of us were all too well aware of this.

As the curfew drew near, we emerged from the quasi-privacy of the curtain for the final good-byes. I had prepared a little speech in Vietnamese for Suu and Tot, but found myself so choked with emotion that it was impossible to speak. After taking a few minutes to recover my composure, I uttered my farewell in English, asking Minh to translate.

"I must leave for America tomorrow," I choked, "but I promise you all that I will return. If Minh and the children are not with me in America by next year, I vow to you that I will be back before a year has passed. I asked to be extended here for six months, but the army refused me. There is so much I want to say to all of you, but I don't have any time or words to express myself. I love you all, and I promise that Minh and the children will join me in America."

With that, I straightened my back and then bowed deeply to Tot and Suu. Tot returned the bow while Suu gave his son-in-law an emotional hug. The two of us looked one another in the eye and shook hands, but neither could speak. For years to come, I would remember Suu in that light. Tough soldier and resourceful provider, but most of all, a tender and loving human being and one terrific father-in-law.

I kissed and hugged the children and walked to the alley with Minh at my side. At the street we held hands, gazing at the moon. Once more, our thoughts were identical.

"When I look at the moon here in my country," Minh whispered with emotion, "I will know that you are looking at the same moon in America, and we will be close."

"I know," I replied softly. "I was just thinking the same thing."

We smiled then, and with a final hug, I walked into the Vung Tau darkness for the last time.

At five a.m. I was awakened by the C.Q.. Time to rise and catch the freedom bird, as the planes home were called. As I walked to the airfield to board the C-130 that would take me to Saigon, Minh appeared at my side. She had arisen early, determined to see me off.

At the gate we embraced once again and I kissed her good-bye. I walked slowly to the tiny terminal, not daring to look back. Entering the building I turned to see Minh walking back to the hospital. Ten minutes later I was circling over Vung Tau on the first leg of the long journey home.

At Saigon I boarded a United Airlines jet with dozens of other returning G.I.'s. The mood in the plane was festive. Most of the men had been in Vietnam for a year or more and their dream of returning to the world was about to come true. For me, the emotions were mixed, but no less strong. I would be separated from the service upon landing in Oakland. There would finally be an end to uniforms and chain of command bureaucracy. As a civilian I would be free to pursue my commitment to Minh. With the thought of her name I felt a pervasive melancholia sweep over me. The emotional farewells of the previous night lingered in my mind, and by trying to remember all of the words and sights, I found the vivid memories to be a delicious form of torture.

My trip to Vietnam had been punctuated with stops in Alaska and Japan. The return journey featured refueling halts in Guam and Hawaii. During the three hour layover in Agana, on the island of Guam, I tried to imagine my father here. He had spent over a year on this Pacific Island during the Second World War. As the sweet scent of frangipani drifted about my nostrils I thought again of my family in Vung Tau. I had yet to tell my family in the States of these new commitments. They hadn't reacted very favorably when I had first mentioned Minh and her family. Now I would have to tell them as gently as possible.

Actually, I mused, there had been little opportunity to do so in the last short letters I had sent home. My mother had carefully avoided mentioning Minh in her letters, and I had taken my cue from them. I had no fear of telling them of Minh and Ngoc and Thu and Tri, but was worried about their reaction. They had strong hearts, I knew, but one never is sure what this kind of news might provoke.

When the jumbo jet touched down at Oakland, I checked my watch. It had been twenty-four hours since I had left Saigon. A mere twenty-four hours, yet light years away in terms of emotions. There would be no more rockets at night, no bed checks or fresh casualties. The stench of burning latrines and diesel fuel would be replaced by the aroma of fir trees and clean mountain air.

The sensations were overwhelming. I had to focus.

Out-processing -- that was the immediate goal. Everything else would have to fall into place in its own good time.

Incredibly, the discharge process took less than an hour. I was given a new uniform for use while completing the inactive reserve requirement, and plane fare to the airport nearest my home. I pocketed the money and took a bus, keeping the balance for spending money. After all, this was America and I was free to make my own decisions. Free at last ....

187

Chapter Twenty-one

In the Oakland bus terminal, I called home to confirm that I had arrived in the States safely and would be home in a few days. I had a change of civilian clothes but opted to wear my military uniform for two reasons. On the practical side, the bus ticket would only take me to Albany, New York, a hundred miles south of home, and I hoped that hitching a ride in uniform would increase the chances of getting a ride. On a more ethereal plane, I was proud that I had answered my country's call, and wearing the uniform home was a rite of passage. I had not heard of uniforms being spat upon and soldiers being harassed. Pacific Stars and Stripes had neglected to print that part of the war news, or I had missed it in their pages.

My first inkling that wearing the uniform might be a mistake came as I sat in the bus station eating a sandwich. A nice-looking young woman approached and asked if I were on my way to Vietnam. With a smile, I responded that I was just returning home from there.

The girl literally hissed as she launched into a tirade against the war, calling me a baby killer and wishing that I had burned up in my own napalm. Taken completely by surprise, I could utter no response.

The girl stalked away, still sputtering in her own self-righteousness. Looking around, I caught the stares of other people sitting nearby. In some of the faces I read cold hostility, in others, naked contempt. There were no flag-wavers or streamers of bunting to greet a returning G.I.. Of course I hadn't expected that there would be, but was a smile or friendly handshake too much to ask for?

Boarding the bus, I took a seat across the aisle from two young men in their early twenties. They stared briefly at me, got up, and walked to the back of the bus.

I'll be darned, I thought, it looks like I've become a pariah, and I don't even know how to spell the word! Snuggling against the window, I closed my eyes and drifted into an uncomfortable sleep.

Some time later I awoke in a sweat. I had been dreaming of Minh, but not the happy reverie I had intended. We had been walking down the market street in Vung Tau when a group of young boys surrounded us, taunting us with lewd and hateful remarks. I had smiled and asked them in their own language why they were harassing someone who had come half way around the world to help them. I hadn't understood their answers, but Minh had. She shouted at them and chased them away. They despised seeing an American with a Vietnamese woman, she had explained.

There had been much more than racial hatred in those dark eyes, I thought, but I was unwilling to explore it further at the time.

Wide awake now, I considered what lay ahead as far as employment. When I had learned my D.E.R.O.S. date for leaving Vietnam, I had written to the State Conservation Department in Cortland informing them that I would be home soon to fill the position for which I had been hired. A week before leaving the 36th I received a puzzling letter from the Conservation personnel office in Albany, claiming that they had no record of my having been hired for a permanent job in Cortland.

Must be one of those bureaucratic goofs I've heard of, I opined. I'll straighten it out when I get back home. Now, I began to worry about the letter. Financially, I was far from solvent, and that job was important.

During my tour overseas, I had kept up the payments on the old Chevy I had bought in Texas. Most of the rest of my meager pay had been invested in a camera or had helped Minh and her family. My bank account was as flat as a beaver tail. Putting finances out of mind for awhile, I concentrated on my fellow passengers. The bus was only half full, but all of the seats nearby were vacant. Coincidence, I guessed.

Rising to go back to the bathroom, I caught the eye of a man working on a crossword puzzle. I smiled and asked how it was coming. The middle-aged man looked me up and down, grunted some kind of a non-committal response, and continued with the puzzle.

Must be from the city, I guessed. Country folks are always

friendlier. As I opened the bathroom door, the two boys who had moved from their seat across from me began to speak in stage whispers designed for me to hear. Their remarks were cutting. I forgot Major Mahoney's advice to just walk away. Angry, I turned on them, asking if they had a problem. They apparently saw something in my face that cowed them, for they meekly answered that they had no problem. Unsatisfied, but unwilling to cause a scene, I let the matter drop.

The remainder of the trip to Albany was quiet. I left the Greyhound terminal in the capital city with my duffel bag slung over my shoulder and a heart becoming lighter with every step northward. Home, and family and apple pie were mere hours away.

My first ride took me as far as Saratoga. The racing season was still on and the roads were buzzing with Lincolns and Mercedes. I walked through the outskirts of the town, drinking in the sights and sounds. It seemed like a hundred years had passed since I had felt this free.

Out on U.S. 9 again, I caught a ride with a coffee salesman. We talked about the weather, the economy, the world series and fishing in the Hudson River. Neither the war nor my uniform were mentioned. I was relieved when I finally stepped out of the car, but a little disappointed. Again, there had been no trace of a welcome home.

The experience in Vietnam had been intense, even other-worldly. It dominated my thinking just now, and making a transition to normal life was going to be more difficult than I had imagined.

The beauty of the sunny August afternoon finally lifted my spirits, and with thumb upraised, I continued the journey home. By sheer coincidence the next person to stop was a native Schroon Laker. For the remainder of the trip we discussed the weather, the economy, the world series, etc., but again there was a careful avoidance of bringing up the war.

I tried to fathom what was going on. Perhaps as the weary people of Vietnam went about their daily business in spite of the war, so too the citizens in America coped in their own way. The war was a fact, but life went on. I realized that it must be a painful subject for many to consider. Until it had become personal for me, I knew that I had been no different from most others in concerns with Vietnam. And now, I could lay no blame on these good people who were not hanging bunting and ribbons for a returning Vet.

As I climbed out of the car, thanking my benefactor, the man stuck out his hand and said, "Glad to see you home safely, Mike."

Walking down the main street of my small home town, I checked my watch. Five-thirty. Dad would likely be having a cold beer in the tavern after working all day in the hot sun. I stepped into the familiar little tavern and my hunch was confirmed.

Dad's handshake was firm and his greeting sincere. The other working men echoed the welcome. Their offers to buy a few rounds were tempting, but I was anxious to see my mother and sisters. I took a rain check. Harrison picked up his son's duffel and led the way outside to the jeep. Moments later a grateful mother was welcoming her soldier home.

Halfway around the world it was six a.m.. Minh walked between the rows of bunks in hootch eleven and stopped at the head of an empty upper bunk. She ran her hand over the bare mattress and fluffed the ragged, flattened pillow. Her eyes dimmed with tears as she thought of her soldier, now so far away. Was he home yet? Was he happy? Did he remember her and little Ngoc? Overcome with emotion, she ran sobbing from the hootch. It would be a week before she could bring herself to come there again.

In Fredericton, New Brunswick, Marc Schneider and his wife Bev came to the window of their renovated old farmhouse. An old white Chevy had pulled into the driveway bearing New York State plates. They walked outside to greet Marc's former college roommate and close friend, Mike Hall.

Marc had moved to Canada after he finished college to take a position teaching at the University of New Brunswick. He and I had corresponded over the past year using tapes, and he had extended an invitation for his old friend to visit after he returned home. A week in the far North Woods fishing for salmon and trout would provide a much needed respite.

After spending a week at home, I had made the twelve hour trip in the old Chevy and was looking forward to renewing our friendship and meeting Bev, whom Marc had met and married in Canada.

She was a most thoughtful and generous hostess. She gave the two old friends time and space for a week, while providing meals and company in an unobtrusive way. She was a practicing veterinarian by profession, but would have made a terrific diplomat.

The fishing was good, but the peace and camaraderie overshadowed any piscatorial success. I talked for hours about my experiences in Vietnam and showed my friends the slides I had taken. They in turn offered patient and receptive ears. Years later I would fully comprehend the importance of the therapy embodied in that simple act of listening, of being there quietly for a friend.

Schroon Lake was a serene cove in the turbulent waters of America in the fall of 1969. Following my return from New Brunswick, I spent another week at home becoming reacquainted with my younger sisters, Mary and Liz. They were engrossed in the beginning of a new school year and full of life, as only teen-agers can be. I drew strength from them and decided that it was time to get on with my life.

I got in touch with the State Conservation Department and learned that the only record of my employment with them was for a temporary job in the Catskills. All records of permanent hiring in Cortland had disappeared. With a fierce determination born in the rigors of the past year, I persisted in contacts with the agency. Meeting with the State Civil Service Office, I ascertained that my name was still first on the most recent exam list for a full-time biologist position. I then contacted my former co-worker in the Catskills, who had taken a job nearby in the Adirondacks, and was hired by him as a temporary biologist aide.

On the night before I moved to the new job location, I sat down with my parents and gently broke the news to them of the marriage. They were surprised, but not shocked. I had told my sisters a few days earlier, but Dad and Mom were not totally unaware that something was in the wind. They had seen a letter arrive from Vietnam and their son disappear into his room with a Vietnamese-English dictionary. Two hours later I had re-appeared in an upbeat mood, the happiest they had seen me since my return. They were still upset that I had made such an important decision while under such stress, but decided to let the matter drop for the time being. Their relief at having their son home safe and sound far outweighed the worries over his marriage.

The first letter from Minh had finally arrived. With the help of the dictionary I had gleaned the sense of the long-awaited letter, but the use of idioms left much to the imagination. It was so frustrating to have my loved one's words in hand and be unable to fully understand them.   What if there were important instructions enclosed? We would need help. In my next letter to Minh, I would ask her to enclose a letter in English from Lieng whenever she wrote.   For my part, I was writing in English and Vietnamese. Lieng would translate for Minh to insure that nothing important was misunderstood.

In Vung Tau, more than a month had passed and still there was no word from Mike. Minh grew worried as each day came and ended without a letter. She guessed that he was busy with his family and job and would write soon. Lieng agreed, but secretly feared the worst.   Minh had been used and abandoned, left with a half-American souvenir as so many other women had been. Why did this madness have to hurt her best friend, she wondered. She had lived with such pain as a child and young woman, why was she given this additional burden to bear? Who could explain? Where were the answers?

The answers arrived in the form of four letters for Minh. Inexplicably, they had been held up in the mail room of her husband's company. The letters were a tonic for the two women. Lieng was delighted for her friend and reaffirmed in her ability to judge character.   Minh was relieved and overwhelmed by the outpouring of love and confidence in the letters. She had not been forgotten!

One letter was ten pages long. It described a marvelous trip to a place called Canada, where her husband had slept in the open air beside rivers with strange names. Names like Renous, Dungarven and Mirimichi. It told of catching salmon fish, splitting them in half and cooking them over coals next to the stream. But most of all, the letter showed her that her beloved was happy, that he was able to find contentment with an old friend.

She had worried about his state of mind before he left. He had become obsessed with the patients in the hospital, she felt, his moods swinging with their progress. He took deaths personally, believing that every victim brought to the 36th should survive, regardless of the severity of his injuries. Minh knew that this was unrealistic, but she was proud of his dedication to his job. And now he was home and happy. She felt a great weight lift from her shoulders. Brighter days were ahead.

Warrensburg, N.Y. -- November, 1969.

"Mike, we have a special job lined up for you."

The speaker was my old friend from Catskill days, and now my boss, Gary Parsons. "We're continuing our study of whitetail deer in the Moose River Plains. We want you to head up a team to trap and tag deer in their wintering areas, using a log cabin deep in the wilderness as a base camp. You and another man will spend the winter in there and we'll send in another helper for weekdays. How does that sound?"

"Sounds great," I replied. "Will I have a chance to get out for mail and an occasional phone call?"

"Oh sure, no trouble at all. Of course, once the snow comes, you'll be fifteen miles from the nearest plowed road. All of the work will have to be carried out using snowmobiles."

I considered the assignment carefully. It would be hard to work out a plan for bringing my family here if I were stuck back in the wilderness all winter, but since most of my efforts would be through the mail, it just might be possible. Besides, I could practically bank my whole pay check since there would be no place to spend money deep in the forest. I might just be able to save enough for the plane tickets.

With the prospect of an exciting new job ahead I sat down immediately to send out another round of letters seeking assistance in re-uniting our family. Thus far, the Immigration and Naturalization Service had been of little help, although they had been prompt in answering my initial inquiries. I had forwarded the list of supporting documents needed to Minh, and hoped that she could have them processed quickly. There was nothing else to do now but wait.

I had been looking forward to deer trapping, imagining an exciting and glamorous undertaking, delving into the private lives of the hardy, adaptable deer. What I found was hard work! Seventy heavy wooden box traps had to be assembled from their components, which had been taken apart and stored at the end of the previous winter. Moving the parts to suitable trap locations along a forty mile line was no picnic either.

The set up work went slowly. Cold temperatures with frigid wind chills near zero turned fingers to ice, making them slow and clumsy. Bolting the traps together and tending to all the small details that insured a smooth operation was tedious business.

I began to think that I would never be warm again. I had never really adjusted to the tropical heat and humidity in Vietnam, and now my body refused to adjust to the bitter cold. From 115°F to -40°F in such a short time was overwhelming.

Twelve hour workdays in the frigid north woods drained energy from a body as easily as it drained a car battery when the lights were left on. Every night I planned to write Minh, and every night I found myself falling asleep in the warmth of the roaring wood stove. Manana, I would think sleepily, tomorrow I will write.

Chapter Twenty-two

A black cat scurried across the alley in front of Minh as she left for work.

Great, she thought, what next? She was having a problem getting the necessary emigration documents together and the outlook was dim. She had taken a copy of her marriage certificate to the U.S. Embassy in Saigon and been unable to speak with anyone who could help her. The Vietnamese office which processed exit visas was also no help. They wanted to see an American passport for Ngoc before they would process anything. The bureaucratic manner of all of the officials she had seen thus far was frustrating and infuriating. And now the darned black cat had crossed her path.

As Minh entered the main gate at the airfield, she became aware of a stir in the air. For weeks there had been rumors of the base closing, but rumors and war go hand in hand. Few of them were ever completely true. Unfortunately, it seemed this one was.

The worried young woman went straight to the orderly room to see Lieng who confirmed everyone's suspicions. The hospital would be closing in less than two weeks.

Lieng could work at the nearby air field for awhile, but all of the other civilian workers would lose their jobs. Minh took a deep breath and headed for the hootch. She was short of money, and with the children living with her and expenses mounting for the baby sitter and document translations, this job was critically important to her.

In the hootch she found Mop sleeping off a bender. He was a sergeant with a very generous girth who often came in early in the morning and passed out on the bed in his clothes. This time, in lying on the bed in his pants, his wallet had fallen open on the floor. As Minh picked it up she saw several hundred dollars in large bills lying loose in the wallet.

It was a miracle, she thought, that no one had come in and relieved him of his money. He was out cold and would not have heard anyone. Thinking that he needed a lesson in taking better care of his finances, she hid the wallet under a tape recorder on top of his locker and continued cleaning the room.

She was at the communal water tap doing laundry when she heard Mop's anguished cry. He was taking the hootch apart, looking for his wallet. When Minh brought the laundry back to hang it, he grabbed her arm and pleaded with her to help him. He was sure that his money had been stolen downtown the previous night, but just to be sure, he wanted help searching the hootch. Minh went along with him for a few minutes, but soon she couldn't take the little-boy-lost expression and the crocodile tears. She told him to look under the tape recorder, and next time, take better care of his money. He was so relieved that he offered her a very generous reward. Minh refused, but he pressed the issue until she was forced to accept a few dollars.

Such a seemingly insignificant occurrence played a major role in Minh's life in the next week. Her actions had flowed from her honest nature but so many of the other housemaids' fingers were light that all of them suffered with a reputation for thievery. Minh's actions as a good Samaritan, though she later admitted to having a penchant for mischief, spurred the sergeant to appeal to the commanding officer on her behalf. When she was discharged from her duties as the hospital closed, she was given a letter of commendation filled with praise for her hard work and good character. This letter of reference would serve her well in obtaining another job with the Americans and in processing some vital papers. It seemed that as a harbinger of bad luck, the black cat had been a dud!

Some thirty miles away, in the town of Bien Hoa, was another small American base. Minh took a bus there, and with the help of the letter of reference, soon had another job. Her duties were the same as they had been at the 36th, but there were no nurses to assist. There was also no way to return home each night, so she worked weekdays and traveled to Vung Tau to be with her children on weekends. A neighbor woman watched the children during the day, while Thu took care of them at night. The arrangement wasn't very satisfactory but it was the best she could do. The small amount of

197

money that Mike was able to send helped a bit, but it was far too little for them to rely on. Minh prayed that this job would last.

Arriving home late one Friday night, Minh found Thu in a state of panic. During the day, Tri's father had stopped by and taken the little boy away. When Thu had tried to stop him, he told her to let her mother know that he had another woman and was taking Tri away with him. He would be in touch some time in the future if he got around to it.

Minh tried to calm her daughter but she was hysterical, unable to recall any further details. Ngoc was hungry, dirty and in tears, his squalls serving to heighten the turmoil in the room. Minh was unsettled by the news but she quickly restored calm within her depleted family. She convinced Thu that there was nothing she could have done to prevent the abduction. Tri's father had come while the old woman from next door was at the market, and even had she been with the children, Minh doubted that the outcome would have been different.

As she hummed a lullaby and little Ngoc-Mike drifted into the peaceful land of sleep, she tried to imagine where Tri had been taken. A tear slid down her cheek and fell on the baby's head. Brushing it away, she resolved to be strong in the face of this latest crisis. If her son was still in Vung Tau, she would find him.

For the next two days, Minh, Thu and Ngoc scoured the city looking for Tri and his father. Minh checked their old addresses and left word with dozens of neighbors and friends to keep their eyes and ears open for her. Visiting the city registrar's office, she found no clue as to the man's address, but she made a friend there with a small gift of money. If the man should happen to come to that office for any purpose whatsoever, she would learn of it.

On Sunday night, before she left for Bien Hoa, her father came to the house. As Minh explained the situation to him, his face suddenly looked old to her. She had never seen her father appear so helpless. He slowly arose, and began to pace the room.

"My daughter," he began, "I will help you find Tri. I'll start in Baria and follow this man's trail until we find your son. My heart is heavy because I know how to find him, but I'm unable to use those methods. My contacts in the intelligence service could find him in short order if I dared to ask them. Unfortunately, the service has been compromised by the V.C. and I might do more harm than good if I attempt to use those contacts."

"I understand, Dad," Minh answered, her face taut with worry. "I just can't believe that this has happened when we are so close to finding a new home in America. Mike's letters have been coming regularly and I know he is doing everything he can to bring us to his country. It just isn't fair."

Suu took his daughter's hands between his own and spoke gently with her. "You have always been the strong one, Con Hai, and I have been so proud of you. Try to stay tough now, in these hard times. I'll do everything I can to help you. I'm sure of your husband, too. He's a good man. He will certainly take you away from this country and I will likely never see you again, but with your courage and strength, you'll make a new life in a better world. I have known that this is your destiny since your birth."

Minh was astonished. Parents in Viet Nam never expressed such open emotions with their children. She had never seen her father so tender, so open .... if only she had known of this deep love for her as she suffered in her self-made exile in Saigon all those years. She wanted to tell her father how much she had loved him all her life, and how much she had tried to be like him. If she had only been born a male, she thought, how much she could have accomplished. Looking into her father's eyes, she could only say, "Thanks."

For the next month, Minh continued to work at Bien Hoa, returning home for the too-short weekends. Her search for Tri went on, but the efforts were futile. He and his father had vanished. Even the seer at the temple was unable to give her a clue. Discouraged, she confided in Lieng one night that she despaired of ever seeing her son again. Lieng could offer her shoulder, but little hope.

And then Minh's luck turned bad. On a sultry tropical afternoon, as she was hanging a load of laundry behind a hootch in the compound at Bien Hoa, a young G.I. bolted into the company street, firing an automatic rifle into the air. He ran by Minh, stopped, and leveled the weapon at her.

Frozen with fear, she tried to reason with him before he pulled the trigger. With a wild laugh, he suddenly fired into the air and threw the rifle to the ground, empty. Pulling a grenade from his pocket, he removed the pin and began shouting and waving it about. Soldiers were running in all directions, diving into bunkers and behind hootches. Minh and another woman were trapped. They dared not run for fear the man would toss the grenade at them.

The M.P.'s arrived within minutes. As they advanced on the crazed soldier, he held the grenade aloft, threatening to blow up the entire camp. When the man turned to face the M.P.'s, Minh scootched down and backed to the wall of the hootch. Her friend, meanwhile, was rooted to the spot in terror, and remained in the open.

Minh retreated cautiously along the wall until she reached the safety of the corner. Scrambling around the hootch, she recoiled in horror. A third M.P. was kneeling beside the hootch, a rifle aimed at the drugged G.I.'s head. Suppressing the urge to scream, Minh called softly to her friend. She looked over, but still couldn't move. The stalemate appeared hopeless.

Minh prayed to Buddha as intensely as she could to help the young man. Suddenly he began to wander again, aimlessly at first, and then in a straight line towards one of the sandbagged bunkers.

The M.P.'s ordered him to halt. He turned around, looked at the terrified woman next to him, and replaced the pin. Sitting cross-legged on the sand, he put the grenade down beside him and started chanting. Before Minh could make out his words the M.P.'s were dragging him off. Her friend, still in a daze, remained by the clothes basket. Minh helped her into the hootch, where they shared a bottle of Coke. Both of them were shaken for the rest of the day.

The black cat had been bad, Minh recalled, but this incident was probably foretold by the owl calling last night. What next?

On her way home that Friday, Minh reflected on the new job. There were so many G.I.'s using drugs here and getting into trouble. Fights and racial tension were daily threats. If she didn't need the money so badly, she would leave and never return.

A week later, she did just that.

Upon arriving in Vung Tau, she found Ngoc screaming in pain. Thu couldn't settle him down. Minh noted some swelling above his right knee and asked if he had been hurt. Thu replied that she had been carrying him when she slipped. They had both fallen, but she had managed to keep him from hitting his head on the floor. Minh carefully touched the swollen leg and Ngoc howled in protest. Fearing the worst, Minh gathered him up and made for the hospital.

The Korean doctor who had been so taken by the little boy at his birth was working late in surgery when Minh arrived at the hospital. After examining the child and learning how he had been injured, he angrily confronted Minh, berating her for leaving the baby with only Thu to care for him at night. The boy had a green-stick fracture of the femur. The break could be reduced without surgery, but a cast would be necessary. In this climate it would mean considerable discomfort for the babe and require close attention from his mother.

Minh explained that she could quit her job to stay home with the children, but then she would be unable to pay for this treatment and any medicine that might be needed.

The surgeon brusquely informed her that this treatment and all future visits were free. Furthermore, he wanted to see the baby once a week until the cast was removed, and twice a month thereafter. Before Minh left, he gave her a bag of vitamins for herself and Ngoc. She was grateful for his generosity and genuine concern, but worried how she would find enough money to meet their needs.

When his patient had left, the kind doctor rubbed his hand across his face, and talking to no one, asked why the little ones seemed to suffer the most in war. He was still angry after having learned that Minh's husband, the father of the handsome little boy, had returned to America without his wife and son. Minh had told him that she would be leaving for America some day soon, but he had heard that all too often since he had been here.

Sometimes life stinks, he thought. I'd like to have my hands around that young man's neck right now. How could anyone leave such a beautiful child behind?

Chapter Twenty-three

I awoke to the sound of choppers. The insistent pulse of their blades seemed to course through my veins, throbbing with increasing intensity. A wailing siren jerked me bolt upright in bed. I had to get to the O.R., prepare the tables for their unavoidable gruesome tasks. I gave an involuntary shudder as my feet hit the cold floor. Lighting the oil lamp, I caught a flash of movement on the fringe of the light.

Just another big rat, I thought. The movement was repeated and a small furry creature leaped through the air, coming to rest on the cot. This was no rat. It was far too small and had strange flaps of skin extending from leg to leg. It was a flying squirrel! The sleek creature had glided down from a crevice in the log walls. Log walls -- the hootch doesn't have log walls.

Oh Lord, I thought, this isn't Vietnam.

Pulling a pair of wool pants on over the thermal underwear, I slowly regained my bearings. I would be trapping deer today, not binding wounds. Adding a sweater over the flannel shirt, I held my hand out to the cot. The squirrel responded with an agile leap onto my palm. His tiny feet tickled my hand as the little rodent with the enormous eyes searched for a morsel of food. Finding none, it scrambled to the floor and disappeared down the stairs.

I rubbed the sleep from my eyes and picked up the picture of Minh and Ngoc from the bedside shelf. I bid them good morning and fixed the image in my mind. She was wearing a white sweater over black silk pants and smiling deliciously as she held our son. My heart ached to see them. Each night I would fall asleep thinking of them, and each night the dreams would turn to nightmares. Remembrances of images fixed vividly in my brain. Images that would not go away. Last night I had seen the aftermath of a young man's haste to finish a dirty job.

Washington was a cook's helper. He was also a bully. At six feet five, two hundred fifty pounds, he was used to getting his way. On this particular steamy afternoon, he had been assigned to burn off the latrine. This meant pulling out the halves of fifty-five gallon drums of human waste and burning them. A spray tank of fuel oil was used as an accelerant. The tank strapped onto a man's back and was equipped with a hand-held pump and nozzle. Fuel oil was sprayed on the burning waste to insure complete combustion. The stench was overwhelming on a hot, muggy afternoon, and not soon forgotten.

Washington, as usual, had tried to bully his way out of the task in order to go downtown to his favorite bar. He had offered me ten dollars to take the duty for him. Not for ten times that, I had replied.

The frustrated fire-tender might have been a good cook's helper, but he was no rocket scientist. He habitually worked harder to get out of a job than the effort most jobs required. On this day, he decided to replace the slow-burning fuel oil with something that would work faster. He partially emptied the backpack tank and refilled it with gasoline. As he sprayed a stream of the volatile fuel over the flaming drums, the fire leapt to the tank and exploded.

I helped the specialists from graves registration pick up the remains. Three memories would never leave me; the smell, the charred ear we found the following day and the jokes about Washington playing Buddhist monk.

But this was Hamilton County, New York and the temperature was twenty-four degrees below zero. I shuffled out to the shed to start the generator. As the Kohler engine roared to life I heard the choppers again. The wind was ripping through the spruce and fir trees with a wavering, chopping sigh that was easily mistaken for the egg-beater sounds of a helicopter. My colleague Dale heard only the wind.

After a hot breakfast, we set out for the days work. Snow crunched noisily under our boots. Moisture in our nostrils froze the tiny hairs together and fingers and toes were at risk. My two toes which had been frostbitten during that wintry swim in the beaver pond years earlier were particularly sensitive to the frigid air. Riding a snowmobile under these conditions produced wind chills near fifty below zero. Woolen face masks with eye slits were standard wear, as were insulated jackets with hoods. Even so, on these coldest days, we were never warm and always in danger from the elements.

During this third week in January, the high temperature was -2 degrees Fahrenheit and the low was -34 degrees. From December 15th through January 28th, the thermometer never read higher than 20 degrees! The woods were in a true deep freeze. The snowmobiles and Tucker snowcat were always breaking down, necessitating emergency repairs on the trail. More than once we were forced to snowshoe back to camp as the recalcitrant machines bowed to the overpowering weather.

As if the weather weren't enough, we were harassed by a small group of local hunters who were opposed to the trapping and tagging project. While pulling the unwieldy sleds with the bait box and yoke, we would be forced off the trail by small groups of men on fast snow machines. Often, these men would ride through at night, kicking the trigger devices, springing the traps closed.

More subtle pressures were felt in town when we would ride out on a weekend night for supplies and a brief stop at the local tavern. Guarded threats would cross the room when whiskey-courage had been built.

The bitterly cold weeks of January and February were punctuated by rare days when the temperature rose above the freezing mark. The melting snow surface would freeze at night, making a very fast icy track the following day. Unfortunately, the thawing and freezing jammed trap doors and triggers, hampering our efforts to capture and mark a record number of deer. With Yankee ingenuity, these minor problems were overcome and work progressed well. The addition of a third crew member on weekdays helped to buffer the two personalities and resolve the inevitable tensions brought on by cabin fever. My two regrets were being unable to talk about the war and the inability to make any progress in bringing my family to the States.

On one Sunday visit to town to attend church, I spoke at length with the priest. The cleric was unable to help with procedures, but promised to write to his local congressman for advice on how to proceed. I had written to the lawmaker earlier but received no response. After the priest's letter, there was an answer within two weeks. The Congressman's office was very helpful, providing names at the Immigration Service for me to contact. The U.S. Immigration Service was also helpful. They provided a veritable mountain of information and forms. After digesting the requirements and procedures necessary to bring my family to America, I was convinced that Minh was right. I would somehow have to return to Vietnam to expedite the paperwork.

The prospect was intimidating. I didn't know if civilians were allowed to travel in Vietnam unless they worked for a legitimate company over there. And where was I going to get enough money for the trip and that of my family? March was a very depressing month.

Now I know how our little flying squirrel felt when the weasel moved in, I thought. The memory of the spot of blood and pile of fur made me wince. The squirrel had been no match for his Goliath, I decided, but my Goliath has yet to see me fight.

Chapter Twenty-four

"Haow naow braown caow," intoned the class. A dozen Vietnamese voices repeated the words exactly as their tutor pronounced them.

The Australian teacher was pleased with his class. He was especially pleased with Minh, and planned to ask her out for dinner later in the week. His class met for two hours, three evenings a week at the small Australian hospital on the perimeter of Vung Tau. He was a supply sergeant who enjoyed teaching the King's English in his spare time. It was also a good way to meet the ladies. He had no interest in the short-time girls at the bars, rather, he hoped to establish a relationship with more secure ties.

"Now Miss Minh," he drawled, in the Cockney-Australian accent which the class was doing its best to mimic, "I want you to tell the class why you are learning to speak English, and I want you to tell them in English."

Minh blushed and spoke rapidly in Vietnamese. The class roared with laughter. As she haltingly began her little soliloquy in English, the teacher stopped her.

"Now Miss Minh," he began with a hint of a leer in his smile, "I just have to know what you said to the class to get them so riled up. Out with it now!"

"Well sir," she explained, "I told them that if I gave my reason for learning English, you would probably stop chasing me and they would lose the joke that they are in on. You see, my husband is in America waiting for me and I want to surprise him by speaking better English."

To his credit, the tall Aussie put his hands together and made a deep bow. "I had no idea that you were married, little lady. I apologize for all the chasing I have done in the past month. But why in thunder didn't you tell me?"

Now it was Minh's turn to apologize. "Well teacher, the class was having so much fun watching you, they didn't want me to spoil it by saying anything. I'm sorry, but we were just having a little fun."

The teacher laughed at himself along with the class and seemed to take the whole joke good-naturedly. And then he made his mistake.

"Now Miss Minh," he queried, "I mean Mrs. Minh, why would a man go off halfway around the world, leaving a good looking young wife behind? Maybe we could get together anyway and talk about it. How does that sound?"

Furious, Minh spit out her answer. "You are just like all men," she snarled. "You don't care if a woman is married or single, she is just another short-time for you."

The rest of her answer was in Vietnamese, and unprintable. She was tired of all the nay-sayers and free advice she had been getting.

Do I look like such a fool, she thought? No one believes that my man will come back for me. Even my father is starting to have doubts. If I listened to all of these prattling tongues I would go crazy.

She liked this friendly Australian. He had taken the time to learn a little Vietnamese and he seemed to genuinely like her countrymen. She regretted her hasty outburst and made a brief apology. Embarrassed, she never returned to the class. Much later she found that quitting those sessions had cost her little -- the English which she had learned was laced with such a heavy Australian accent that no one could understand her when she spoke.

It would soon be a year since her husband had left and yet, it seemed they had made no progress in their quest to find happiness together. The list of documents Mike had asked her to supply was proving to be a formidable barrier. Birth certificates, death certificates and biographic data forms were not too difficult to round up, but other requirements could only be met by greasing many greedy palms, and she had no money for that.

The tougher papers to complete included a chronological record of all her residences since birth, a police certificate of good conduct covering her entire lifetime, a background investigation by the U.S. Embassy Security Section and on and on ad infinitum.

She had written to Mike for money and he had always sent a

207

little, but now she needed much more to pay for the paperwork, in addition to supporting herself and the children. And a new problem had arisen. Her friend's husband had been acting as the go-between when she received letters and money, but now he was withholding them. For certain favors he would turn the letters over to her, but if she told her friend of this, the letters would be lost forever and other more dire consequences were promised.

She was in a quandary. She could never comply with his wishes, nor could she hurt her friend. Her options were limited. Even her cowboy acquaintances downtown were of little use since this man ran with a rough crowd which was quite capable of creating serious mayhem. Boxed in, she went to the temple to pray. Perhaps she would once again find her help from above.

In the meantime, deep in the Adirondack Mountains, winter was winding down and I was praying for an early spring. I needed to take time to gather documents and explore alternatives. I had provided financial statements, affidavits of support, birth records and biographic data forms as requested, but now I needed the freedom to follow up on these submissions and try to expedite the immigration process.

As I tried in vain to sleep one night, my thoughts turned to Vietnam. Was Minh safe? The war was still raging and civilians were bearing the brunt of the destruction.

Were the children getting enough to eat? I knew that Minh was no longer working and needed money.

Had she been able to find the necessary documents? The morass of red tape and bureaucratic wrangling could be so intimidating.

Would little Mike remember his Dad? I imagined my son growing up, taking his first steps and all of the little childhood firsts that I was missing.

I had to find a way to get them here soon.

At last the weather warmed and the deer began to search out food and shelter away from the trapline. We secured the traps and started preparations for closing the camp. The season had been busy and successful. I was grateful for both, since the hard work had kept me too busy to submit to brooding and too much needless worry.

In Vung Tau, a worried Minh was making a decision. She had discussed her dilemma with a monk and was about to confront the enemy, armed with confidence that Buddha was with her. Still, she wished the fabled Trung sisters were at her side with their magic swords. She was playing in the big leagues now, and knew that her friend's husband was vindictive. He might be capable of almost anything.

Meeting him at a pre-arranged location near the market, where there were many witnesses, Minh steeled her resolve and spoke first. "My good friend's husband," she began, "I want to thank you for all of your help during these past few months. But I want to ask why you are doing this to me now. I have never hurt you or encouraged you, yet you have placed me in this uncomfortable position. And, my friend Thuy has written to my husband for me and says that maybe you have kept back many letters and money before this. Can you explain this to me?"

Denying any wrongdoing, the man insisted that Minh meet his conditions before he would give her any letters or money. His face betrayed his uneasiness, however, and Minh pressed on. "I can't do as you ask," she told him, "because it's immoral and disgusting to me. Now I will tell you what I'm going to do. First, I'm telling my friend all about this ugly thing. Next, I'm going to the police and then to your boss. After that, I will tell my husband and he will hunt you down when you return to America. He is a mountain man and will hunt you down like a crazy dog and kill you. I'm not scared of you and neither is he."

The man was taken aback at this determined stance. He had not expected any resistance. Reluctantly he agreed to give back the letters and money and leave her alone. He had only been bluffing about any harm befalling her or the children. It had been the alcohol clouding his brain, he explained.

Minh remained civil, accepting his apology. She would not tell his wife, but if he ever tried anything again he would regret it.

He knew that she meant every word and would follow up on her promise. Her reputation for toughness was proven.

He gave Minh the letters and most of the money that same day.

The letters proved to her that she had not been forgotten. Lieng and Thuy translated them for her and tears streamed down their cheeks as they heard the outpouring of love, and anguish of separation described on those pages. They realized then that they had not seen the last of Minh's medic.

Chapter Twenty-five

In my small apartment in the mountain town of Warrensburg, I was waiting for responses to my latest inquiries. I had written the Immigration Service, Vietnamese Embassy in New York, American Embassy in Saigon and International Social Services in New York City. I had sent telegrams to my congressmen and begun looking for help to finance the struggle.

By mid-April, nothing had materialized. The answers to all of my letters were polite, stating only that the matter was under consideration and I would be informed when anything was resolved.

I was busy at work during the day, but the nights were long and filled with memories of Vietnam. The intensity of that year would not leave my subconscious. I would awaken at two in the morning, certain that I heard choppers approaching. On occasion, I would get out the battered old typewriter I had used in college, and peck out remembrances and anecdotes that were swirling through my mind.

Sometimes a couple of beers would stimulate the memory, and sometimes confuse it. In the morning light, reading those beery efforts, there seemed to be a melding of my experiences and those of friends and acquaintances.

Would I ever be able to totally separate them, I wondered? It didn't seem to matter, as the writing, painful though it was, acted as a catharsis for the pent-up emotions that could not be expressed outwardly. A small notebook began to fill with my ramblings.

O ver and over, each dawn brings renewed hope
P erhaps today will bring the anticipated letter
T omorrow is a refuge and reserve
I nstead of despair there is desire
M ist of the night dissolves with each day's light
I f there is no letter today, surely it will come later
S oon becomes a friendly work companion
M ost never realize the powerful force that is OPTIMISM

Medcap

The line was endless. Tall and small, they queued in a patchwork of ragged shirts and bare feet. Every disease and ailment of mankind seemed to be represented. The needles kept the shammers and curious from the line, but nearly all needed treatment of some kind. Candy and balloons quieted the most persistent squallers.

Amid the drab crowd, a raven-haired beauty was as conspicuous as the first evening star. She was no more than fifteen, but there was a serenity, a look of detached peace, which set her apart. She offered a cup of coconut milk. Smiling demurely, she softly spoke, "Bac-si dep lam. Co the toi giup ong?" Handsome doctor, can I help you?

There was no typical shyness about her. Old and wise at fifteen, her parents had disappeared during a raid on the village a month earlier. She knew they would never return. And a stomach gets hungry whether there is money for food or not. Would I care to buy a reed sleeping mat or a newly-woven basket?

The next morning I saw her again. This time her peaceful expression came from the demerol and atropine. The grenade had done its deadly job well. Nguyen Thi Mai -- good-bye!

And the meek shall inherit the earth. But if the meek are killed, who will be left? Can the left hand heal while the right hand avenges? If loved ones are dying while a man turns the other cheek, what will remain to inherit?

Justice is not of this world.

Innocence and hope, meekness and humility must wait for a higher justice.

Patience must be the watchword, else futility will overcome, and reason depart.

All Clear

And he leaned back and grinned and gave the thumbs-up high sign, which meant everything is fine, and good luck, and dear God I'm scared, but if I put my thumb up I'll be confident and forget what is down there.

He laughed a lot and kept promising to let me remove the wart from his back sometime when he was good and drunk. And every time the subject came up, which was at least once a day, we shared the private joke about sterile technique, which it was obvious I hadn't mastered.

And then the pilot shouted that the ground report was clear and we were going in. Clear, clear, clear. That was the word every time and there could be no question of fire-fights, or mistakes or doubts. They're dying so who the Hell are we to worry about ourselves? That was Bill's routine every time.

Devotion to the cause, or succumbing to the damned propaganda, the result was the same. Which fate was worse -- holding back and coming again and again -- or giving it all for a few, and then coming no more, evermore?

But it's clear below and the choice is out of our hands. And the clear lie is perpetuated as we go in again.

One minute and thirty seconds. No records broken this time but there are two litter cases and three ambulatory, and confusion on the ground. This time the clear is gone and the air is heavy. Victor Charlie is alert and not so dumb, and the clumsy bird can't lift off for one minute and thirty seconds.

Then clumsy goes and the tourniquet slips and air slips beneath us, and clumsy is no more, but lifting and dodging and climbing, and the spats and pings are surreal.

Where is it -- but the clip is gone and before he can turn to swear he question he is jolted and slips very quietly, slumping against the opening.

An eternity before he is gone, his head turns, but there is no face, only red and cartilage, and then to the clear, all clear ground below.

Duty, honor and country, and death before dishonor. Platitudes without number are fine and inspiring, and must be defended by The Legion and Vets. Words can be so important and exaggerated memories and lies are fine over the beer. Death is far behind and spoken of reverently, but the radio said "all clear," and Charlie's gone, and all is right with our world.

Her son was a door gunner, and a dreamer would be home in three weeks, and he is still falling to the swamp-mud home, and vows and prayers are forgotten. They're running and we're over them and low and diving and they stumble, and one looks up before he dies. And dear God, she didn't have a weapon.

Hostages or innocents or guerrillas, they are yellow and little and they run, so they must die.

Insert the needle, and the plasma and Ringer's flow. Life is renewed. But these fingers pulled the trigger, and is the score even? Is the white life, the all-American boy, worth more than the three yellow lives? The enemy?

What the Hell are you man, some liberal, pinko hippie? A peacenik gook-lover? Bill is lying in the mud, faceless, and you choke and quibble and fumble with the infusions and gauze. Not bad shooting for a medic. You got all three.

Oh Lord, why? Colonel, the transfer proved your point. Request my previous assignment. My sweet Jesus, how can I explain? How can I live with myself? How can I heal?

Cut'em up, sew'em up. You must be proud to be on the healing end of such an unjust and terrible conflict. War is Hell, young man, but you're home safe now, so all is well with the world. Forget the blood and gore, the hospital smell and the daily corpses and mutilated. We shouldn't have gone over there in the first place. We don't belong there.

Thou shalt not kill.

My hands. Oh God, I'm sick. It's unspeakable. To lose a face from shrapnel or a heart from within -- both bring an end to life.

25 April, 1970
The Last One Died Tonight

The commentator said that war changes people. That no one survives unscathed the experience that is war.

Don't they?

Or does war merely strip away the glossy facade of each one of us and expose the stark individual within?

Who can say that he really knows the young man who just now forsook his safety -- overcame his inborn fear of dying -- to help a stranger? Who dares to claim that he knows the dedicated surgeon who yesterday blandly allowed a man to die because he was only a gook .... an extra cup of coffee with an old friend meant more than an immortal soul? And what of the all-American boy who murdered the two helpless prisoners?

I have drunk beer and gulped coffee with them all, from skilled surgeons and professional athletes to dropouts from the human race. My black friend of last night who beat me at chess, tonight threatened to cut on me while he was with the brothers.

213

Our carefully contrived facades fade under hypnosis or too much alcohol. War too, has this effect on a practiced exterior. The thieves, whores and black marketeers whom war has "created" were only lacking the excuse -- the stimulus of war -- before they began to ply their odious trades. The pent-up fears, frustrations and inner hostilities that caused the men to massacre an innocent village would appear in all their ignominy under other conditions of stress as well.

The real being waits for its release, to spend itself in a short burst of pure emotion, and brief it must be, for the covering personality -- the glossy facade -- is fast to recover. The secret dreams, fears, passions and emotions so carefully held within are so stark, so real, and often so different from that outside shell, that their appearance seems to be a change in the man that everyone has known.

But has he changed, or has he merely given himself and others the opportunity to really see him for the first time?

Prejudice is - being rejected by Americans and Vietnamese alike, and delivering the baby yourself.

Tolerance, and yes, even love, - is being accepted by the Koreans and receiving their hospitality and help.

Hate is - the look from a ten year old boy as a G.I. walks off with his sister.

Love - is the look from that same boy after you have lanced and dressed his painful boils, and comforted him in his own language.

Futility is - being white in a yellow country.

True generosity - is an invitation to dinner with a hungry family of another race and color.

Pain surpasses all boundaries of color and race.

No one dies of a bullet wound peacefully.

Hate and prejudice are so easily overcome with kindness and understanding.

Absence of a pedal pulse may well indicate an A-V fistula, but for the real lessons learned, brotherhood and the overall purpose for mans' existence must be constantly kept in sight.

Happiness is - believing in life everlasting and working to obtain that reward.

Happiness - is hearing a fetal heartbeat and rejoicing that here is a wanted child. Life is created willfully, and two lives join eternally to provide for him.

Happiness is - a perfectly developed child with a healthy squall, no matter the two o'clock feedings.

Anguish and desperate worry are separation.

Love, regardless of the depths it must be drawn from, never fails to confound and overcome the opposition.

Chapter Twenty-six

The hook-jawed brown trout slashed at the crippled minnow as it drifted by him. An instant later, with a hook firmly embedded in the corner of his mouth, the big trout leaped from the safety of the pool and churned through the rapids. The line ran taut and the trout, feeling the pressure, swam upstream towards the fisherman. Five minutes later the exhausted brown was lifted by a net and carried to the side of the current.

Wading carefully to the bank of the upper Hudson River, the fisherman dispatched his prize and headed for his car. This will be a great supper, I thought.

On this beautiful May afternoon my heart felt as light as the billowy clouds hanging in the azure Adirondack sky. My life was coming together. All was in readiness for a journey back to Vietnam. I had my passport, entry visa and plane ticket in an envelope on the shelf. All that remained were the immunizations required for entering and returning from Southeast Asia. I was to receive them ten days before departure. Minh was expecting me on May 22nd.

My cousin Johnny had loaned me enough money for the plane tickets, and my boss had provided the time off from work. Although I had worked such long hours all winter back in the Moose River, there was no money for overtime. The boss stuck his neck out a mile and let me take compensatory time, even though I would be shown on the books as present and working. It was really a bureaucratic Catch-22 since I had legitimately worked hundreds of hours over the standard forty hour week, but there was no mechanism at the time to compensate me for it. Should anything happen to me while I was in Vietnam, the boss would have a ton of explaining to do. Thanks, Carl.

In Vung Tau, Minh had finally gathered all of the necessary

216

paperwork and was eagerly anticipating her husband's arrival. Her joy was tempered by the absence of Tri. She had received a letter with no return address from Tri's father, with a short note from Tri enclosed. He was fine, he said, and enjoyed living with his father. Minh was doubtful, but there was nothing she could do.

In order to complete the long immigration procedure, Minh and her American spouse would have to travel to Saigon to visit the U.S. Embassy and the Vietnamese Visa office. She had been there already, but now her husband would be with her and the paperwork could be completed. From the minute she received his last letter, detailing his arrival, she had been singing around the house and skipping down the street. Nothing could stand between them now.

At the doctor's office I received my immunizations and some bad news. One of the shots had to be administered in three doses, ten days apart. There was no way I could leave on schedule.

That night I dejectedly wrote to Minh explaining the delay, hoping that the letter would reach her in time, since most mail took ten days to two weeks to be delivered to her address in Vietnam.

For the next few days there was no joy in Warrensburg. On the third day I dug out the immunization record and studied it carefully. Each page detailing the record of shots had been signed and sealed by the doctor. If I could add two dates and copy the signature the booklet might just pass a cursory inspection. The doctor had signed in a scrawl, very easy to duplicate, but the seal would take a bit more work.

Blotting some red ink on a piece of scrap paper, I practiced smearing the page until a reasonable blurred seal was outlined. I transferred the blotchy seal to the certificate and added a scrawled signature.

Not bad, I thought, as I studied my handiwork. Now let's hope the customs and immigration checks aren't too detailed.

On May 21, storm clouds rose over Vung Tau. As Lieng read my letter about the delay, Minh steamed like a volcano. Her friends and neighbors were full of I-told-you-so's and clicking tongues. So sorry, Mama-san, but you should have expected this. He's backing out just as we predicted.

Minh didn't believe that for a moment, but she was utterly disconsolate over the delay. To have her hopes brought up so high, so many times, only to have them dashed at the last minute, was too

217

cruel. She prayed before bed, cried herself to sleep and made life miserable for everyone around her for the next two days.

Catching a ride to Albany, I boarded a plane to New York where I connected to San Francisco. From there it was on to Hawaii and Vietnam. On May 22nd I stepped onto the tarmac at Tan Son Nhut airfield in Saigon.

I had returned. Back to a world I thought, and at one time earnestly hoped, I would never see again.

Though I had expected the oppressive heat and humidity, it was still a shock leaving the air-conditioned plane and hitting the oven-like temperature of Saigon.

Nervously waiting in line for the customs check, I prayed that my amateur forging would go undetected.

No problem. The check was a brief formality. Musing over this as I left the line, I realized that the acid test would come as I departed and the immunization record came into play. Carrying my single small bag of clothing, I made straight for the check point for all military hops in-country.

"Sergeant," I declared, in my best official voice, "I need a hop to Vung Tau. Can you fix me up?"

"Sure thing, Bud, just give me a copy of your orders. We have a chopper heading that way this afternoon."

"Well, Sarge," I replied, "I don't exactly have any orders with me. I was sort of hoping I could catch a quick ride and leave it at that."

The air sergeant gave me a quizzical look, glanced all around, and in a conspiratorial tone told me to come back the next day. Unauthorized rides could be arranged, but they took a bit of doing.

"How much doing?" I queried, reaching for my wallet.

"Nothing like that, Jack," the airman answered. "I mean a ride could be fixed tomorrow, but I don't charge for the service. There's just no way I can work it out today. Sorry, man."

Thanking him for his candor, I left the counter and made my way to the Air Vietnam terminal. The local airline was notorious for broken schedules and broken planes, but it would be the fastest way to reach the coast. I didn't want to waste a day waiting around here when there was so much work to do in such a short time. Besides, my visa was good for only ten days.

A smiling young woman behind the counter asked how she could help me. Her eyes shone with friendliness and I found myself staring at her. She looked so much like Mai, the girl who had helped me on the Medcap, that I couldn't take my eyes off her.

When she spoke again I was momentarily flustered. I broke into a sweat and my temples began to pound. The girl's resemblance to the unforgettable memory of Mai lying on the operating table had triggered a totally unexpected reaction. Wiping the sweat from my face, I recovered enough to ask for a flight to Vung Tau.

"I'm sorry, sir, but we have nothing going there until tomorrow."

"I'm sorry too. Could you tell me if there is a bus station near here? I really can't wait until tomorrow."

She directed me to an address about half a mile from the airfield. It wasn't a station, but a regular bus to Vung Tau stopped there and I could buy a ticket from the driver.

With a last apology for staring at her, I picked up my bag and started for the gate. Suddenly, I remembered that I hadn't asked if the woman knew when the buses ran. Walking back to the counter, I felt uneasy, like someone was watching me. Looking around, I saw no one, but the feeling persisted.

At the counter, the clerk told me that she thought a bus might be leaving about four that afternoon, but she wasn't sure. Thanking her again, I headed for the gate. As I stopped to look for a food stand, a hand came from nowhere and rested on my shoulder. I spun around nervously to find an elderly man with a cane and bowl.

Just a beggar, I thought. Relieved, I gave him a small offering and continued down the road. I hadn't expected to feel so nervous.

The bus stop wasn't too far so I opted to walk. Sauntering more casually along the road I drank in the familiar scenes. It seemed like only yesterday I had been bowing to passing ladies in their long, flowing ao dais, and waving and joking with cyclists and pedestrians. It was hard to imagine some of these smiling, open people as Vietcong terrorists, but I had seen firsthand the reality of their terrorism and knew full well the folly of taking anything for granted in this topsy-turvy land.

I found the bus stop by one o'clock. There were several open-air food stands nearby, offering a variety of ptomaine delights. I couldn't forget that nauseous bout with dysentery, and ordered a steaming bowl of "Hu Tieu", the spicy noodle soup ubiquitous in this country. Preferring not to ask what the tiny pieces of meat in the soup were, I noisily finished the bowl and topped off the meal with a heel of French bread and a warm coke. No sense risking my stomach with local ice so early in the trip. Hopefully, the soup had boiled and steamed long enough to render it harmless.

Across the street was a grassy plot under several large shade trees. I ambled over and stretched out for a rest. The owner of the little cafe promised to wake me before the bus arrived. While I had no intentions of actually sleeping, I was leaving nothing to chance.

With eyes half-closed, I reflected on my departure from the mountains. My family had wished me Godspeed and promised to pray for a successful enterprise. Dad hadn't said much, but he was behind me 100 percent. Mom was another story. She had been reluctant to accept this marriage and was surprised to learn that I was indeed returning to Vietnam to recover my family. I was afraid that she would not accept Minh when she eventually joined me, but had made up my mind that regardless of anyone else's feelings, Minh and I would make a good life together.

A few days before I left, Mom asked to speak with me. She let me know that she had had misgivings when I had first told her of my wife and son, but now things were different. She was proud of me for returning to get my family out of harm's way. When I returned to America with them they were to come for a long visit and be welcomed into the family. She explained that she harbored no resentment of the union, but had merely questioned my judgment when I was under such stress. If I had such strength of purpose now, she was absolutely certain that I had made a good decision.

A group of small boys broke into my reverie.

"Hey G.I., you got money? You got cigarettes?"

"Sorry boys," I laughed, "but I'm broke. Titi money and no "hut thuoc." Check this out," and I tossed a handful of gum into the air.

The boys scrambled and jostled for the "chewn gum" as they called it. I had brought it for just such occasions. They were a delightful crew, eager to try out their few words of English on a friendly American. I, on the other hand, was impatient to brush up on my very rusty Vietnamese. By the time the bus arrived, there were no fewer than two dozen Vietnamese crowded around me on the tiny plot of grass, all mesmerized and amused by my attempts to tell stories in their language.

I told them of bear hunting and fishing in America and of my

220

work as a medic in Vung Tau. They were most interested in the story of my quest to find Minh and the children and bring them back to America. An older woman wept softly as I described the ordeal of finding a place to have our baby. She began to tell her story, but even with my constant interruptions of "lap lai, lap lai," she didn't slow down or repeat enough for me to catch the gist of the tale. One of the small boys spoke just enough English to convey the story to me, however, and I was able to smile and tell her how sorry I was that her daughter had left for America and never been heard from again. I wrote down the name and address and promised to do what I could to find her, all the while knowing that San Francisco, U.S.A. with no street address or last name would not be enough.

The bus, when it arrived, reminded me of the old buses loaded with migrant workers from the South that came to Central New York for the fall harvest season. They would wheeze up the hills, threatening to cough to a smoky halt just before reaching the crest. This bus must have made a few stops prior to reaching this last stop on the outskirts of Saigon, for there wasn't a seat that wasn't crowded far beyond capacity. The driver shouted that there was no more room and was about to pull out when someone yelled back that there was an American who wished to board.

The bus fell silent as every dusty window became a porthole for the passengers to stare at this extraordinary sight -- an American asking to ride through the countryside on a civilian bus. The door opened and the driver beckoned me forward. With much ado, a seat miraculously cleared long enough for me to squeeze my backside in before the crush of humanity closed in once more.

With gears grinding, the ancient bus lurched forward, eliciting cheers from the children as they were bounced from one lap to another. My seat had been designed to hold two small passengers comfortably, but I shared it with an old lady and two boy scouts in full uniform. They had placed their knapsacks on the floor and hooked their feet through the loops, to maintain possession. I did likewise with my bag.

The boys spoke English quite well and were only too happy to have a captive audience, so to speak. Whenever I tried to respond in halting Vietnamese, the old lady would sniff and scowl. The scouts, on the other hand, were much too eager to correct my poor pronunciation. After a while, both sides agreed to a truce. No more grammar lessons for today.

The heat in the bus was stifling and sweating bodies did nothing to improve the air, but the windows couldn't be opened because of the dusty road. The scouts had told me that the trip should take about two hours if all went well. They didn't mention what not going well might mean. With visions of flat tires and engine trouble flitting through my mind, I closed my eyes and tried to sleep.

When I awoke, the passengers were buzzing anxiously. The bus had come to a halt and it quite obviously wasn't in Vung Tau or any other town. The sound of gunfire brought me to high alert.

The driver walked back through the bus trying to quiet his passengers. They complied too easily, I thought. Before I could ask the two boys what was happening, the heavy staccato bursts of a machine gun brought goose bumps to my arms.

We were in trouble.

The machine gun was behind us and more firing was coming from the front. Peering out the dirty window I could see nothing. Without warning, the old lady grabbed my shoulders and pushed towards the floor. She motioned for me to get down on all fours. As I did so, she and the scouts put their feet on me and arranged the bags as a cover. A piece of cloth and more bags appeared and they were added to the pile.

On the floor, I began choking from the stifling heat and dust. The blanket, or cloth, smelled of stale urine and mold, and someone hadn't washed his or her feet in ages. Just as I felt that I had to come up for air, the crash of a mortar round shook the bus.

Children screamed and cried. The old lady grunted something and dug her heel into my neck. Somehow I found enough air to remain where I was.

Moments later there was another volley of automatic weapons fire and the sound of grenades exploding. The firing increased in intensity, but seemed to be moving off.

After what seemed hours, the bus began to move. It crept slowly for about a minute, and then the engine revved and the old crate shot forward at a speed belied by its ancient appearance.

The scouts tugged on my collar and I emerged from my squalid little cave among the smelly feet and bags. The old woman was grinning at me with betel-stained teeth and smoothed my hair with her gnarled fingers.

"Khong sau, My," she offered. Don't worry, American.

I thanked her for her concern and asked what had happened.

"The bridge near Bien Hoa was under attack by Vietcong," one of the scouts answered. "The army was fighting with them when we got there. Usually this doesn't happen in the daytime, so something big might be coming."

"Isn't this road secure, though?" I asked.

"Oh sure," the scout responded, "but sometimes the unexpected occurs. When something like this happens, you just have to make the best of it."

I considered that answer. For such a young boy, he surely had a useful philosophy. It sounded almost like Major Mahoney's advice so long ago. For the remainder of the ride I spoke with the nearest passengers. I was happy to tell them what I was doing here, but cautious enough not to mention Minh's name or show them any pictures. No one was above suspicion.

As we pulled into Vung Tau, I thanked the old woman again for her concern. She answered with a wry smile playing at the corners of her mouth. I didn't understand her words and asked the scouts what she had said.

"She said," they replied, "that we covered you up in case the government soldiers were defeated and the V.C. boarded the bus. If they had found you we might all have been shot. She said that you are a good man, and a happy one, but she was worried that her grandchildren would be disappointed if their grandmother was killed, and so she hid you for her sake, and not for yours!"

I laughed and bowed to the old woman.

"Cam on, Banoi. Ba di manh." Thanks anyway, Grandmother. Go in good health.

The bus finally reached familiar ground. When the road intersected Nguyen Thai Hoc Street I signalled the driver to stop. Stepping off the bus, I was enveloped by an eerie feeling of Deja-Vu. A year ago I would never have dreamed that I would see this part of the world again, let alone this street. I was overcome with what could only be described as acute melancholia. The smells and sights washed over me as if I had stepped into a former life, back in time.

I had done just that, I thought. But this time I had the power to effect a change. I was free of army rules and felt that I finally had control of my destiny. And now to find Minh.

Chapter Twenty-seven

Once again on the dusty road I had walked so many times in the past, I was torn between walking slowly to make this dream last, and grabbing the first lambretta to rush to a speedy reunion with my wife. The latter option won.

Bouncing along in the three-wheeled, spring-less contraption, I could discern no changes in the landscape. The Buddhist temple and adjacent banana grove appeared exactly as I remembered them. The dogs were still gaunt and the children still charming. Had I really been gone a year?

I gave the driver a generous tip and dismounted into the alley leading to Minh's house. Walking by the neighbors' houses I was greeted like a long-lost relative. Smiles and shouts of welcome buoyed my spirits.

Maybe I really haven't been gone that long. At the entrance to Minh's house I hesitated for a moment, trying to picture her as I had last seen her. My palms grew sweaty and my heart raced. Ten months of separation melted away like April snow. The moment of truth had arrived.

Two children ran through the open doorway to greet me. I didn't recognize either one. A man appeared next, wearing a ragged pair of shorts and a quizzical expression.

"Lam gia ong?" he asked. What do you want?

Taken by surprise, I couldn't reply. Finally I asked for Minh.

The man had never heard of her.

My worst repeating nightmare flashed through my mind. I had returned to Vietnam to claim my bride and she no longer wanted to see me. She had moved to another city and was in hiding.

Recovering my composure, I explained that Minh had lived here during the past year and I had come back from America to see her.

The man exclaimed that he didn't know what I was talking about, but I was welcome to come in for a Coke or beer.

With growing anxiety, I turned to look for a friendly neighbor who might be able to explain where Minh had gone. As the nightmare constricted my chest, forcing my temples to pound, a teenage girl appeared and shyly asked if I were seeking Chi Ba. I was about to reply no when I recalled that Minh's family and friends called her Chi Ba, referring to her position as the third child in the family.

With great relief, I nearly scared the young girl to death with the fervor of my reply. I told her that I very definitely was searching for Chi Ba, and did the attractive young lady know where she might be? The blatant flattery drew a blush, but the girl remained poised enough to answer. Minh had left word to send for her if her American husband showed up. The girl promised to return in a few minutes with Minh. In the meantime, I was to wait at her house.

Excited to be included in this romantic reunion, the girl sped away on a bicycle, shouting the news to the entire neighborhood as she passed.

A regular Paula Revere, I thought, grinning at her enthusiasm.

For half an hour I was grilled by the neighbor women. They wanted to know if I would be taking Minh back to the States, how long I would stay in Vung Tau and a thousand other details. I tried to humor their curiosity, but my mind wasn't on their questions. And then I heard a commotion in the alley. A small pony cart was slowly clopping this way. The teen-aged messenger sat beside the driver, and beside her was a vision I had dreamed of for almost a year -- Minh was wearing the same blouse and slacks she had worn when she said good-bye at the airfield, a lifetime ago.

Though she was usually reserved in public, this was no routine meeting. Minh jumped from the rig and threw her arms around her man's neck, kissing him and hugging him for all she was worth. I of course, responded in kind, much to the delight of the rapidly growing audience. Minh's eyes misted and then tears of joy streamed down her cheeks.

Paula Revere cried openly, as did several of the other onlookers.

Minh thanked them for their hospitality and climbed back into the cart. I sat beside her. With a cluck to his little horse, the driver headed the rig out to the street.

We arrived at Minh's new address in a matter of minutes. This time, she tipped the driver generously and even gave him an extra ten piasters to treat his horse. The man smiled knowingly and offered to drive us anywhere we wanted at any time of the day or night. As Minh sent him on his way, I couldn't take my eyes off her.

If this is a dream, I thought, please don't wake me up.

"I'm sorry I wasn't there to meet you," Minh began, "but your letter said that you wouldn't be here for another week."

"I'm the one who is sorry," I answered. "After I wrote you about the shots, I decided that I just couldn't wait any longer, so I faked the doctor's signature and here I am. Did I surprise you?"

"You most certainly did," a voice from the house answered. "And it's a darn good thing you got here when you did. She has made life unbearable around here since you wrote that there was a delay. I won't say any more, but you know how she can get, right?"

I diplomatically sidestepped the question and gave Anh a big hug.

"How long have you been living here with Minh?" I asked.

"You mean how long has she been staying here with me," Anh retorted. "She ran out of rent money at the old place, so she came here with me to help share expenses. And once more, thank you for coming when you did!"

I couldn't help but laugh at Anh's complaint. I had known her when she worked with Minh at the 36th, and she had never been a shrinking violet. She was a cousin of Lieng, and had been a good friend to Minh in the past.

Behind her in the house, I heard a little cry. I entered to see Thu and Mike Jr. on their way out. Little Mike was startled and began to cry when he saw the stranger. I picked him up and he cried all the louder. Handing him back to Thu, I felt a knot in my stomach. I had been afraid that my son wouldn't recognize me.

Minh read the concern on my face and tried to reassure me. "Don't worry, Minhoi. He knows who you are. I think he was just startled when you came in the door so suddenly. I've been showing him your picture everyday and we talk about you constantly with him. Give him a few minutes to calm down and you will see."

Unconvinced, I merely nodded and continued to fret.

"Hey Ngoc, Ba lai Ngoc. Ba lai." Your father is here, Minh repeated.

I called to my son and he shyly came to me. Picking him up and kissing him, I felt the knot in my stomach rise to my throat.

I was speechless. This little stranger in my arms was really my son. It had been so long since I had held him, and now he had grown to toddler size. I handed him to Thu and the three of us shared a bear hug before Minh announced that it was supper time. A few minutes later Lieng arrived and the reunion continued. After all the letters and delays and complications, the dream had been realized. More than ever, I was convinced of the power of prayer. I knew only too well that I had not made it back to America unscathed, and then back to Vietnam, without some big league help. And that help was still needed if I were to consummate the final details of this quest.

The following morning, Minh and I took the bus to Saigon. As we passed over the bridge at Bien Hoa, I related the story of the firefight. Minh was angry with me and with herself. She told me that I should have called Lieng at the airfield in Vung Tau. Then I could have waited until someone came to meet me.

"Minhoi," Minh continued, "we have to stop at the lawyer's house first. He has been helping me to get everything together. He specializes in assisting Vietnamese in going to America. Lawyer Kim is a crafty fellow though, so you had better let me do the talking."

Unsure whether I had been insulted or just warned, I nonetheless recognized good advice when I heard it. When the bus arrived in Saigon Minh hailed a taxi and soon we were weaving through the worst traffic I had ever encountered. More than once I closed my eyes as a near accident loomed before us. I took note that the lawyer did not live in a very prosperous neighborhood. I wasn't sure if that was a good sign or not.

Mrs. Kim welcomed us into her home. Her husband was out on business but would return within the hour, she explained. Would we like to take a shower or nap?

"Well Minhoi," I crowed, "it looks like you picked the right lawyer. This is real class, letting us use his home this way."

"Don't speak too soon, Minhoi," Minh replied. "We should receive first class treatment for the money he is charging."

Before I could answer there was a knock on the door. Mrs. Kim was inquiring to see if we were ready to eat. Minh announced that we would be there in a moment.

"Don't forget," she reminded me, "let me do the bargaining."

"Welcome to my home, Mr. Hall and Mrs. Hall. I do hope you are hungry, as my wife has fixed a small meal for us. I am Mr. Kim."

As I shook the lawyer's hand, I knew immediately where I had met him before. He was every used car salesman I had ever dealt with. His demeanor and smooth talk left no doubt in my mind that Minh's cautions had been well advised. Despite the humble attitude and self-effacing mien, this was not a man to take lightly. Behind the cloying smile was a mercenary spirit which was far more experienced in these affairs than the country boy from Schroon Lake. I couldn't wait to observe the battle of wits between this clever barrister and the street-wise Mamasan.

The "simple" meal was in actuality a smorgasbord of delicious oriental delicacies. Mr. Kim steered the conversation away from business, preferring to discuss politics and family life in the United States as compared to Vietnam. Mrs. Kim was charming and intelligent, also directing any reference to business into a dead end.

Round one to the lawyer.

After the meal, Mrs. Kim took Minh aside to show her some family pictures and heirlooms, while her husband took me to the next room for a glass of brandy. A glass of brandy and a proposition. If I could pay the final installment of $300.00 today, all of the necessary paperwork could be completed and the visas obtained the following day. I agreed that that would be very favorable.

Round two to the lawyer.

"I have the money in Minh's account," I explained. "I thought she told me that she had made the last payment to you but I could be mistaken. I'll speak with her and get the money today."

"That will be fine sir," responded Mr. Kim weakly. He had caught an edge in my voice that warned him not to pursue the matter. He had dealt with Minh already and was aware that as much as she wanted to join her husband, she was still a very shrewd woman. It was obvious that she had taken charge of the finances in this arrangement.

Well, he thought, I've made enough profits on less sophisticated couples. Instead of double charging here, I'll call this one even and stick to the original deal.

We accepted the lawyer's invitation to spend the night as his guests. Before we returned to Vung Tau, however, Minh wanted to visit her older sister in the Gia Dinh section of the sprawling city. Hailing a cab, we parted with the Kims.

As the streets grew narrower, I became appalled at the poverty we were viewing. I was used to the poor living conditions in much of Vung Tau, but had never dreamed of the unbelievably over-crowded squalor we were now passing by. The war had driven tens of thousands of people from the countryside to the city, but there were no systems or facilities to handle the glut of refugees. Thousands of these people were living on the street with no roof over their heads or hope for one.

My heart went out to them. To watch a fellow human's dignity fall away as he begged for a scrap of food or fought for garbage in the gutter left me feeling empty inside. I yearned to take each of them by the hand and give them a coin or offer words of encouragement, but reality dictated otherwise. These unfortunates, bedeviled by war, could just as easily be me or my family, except for an accident of birth. They would be remembered in my prayers. I hoped that wasn't a cop-out.

Minh's sister Tran lived in a small two-bedroom apartment with her husband and six children. Though she was still severely debilitated by the chronic asthma, she made Minh and her husband welcome. She hadn't seen her sister in quite a long while and had never met her husband.

The children were fascinated by the hair on my arms and legs. They entwined their fingers in it and boldly pulled it as if testing its authenticity, like children test Santa's beard in department stores at Christmastime. While Minh visited with her sister, I played with the children. We were getting on famously until Tran's husband came home.

He hated Americans and made no secret of it. As a captain in the army he had to deal with many overbearing American counterparts and painted all Americans with the same tainted brush. He was civil to his wife's brother-in-law, but not pleased with his presence. Minh stubbornly refused to cut her visit short and the tension in the room became so heavy that even the small children became aware that something was wrong.

The oldest daughter made some tea and I tried to break the ice with my best imitation of lawyer Kim. As I pretended to be a grasping bureaucrat, demanding more money at every turn, the kids couldn't control their laughter. I didn't know if the imitation was that good, or my pronunciation that bad.

When they finally said good-bye, Minh's brother-in-law grudgingly admitted that Minh might have found a decent husband. It probably wasn't his fault that he had been born an American. Minh took the back-handed compliment adroitly and wished her sister's family farewell. She had no inkling of the part that fate had decreed for her husband to play in the future affairs of her sister's family.

After a good night's sleep at the Kims, Minh and I caught an early bus to Long Binh. Arriving at the main gate, we were both denied entry; Minh because she had no base I.D. card, and I because I was a civilian without any special authorization.

While Minh waited at a nearby cafe, I went to the next gate. The base at Long Binh was enormous, sprawling for miles across the flat, sandy plain, and there were dozens of gates. Refused at the second gate, I stopped to ponder the situation. I couldn't come up with any kind of paperwork that would pass me through the main gates, so another approach would be needed.

Whispering a prayer to St. Michael, the bold archangel and my namesake, I walked half a mile to the next gate, defiantly strode up to the guard and saluted smartly. "Get me a jeep and driver right away," I demanded. "I'm late for an operation. It's a transfer from the 36th Evac. in Vung Tau."

"Yes sir," replied the guard, too eager to serve to realize he had been duped. He motioned for another soldier to come over and relayed the order. The Spec. 4 rushed off and within minutes a jeep pulled to a stop by the gate.

"Get me to the hospital as fast as you can."

"Which hospital, sir, the 24th Evac.?"

"No, Specialist," I answered, "the one by the beer tent."

"I'm sorry sir, but there's no hospital by the beer tent," rejoined the confused driver.

"I know that, my friend, but I'd like to buy you a beer for offering me this ride. I'm not really on my way to surgery."

After a brief explanation, we found the beer tent. Alas, the tent didn't open until after noon.

The specialist offered a ride to the administration headquarters and I gladly accepted. My satisfaction at entering the base was short-lived, however. The documents I sought were not here. I would have to write to the Department of the Army to obtain a copy. Discouraged, I headed for the gate where Minh was waiting. I had no trouble exiting the post.

Minh was philosophical about the setback. Maybe the paper wasn't absolutely essential, she offered. Maybe a sworn statement would be sufficient. I wasn't sure, but the idea had possibilities. This wife of mine was O.K..

By early afternoon we were back in Saigon. Not stopping for lunch, we picked up Mr. Kim and proceeded to the American Embassy. To my surprise and pleasure, Minh's suggestion of a sworn statement was acceptable to the consular official. Everything else appeared to be in order, he conceded. There would be a final interview with another officer and that should wrap it up.

Mr. Kim had other cases to work on, and told us he would see us later on at his house. He congratulated us and swept off down the hall.

The interview was conducted by a woman who, coincidentally, came from upstate New York. I had been through her town on many occasions. She gave the appearance of a long-suffering public official, but any rapport I had hoped for was dashed when she admitted openly that she didn't like to see these "mixed" marriages. She would do everything she could to help us, now that we had come this far, but it would take about $400.00 for her to pay off the "corrupt Vietnamese officials" in order to obtain a timely set of visas.

I explained that I had already paid the graft and my lawyer had taken care of that part of the paperwork. The vice-consul bristled at the hint that she was being less than honest with us. "I don't think I can be of any help," she whined.

Not wishing to do anything to jeopardize the gains we had already made, I apologized for any implication of wrongdoing. I certainly hadn't meant to do that, I said.

The woman relaxed a bit and asked to see the papers once more. She signed a few forms and witnessed our signatures. The embassy requirements had been fully met. She wished us luck in obtaining the exit visas from the Vietnamese government, still maintaining that it would be expensive, and that she had just been trying to help by using her contacts at the visa office.

I decided to give her the benefit of the doubt, though I would always wonder about her true motives in asking for the money.

Thank God she had relented, I thought later on, for Minh and I were nearly broke and couldn't have afforded her price.

When we reached the lawyer's house there was a message waiting for us. Mr. Kim had been called away but would see Minh again in a few weeks. He had already explained that the final approvals, passports and visas would take about six to eight weeks. The disappointment over not traveling to the States together had worn off soon after we had been informed of it. I would have to leave in a couple more days, but my involvement in the whole process had been completed. Minh and the children should be able to follow soon.

After a grueling two days, we stepped off the bus in Vung Tau, tired and hungry. With precious little money left, we decided to go home and scrounge the cupboard for whatever might be left over from the day's meals. Entering the house, we were greeted by Suu.

"Con lai roi," he said simply. You came back. That summed it all up for him. His son-in-law had returned as he had promised. It was a good sign. He gave me a hug and a heartfelt handshake. He had expected us to return that evening, and had already prepared a meal. He well knew the frustrations we had been going through, and felt that a good dinner would be just the right tonic. His insights were right on target.

After supper, tired as we were, we went over the paperwork with Suu. It appeared that only one more document was needed to complete the package for the exit visas. Suu volunteered to go to the provincial capital of Long An to retrieve the form. He would leave in the morning.

The next day we took the children for a walk at the beach. Thu stayed close to her mother while I tried to win my son's confidence. By lunch time I declared myself the victor. Little Mike was delighted with his father's attention. The afternoon flew by and soon we were on our way back home. We walked hand in hand, imagining our future together. At the house our mood was quickly sobered. Suu had returned with the document we needed, but the price was nearly too costly.

He had ridden a bicycle between Long An and the small town

233

where Minh had been born. On the way back he had encountered a roadblock. It had been a rare daylight encounter with the Vietcong which Suu had not anticipated. As he pedaled closer to the two V.C. he thought about the papers he was carrying. He didn't want to give the communists any excuse to threaten his daughter, so at the moment he approached the men, he waved and then accelerated as fast as he could. When they shouted for him to stop, he swept on by and headed for the side of the road.

Pretending to pull over, he glanced back and saw them relax. With a sudden burst of speed, he continued on, weaving from side to side. The fact that they were ill-equipped and poor shots saved his life. If they had been provided with automatic rifles the outcome would likely have been different. As it was, Suu's flapping shirt had incurred a bullet hole and that was the extent of the damage.

Sleep did not come easily that night. Minh prayed that no harm would come to her father or her husband. I prayed that Minh and the children would be safe, and Suu prayed that his daughter and her family would make it to America soon.

As much as she wanted to be with me, Minh urged me to return to America quickly, before anything happened. For my part, I worried that if Minh was so concerned about my safety over here, it was logical for me to be worried about her.

Our last full day together passed quickly, and then it was time to leave for Saigon and Ton Son Nhut airport. Saying good-bye was as difficult as it had been the first time. Only Minh accompanied me on the bus ride to Saigon. I told her that we would be together in another two months, but there was still a lump in my throat and that uneasy feeling that something could still go awry.

Minh felt the same, but was determined to be strong. With all of the prayers we were saying, God or Buddha would have to be deaf not to hear them, and she felt sure that that wasn't the case. I had told her that with God on our side, who could beat us. She took comfort in the thought, but deep inside there remained a queasy little doubt. Heaven would probably win, but the bureaucrats would make a race of it!

She remained at the airfield for an hour, watching several jets power up into the sky, until she was certain that her husband was on one of them. She would spend a lot of time watching their mutual friend, the moon. He had carried her love in his beams to her husband so far away during this past year. Could he do less now, for these few remaining weeks? Slowly, she trudged back to the bus stop. Her spirit was more than willing to accept an optimistic view, but her body felt so weak. She prayed again for the strength to hold on a little longer.

Chapter Twenty-eight

"Sorry, Mike, you no longer have a job here in Warrensburg," the note informed him. "See me as soon as you return from Vietnam. Gary."

With feelings of outrage and helplessness fighting a duel in my head, I hurried to my supervisor's office.

"Hey Gary," I demanded, "What's going on? I got back from Saigon yesterday and found your note on my door."

Gary grinned and walked across the room. Shaking my hand he congratulated me on my new job. A biologist's item had become available in Cortland and I was the leading candidate.

After nearly a year had passed, the system finally must have caught up with my protest over the loss of job rights. Maybe life was going to throw me the high fast ball I liked to hit. This was terrific news. I couldn't wait to write Minh and tell her. The additional money would come in handy, too.

A week later I packed my few belongings into the old white Chevy and headed for central New York and the future.

Meanwhile, in Vung Tau, Minh was impatiently waiting to hear from lawyer Kim. He had promised to contact her for the final paperwork but it had been nearly a month without a word. She decided to travel to Saigon to straighten things out but ran smack into the old problem -- no money. What little Mike had left over from the plane tickets had not lasted very long for her. Just when all appeared lost, her father arrived. He gave her enough money to get to Saigon and return home, but there was nothing left to pay any additional fees.

Arriving in Saigon, Minh went directly to the lawyer's house. He was not surprised to see her.

"Chi Minh," he cooed, "it's so good to see you. I have been working very hard on your case, but without more money it has been impossible to make much progress. Just $400.00 more and we can have everything in readiness."

"Ong Kim," Minh replied, "the well is dry. We have no more money. You promised to have all of the papers ready last month and you said nothing about additional costs. I think you are trying to cheat me."

At that the lawyer blanched and began to sputter.

"I'm not in the habit of being accused of fraud, Chi Minh. I would advise you to be very careful with your accusations. It would be a shame if all of your hard work so far resulted in lost papers. You had better cool off."

"I can't cool off as long as you keep trying to rob me," Minh retorted. "Now I want all of my papers and I want them right now. I'll finish this by myself!"

At that moment Kim's wife came into the room with tea. "Let's all sit down and relax," she quietly suggested. "I'm sure we can work out any problems that have arisen."

She had taken a liking to Minh and was willing to incur her husband's disfavor in entering this business unbidden. Kim scowled his disapproval but sat down and drank his tea. Moments later he left the room and bustled about in his office. When he returned he had a sheaf of documents tied with a blue ribbon.

"I save the blue ribbon for my best clients," he exclaimed with a sudden change of mood. "Here are all of your papers, Mrs. Hall. My wife will accompany you to the visa office and help you in any way she can. Good luck to you and your husband."

The following day, Minh and Mrs. Kim visited the visa office. By mid-morning she was able to see the proper official and present her case. He checked all of her papers and pronounced them complete. There were no additional fees or requirements. She should have the exit visas for herself and her son within two weeks. Unfortunately, a visa could not be granted for her daughter Thu. The death certificate of Thu's father was incomplete and unacceptable. The location and time of death were not specified and the document stated that his death had not been confirmed by an officer.

Minh was taken completely by surprise. She had never received her husband's body, but that was common when the fighting was heavy and in remote locations. The army had certified that he had

237

been killed near the Cambodian border and up until now no one had questioned the certificate. She asked the official what kind of document would be acceptable.

He answered that an official death certificate had to be accompanied by an affidavit from the commanding officer of the soldier's unit. Until that was produced, Thu could not leave the country, and that was final.

Minh pleaded her case again but her efforts were ignored. This was one bureaucratic rule that could not be bent, broken or bribed. She left for home with a heavy heart.

Arriving back in Vung Tau she related her problem to her father. He had not heard of this rule before, but would look into it and try to procure the necessary document. He left for Saigon immediately.

Suu returned to Vung Tau a week later. With shoulders hunched and a downcast expression, he explained that he had spoken with an old friend in the military high command in Saigon and been advised to go to the army headquarters in Tay Ninh, where Minh's husband had been stationed. He had done so, but they had no record of him there. They readily admitted that many of the records had been lost or destroyed and therefore could not be duplicated. They sympathized with Suu but could do nothing to help him.

Remembering her husband's little maneuver with the shot record, Minh asked her father if he knew anyone who could whip up an adequate facsimile of the certificate. He replied that he did know such people, but since the government was already aware that she was missing the document, it might prove dangerous to risk a forgery. They had reached a dead end.

On the same day as Suu's return, the visas arrived for Minh and little Mike. A friendly official who had arranged for Minh's overnight stay in Saigon had been coming to Vung Tau for a short vacation and brought the visas with him, saving Minh a trip to Saigon. He cautioned her to use them as soon as possible since they could be canceled at any time.

Minh was in a quandary. She couldn't very well leave Thu behind, but on the other hand, if she delayed for very long, her chance of leaving could be jeopardized. She agonized over her decision for days, but in the end, her father convinced her to grasp the opportunity at hand, for it was fragile. He and Tot would take care of Thu and find a way to send her to America soon. And they would keep searching for Tri.

Minh knew her father made sense, but the choice was still the most difficult she had ever faced. With mixed emotions, she sent a letter to her husband informing him that the two visas were ready and that he should arrange for the airline tickets with the travel agency.

In Cortland, I tore open the long-awaited letter and slowly read the translation that Lieng had provided. I read the letter over and over but it still said the same thing. Thu could not come over at the same time as her mother. They would have to make later arrangements. I knew what Minh must be going through, and longed to hold her and comfort her. Finally, I accepted the tragic news and went to the travel agency to complete the final details.

My excitement was once again tempered by bad news. I had been denied the pure joy of leaving Vietnam and the war behind that so many G.I.'s had experienced because I had been leaving my new family behind. And now the sorely anticipated reunion would be marred by the absence of Thu and Tri.

In the meantime, Minh was making her final preparations. She had been experiencing much distress with a severe case of hemorrhoids and her friends finally convinced her to enter the hospital for an operation. After all, they reasoned, didn't she want to greet her husband with a healthy body. She really shouldn't burden him with the operation after their reunion, and so, to have the operation here would be in her best interest.

While her parents watched the children, Minh entered Le Loi hospital for the surgery. The surgeon was not a good technician and Minh spent a very painful week in the hospital. The operation took every cent that she and her father could scrape together. She went home on Thursday, penniless, and left for Saigon with Mike Jr. on Friday. With a small suitcase and a smaller boy, she boarded the plane, ready to brave the unknown.

She had been told so many stories of what life in the U.S.A. would be like that now she began to feel the first pangs of doubt. Would she be treated like a slave by her husband? Would she be shunned and ridiculed by the Americans? Would she be accepted by her new family in America? Hundreds of questions raced through her mind as the giant airplane taxied down the tarmac. First and foremost, would this enormous plane ever be able to lift off and remain in the air?

Minh had flown only once before, and that had been a short hop in a drafty old C-130 cargo plane with no seats. This would be an entirely new experience, and a painful one if her sitting could not be relieved by occasionally strolling up and down the aisle. No one had prepared her for this first flight and her English was still limited to a few words and phrases.

She survived the takeoff but the next several hours were some of the most painful she had ever spent. Her discomfort increased until she thought she couldn't stand the pain any longer. Only the thought of her husband waiting for her gave her the strength to hold on. That thought and the endurance she had learned in a short lifetime of overcoming hardships strengthened her.

Halfway through the flight to Honolulu, food was served. Minh dared not eat or drink since she knew she would never be able to wait several more hours to use a bathroom. No one had told her that the giant planes had such facilities! To worsen matters, her little son was sick. He had a slight fever and a roaring case of diarrhea. Minh had packed a few small cloths in her bag to take care of this problem, but the cloths ran out long before they reached Hawaii. She was able to change her little son on the empty seat beside her, but in so doing she became soiled herself. She was so embarrassed by the smell that she purposefully avoided asking the stewardess for help.

In Honolulu she would have a one hour layover, but most of that time would be spent clearing immigration. A helpful fellow traveler gave her directions to the immigration and customs check but a not-so-helpful Vietnamese girl, wishing company while waiting for a later flight, gave her the wrong time of departure, consequently, she nearly missed the re-boarding call. In all the confusion, she never found a rest room and had to endure the long flight to San Francisco in the same soiled condition.

In San Francisco a friendly Hawaiian steward recognized her problem and escorted her to a rest room. There she was able to clean her son a bit but there was little she could do for herself, since her suitcase with her only change of clothing was still on the plane. And then she realized that she had to change planes in San Francisco. How could she retrieve her bag?

Dashing from the ladies room she nearly ran into the friendly steward. In her best pidgin English, she tried to explain her predicament. The steward grasped the meaning and told her to wait at the nearby information desk. A few minutes later he returned with the bag. It hadn't been hard to locate, he explained, he had a nose for such things. The humor was lost on Minh, but the effort was much appreciated. A few minutes later she was boarding another plane for the last leg of her incredible journey.

As Flight 118 of American Airlines landed at J.F. Kennedy airport, a solitary figure turned up his collar to ward off the chilly mist. At 6:10 A.M., the fog-shrouded field offered a damp and cold welcome.

I had arrived the evening before to be certain I would be on time to meet my small family. The trip on the Long Island Expressway between the motel and the airport had been as exciting as I had been warned, and my nerves didn't really need any extra stimuli at this point.

As the passengers deplaned outside the terminal building I edged closer to the stairs. There was no sign of my wife and baby. I was certain that there had been some kind of slip-up. With all of the plane changes and lack of English skills, I was just certain that the wait had been in vain. The last passengers exited the silver craft and the crew started down the gangway. I felt my heart sinking as I tried to remember where I had seen the Traveler's Aid booth. Just when I was convinced that there would be no reunion that day, I heard someone call my name.

"Mr. Hall? I have someone here to see you."

I looked up to see a pretty stewardess guiding a tiny green figure down the airplane gangway. Minh was wearing a green dress cut just above her knees and carrying a small blue bundle. The bundle squirmed as Minh drew near and a fat round face peered out. Ngoc-Mike Jr. was home.

Minh left the stewardess with a smile and flung herself into her husband's arms. She was dirty, smelly and in considerable pain, but the trials of the long trip were over. Oblivious to the clapping hands of the crew which surrounded them, the young couple clung to one another and their son. There was no more army to deny them nights together. There was no more bureaucratic red tape to separate them. For the rest of their lives they would remain together. Minh's tears of joy were matched by the stewardess as she handed the battered little suitcase to the happy young couple.

The five hour trip to Cortland was broken up by a brief visit to my cousin, Johnny, who had loaned me the money for the plane tickets. Minh was welcomed with hugs and kisses from Johnny and his wife, and it is certain that no one knew how much that welcome meant to Minh. She had been so worried about her acceptance in this new land and now her fears were beginning to melt away. But if her fears were subsiding, her pain was not.

In the bathroom she found that she was bleeding from the as yet unhealed operating wounds. She would have to tell her husband sooner or later about the operation, but she was still too embarrassed to bring it up. Cleaning herself as best she could, Minh suggested that they continue on. With heartfelt thanks to her husband's in-laws, she climbed into the long, white Chevy for the trip home.

Home, she thought, will I ever see my home again? Will I ever see my Mom and Dad again, or my friends in Vung Tau? As she pondered these questions her head slipped onto her husband's shoulder and she fell asleep. She hadn't slept or eaten in over thirty hours.

Minh awoke as they followed Interstate Route 81 around the hillside leading into Cortland. The lights of the small city twinkled in the hub of the seven valleys. As her husband explained where they would live Minh breathed a sigh of relief. There were neighbors and stores and streets. She had been afraid they would be somewhere out in the mountains, for after all, her husband was some kind of conservationist, wasn't he?

Pulling into the driveway beside the trailer, I noticed a large cardboard box on the front steps. Helping Minh and Ngoc out of the car, I curiously picked up the box and peeked inside. A brightly colored, homemade greeting card was surrounded by a large array of fruits and vegetables. "Welcome to your new home, Minh." read the card. It was signed by Ben Bradley and family, my boss.

In the trailer, as she helped put away the fresh bounty, Minh was strangely silent.

"Is something wrong, Minhoi?" I asked.

"No Minhoi," she answered. "I was just thinking how nice everyone has been to me. I didn't know what to expect. I didn't even know if people over here on the other side of the world walked upside down, like some have told me. Some of the stories told by

242

girls returning to Vietnam made America sound like Hell. I was so unsure."

And still you came, I thought. I knew that I would never stop loving this woman. Whatever lay ahead of us, I was sure of that one thing. Tomorrow we would begin whatever process was necessary to bring Thu here with us, but tonight, we would be together at last. As my heart overflowed into my eyes I heard a cry from the next room. Mike Jr. wanted some attention, and he wanted it now.

Chapter Twenty-nine

Minh's years in America were filled with the joy of being with her husband but tempered by an emptiness as she thought of her son and daughter and the rest of her family in Vietnam. The prejudice that we had anticipated rarely materialized as we shared the normal ups and downs that accompany family life.

As the years passed our family grew. On Christmas day in 1971 Minh gave birth to Marie Jean, named after the mothers of Jesus and me. In Vietnamese she was called My. She would grow in grace and beauty and become a source of pride for her parents, as would our son, Mike Jr.

Over the next four years we had two more children; Martin John, born in 1974 and called Thanh, and Maureen Elizabeth, born in 1975 and called Tam. A neighborhood wag one day noted that all six people in the family had names beginning with M. He promptly dubbed us the M & M's. Unfortunately, the nickname stuck for many years.

Shortly after Maureen's birth Minh was taken ill. Unable to make a diagnosis, the doctors nearly lost her twice in a three day period. During her hospitalization, my sisters, Mary and Liz, came to help out. They kept the household running smoothly until Minh was on her feet again. Realizing how much family meant, I wondered how much it must hurt Minh to be so far away from her family, unable even to communicate with them except by using codes.

With my wife sleeping beside me in our bed for the first time since her hospital stay, I lay back on the handmade pillow and reflected on our last five years. I smiled as I recalled Minh's first look at snow. She had never seen the temperature drop below 70° in her life. So far she had taken the changes like a trouper.

The smile faded as I remembered the difficulty she had in

adjusting to American food. She would have continual stomach trouble until our discovery of the Oriental markets in New York City and Syracuse.

Suddenly, Minh rolled over, kicking me sharply. I slid out of bed and went to the kitchen for a beer. Sitting in the darkened living room I broke into a wide grin, recalling the day we moved from the country to our first house on Hamlin Street.

Minh had filled a brand new galvanized garbage can with layers of fish and salt as the first step in making a traditional Vietnamese delicacy, "mam ca".

The mixture had been "working" for about six months when moving day arrived. Three of my colleagues from work had volunteered to help out and were busy carrying goods down the narrow stairway. Shelly and Dave had the heavy can between them on the stairs when the bottom gave out. The potent sauce spilled out onto the stairs, covering their pants and boots. The odor was just as you might expect from six month old fish! Shelly commented weeks later that it would have made a great fox lure. He and Dave offered to help us move the next time, but he was quick to ask if there would be any more "mam". If so he would pass. "Nuoc mam, no hands" became the office byword for some time to come.

Glancing at the photos of Minh's parents on the wall, I was struck by the shadows cast on them by the street light. How sadly appropriate, I thought, for their absence cast a pall over Minh's happiness here with me. Slipping quietly back into bed beside my sleeping wife I prayed that we would somehow have a reunion soon. If Thu and Tri could join us I was sure my wife's happiness would be complete. With that prayer on my lips I drifted off into sleep.

In the spring of 1975, the fall of Saigon to the communist troops was imminent. Minh and I were growing edgy. We had finally been able to secure an exit visa for Thu through the auspices of the International Social Services. She was scheduled to leave in late April or early May, but that might not be soon enough. The Communists were moving fast. Tri's whereabouts were still being concealed by his father and we could only pray that God would be merciful and answer our prayers.

One week before the fall of Saigon and the iron curtain of communist oppression, Thu arrived at the Syracuse, N.Y. airport. Once again the Lord had demonstrated his power in our lives.

During the next fourteen years our family grew closer together. Thu married and left for North Carolina with her Marine husband. Shortly thereafter she was diagnosed with cancer. Before her operations and treatment, Minh prayed that if God would heal her daughter she would join the Catholic Church. She had been going to Sunday Mass with her family anyway, but her Buddhist beliefs also remained strong.

It would be a tremendous act of faith to move on to new religious beliefs. It would also be a very significant leap from her past life, a ritual cutting of some very strong ties to her former life.

After two operations and chemotherapy the cancer went into remission, and Minh, true to her vow, joined the church.

On a cold December night in 1990, Minh and I were cuddled in front of the fireplace, watching the crackling fire. The shooting sparks reminded her of long ago rockets and flares, and she saddened. Sensing her mood, I began teasing her into a smile. She humored me, and leaning against my shoulder, reflected silently on the events of the past few years.

She had learned to hunt and fish, American style, drive a car (usually filled to the top with noisy children), cook for several hundred students on her job at the local college and manage the household finances. She was still independent and strong-willed .... and completely devoted to her family.

She had become an American citizen as soon as she was eligible but maintained her loyalties and love of both countries. She continually taught her children to be proud of their dual heritage and encouraged them to learn about life in Vietnam.

There was still a sword in her heart when she thought of her family in Vietnam. Tri's father had died but all efforts to bring her son to America had been thwarted. It was likely that her father's previous connection with the French and staunch anti-communist stand had been discovered, and any attempt to aid her family brought only frustration.

Her brother Hoai, who became a Buddhist priest, disappeared in an area with heavy fighting just prior to the communist takeover. He was never seen again.

Her youngest brother, Duc, of whom she was so fond, was killed in battle by the Vietcong at the age of nineteen. He had been drafted when he turned sixteen.

The husband of her older sister Tran was sent to a re-education (read concentration) camp after the war and spent seven years incarcerated without any contact from his wife and seven children. Upon his release he was denied employment and constantly harassed by the communist government.

Finally, in a desperate bid for freedom, he took two of his oldest sons on a perilous journey by sampan, hoping to reach Thailand. Their ancient motor died and they spent a week drifting helplessly at sea. Two days after their food and water were exhausted a German freighter spotted them. They were taken to an incredibly overcrowded refugee camp in Singapore where they languished for a year.

Minh found it ironic that her brother-in-law who so disliked Americans wrote frequently from the refugee camp asking for help from her and "that American", whom she had married. Unable to crack the formidable barrier of red tape, Minh helplessly watched as her sister's husband and sons were sent to Germany, the country of origin of the rescue ship. She worked tirelessly to help her sister during the next two years and at last Tran and most of her children were able to join Sanh in Germany.

And then, by a horrible twist of fate, Tran died only a few months after her reunion with her husband. Unable to emigrate to the U.S., Sanh remained in Germany with the children.

Minh's darkest day in America came when she received word of her father's death. Her father, to whom she had been devoted; her father who was a heroic presence in her life and the life of his country; her father, who she would never see again because of lines on a map that divided countries and peoples.

A popping ember in the fire brought Minh back to the present. Looking now at her husband she knew that together they had overcome much. It would only be a matter of time before they would find a way to bring Tri and his recent bride and infant son to America.

In the meantime, our other children kept us young, on our toes and perpetually broke. Mike Jr. was working for an insurance company in Maryland and living a very independent life. Marie was a freshman in college, doing well in her studies and sports. Martin and Maureen were in high school, heavily involved in sports, studies and all the sundry activities of teen-agers in America and looking forward to attending college.

Minh smiled contentedly. There must be a way to preserve the memories of her lifetime. She wanted a legacy to pass on to her children. Leaning over, she whispered in my ear, "Minhoi, why don't you write a book about our life? You could start with my childhood in Vietnam and follow through until now. Do you think you could?"

"Well Minhoi, if I did write such a book, and it was made into a movie, I would get a beautiful, hot young movie star to play you and I would play myself, just for realism, of course. How does that sound?"

"Minhoi, you just write the book and we'll worry about the movie later," and with that she gave me a playful shove and broke into a hearty laugh. The same laugh I had heard twenty-three years ago on a sultry summer night halfway around the world.

Chapter Thirty

And now Minh's Christmas wish has come true. I have recorded the story of her life in this book. Our children will have the legacy she desires for them and I have acquired a very special gift - a more complete knowledge and understanding of the beautiful person I married .... Doan Thi Minh - Hall.

For weeks after that fireside request Minh and I spent every night with notebooks in hand - she recounting the memories of a lifetime, and I probing and recording. No marriage encounter could ever bring a couple closer together than this sharing of our pasts, unfettered by false images or posturing.

The conclusion of this love story has yet to be written but the latest chapter must be recounted. On a frosty morning in January of 1992 a letter arrived from Vietnam. Minh's mother was seriously ill and despairing of ever seeing her daughter again. The letter was uncensored and its poignant message clear. If only we could see Tot once more ....

The evening after the fateful letter arrived Minh had a phone call from Lieng, who was living in Indiana with her two children. "Minh, let's go home to see our families. I'm broke like you but what the heck. Will you go with me?"

Reluctantly, Minh turned down her best friend's offer. "Lieng, I want to go back so badly, but we have no money and soon we will have three kids in college. Besides, I still don't trust the communists. For twenty-two years I have dreamed of returning home and every dream ends with me disappearing somewhere in Vietnam and Mike getting a letter that I was killed in an accident. I'm sorry, I just can't go."

As I listened in on that distressing phone conversation I knew that there was only one thing to do.

"Minhoi, we're going to Vietnam." There, I had said it, and this time I would brook no argument. If Minh's "kinh dao" water buffalo stubbornness was nearly impossible to overcome, my Adirondack-born persistence would be totally impossible to withstand.

"Sweetheart, your dream can't come true if we change it. I'm going with you. I desperately want to see your family and get to know them and I will never be happy until that day. If I am with you in Vietnam then I can't get a letter saying you have disappeared."

Perhaps the logic was slightly flawed, and maybe my skills in presenting point by point arguments weren't the best, but after a long night of discussion and tender persuasion Minh agreed to make the long-awaited journey. We could extend the second mortgage on the house and live like paupers after the trip. For our safety and that of the children we would rely on God.

With the decision made, a thousand details came into focus. And each detail became an obstacle. For three months we worked diligently, task by task, until all was in readiness. During this time we found unbounded kindness and support from friends and neighbors, family and strangers. Co-workers and extended family members offered encouragement and cautions. We discovered a pool of love and concern that we had never known existed. We were truly blessed.

With so many of the chores completed we began to focus on broader concerns, on the return to Vietnam and the thoughts, hopes, fears and ghosts surrounding this trip into the past.

For Minh, the journey would culminate in a long-awaited reunion with her family whom she had not seen since she arrived in America in 1970. For me, the trip would be my third to that sweltering green land which still held so much of my memory captive. I could only hope - and pray - that this sojourn would be far less adventuresome than the previous two.

Minh and I earnestly desired to be a part of the healing that is essential if the hate and horrors of the war were to be put to rest. We didn't know what would happen when we again faced the communist red flag with the yellow star. We couldn't really predict our reaction to the expected bureaucratic demands from those we once called "enemy". Would we be able to separate the long-ago deeds from the doers as we surely recalled the incredible pain and

250

suffering inflicted during the war? And perhaps most important of all, could I keep my outspoken wife out of serious trouble if she responded to the forced rulers of her country with her usual feisty retorts?

And now time is flying by. We're leaving soon and there is so much to do before we depart. I will write this chapter of our lives as we live it and hope that it becomes a happy ending to this story.

We have made all of our travel arrangements through a company in San Francisco specializing in tours to Vietnam. We plan to leave together with two of Minh's Vietnamese girl friends and some of their family members. We will travel to Vietnam as a group and then go our separate ways. Hopefully we can arrange to meet in Vung Tau to spend a little time together. Our trip will be marred from the outset because Lieng can't get enough time off from work to join us. We are saddened by this turn of events and hope that it doesn't prove a portent of things to come.

Our passports are now atop the growing pile of luggage and our systems are full of antibodies from the many immunization shots. We'll need plenty of help to ward off typhoid, tetanus, plague, malaria and myriad other nasties.

Minh has been haunting garage sales searching for good used clothing at bargain prices. Durable clothing and medicine are the two biggest needs of her family with which we can help. We are allowed to bring two bags apiece, each weighing up to seventy pounds. We'll crowd the limit to make up for the abysmal luck we have experienced in sending assistance
over in the past. It was a rare instance when anything reached the individuals for whom it was intended. For many years it was actually necessary to write letters with coded messages to keep the true meanings from the censors. Unfortunately this often created discouraging misunderstandings between Minh and the family.

We hope there is a more open country today.

Still, it's hard to forget the way things were. For our journey to be successful we will need to maintain a sense of humor and grow eyes in the backs of our heads. We have been told that Americans are welcomed and looked after in the larger cities in Vietnam but that travel and safety in the outlying regions is less predictable. Minh's mother and a sister live two hours southeast of Saigon by car in the dry season but three hours by car plus half an hour by boat in

251

the monsoon season.   Naturally our trip falls during that rainy period.

To further stimulate our already over-stimulated imaginations, Minh's older sister and mother write that they have not seen an American or any westerner in their small Mekong Delta town since 1968. We will be the first. Oh joy!

We know that there are a number of risks in making this trip but we realize that it could help us to heal so many wounds. For my part, I see so much confusion and misunderstanding when Vietnam is mentioned.

A young girl running down a dusty street, naked and crying in pain and terror; a kneeling man executed by a bullet to the head on a Saigon street; silvery coffins bearing young Americans disgorged from returning airplanes .... these are the sights we remember from television coverage of the war. And much more, as each of us in his own way recalls the memories of that tragic period in our history, though history may be a misnomer since so many in our country have yet to put the war behind them. So very many of us who served in Vietnam and those who served in waiting at home are still emotionally tied to Vietnam.

We all react to the mixed news reports concerning the M.I.A. issue or the prospect of establishing normal relations with Vietnam. The effects of Agent Orange are still profoundly felt in the cancerous legacy bequeathed to both of our countries. Memorials and parks dedicated to veterans of the war are still being established on a regular basis today, nearly eighteen years since our troops left that troubled land.

I sometimes hear a careless remark about veterans, particularly Vietnam veterans, who are questioning the way they have been treated or are trying to put their lives and sacrifices into perspective. "Get a life," they're told.   "Are you going to live in the past forever," they're asked?

The answers don't lie back in Vietnam for most of us. They lie in all of our hearts and minds. Undergoing such dramatic and traumatic experiences form the most remarkable influences in our lives. Few of us fail to recall our best nights on the town, even down to the mornings after, yet these lasted only a few hours. Isn't it only reasonable to expect that the drama of wartime experiences will be retained likewise, and with a heightened influence? Patience, tolerance and time will go a long way in offering a healing space among our veterans and between our countries.

Whoa! Sermon is over.

Departure day is just around the corner and I haven't even purchased a stock of "chew'n" gum for all the kids that will likely mob us wherever we go. Come to think of it, it won't be a bad strategy to keep plenty of people around us during our stay in the boonies of the Delta.

So now we're making the big leap, the freedom flight in reverse. So many friends ask us why now. Why not wait until we have an embassy or some diplomatic presence that can bail you out of a sticky situation?

The easy answer is that Minh's mother is old and ill, and there may not be a later for her. The tougher response swirls through our daily lives and is never absent from our subconscious minds. There is something calling us back that is at least as strong as family ties, at least as strong as the financial and other concerns holding us back.

It may be the recognition that for each of us a very significant part of our lives was spent in Southeast Asia. For Minh, it is important to return to her homeland to pay her respects at her father's grave and complete the mourning process. And she must reconcile with her mother. Her mother, who beat her so often; her mother who never understood her; her mother who was never keen on her marriage to an American; her mother whom she still loves unconditionally.

For my part, there is the compelling, teasing feeling that draws all of us back to view our pasts. There is the titillating sensation of going back to a time when life was lived at a frantic pace and danger and death were not strangers.

There are ghosts to be faced.

Ghosts of the innocents we fruitlessly labored to save that terrible Christmas Eve, and ghosts of young men who became old before our eyes.

As our departure draws near I find myself walking Cortland's streets at dawn, drinking in the sights and smells and sounds. I am furiously willing my brain to imprint these memories. I'm not sure why.

Vietnam, we will see you soon.

Chapter Thirty-one

"Look, Minhoi, there's Singapore below us. Can you believe it?"
Minh nodded sleepily and turned her back to me. The intense
emotions and tensions leading up to this dream trip had left her
exhausted and the seats in the TWA jumbo jet left much to be
desired when attempting to sleep.

I am wide awake. Wired might be a better term. My pre-flight
jitters have been calmed by the steady thrum of the jet's engines and
this second leg of the journey from Tokyo to Singapore has been
smooth. It doesn't hurt that it is being used as a training flight for
a group of novice Japanese airline hostesses. They have obviously
been selected for their beauty as well as competence, and their
enthusiastic hovering over the passengers is an absolute delight.

Changi airport in Singapore is breathtaking and as efficient as it
is beautiful. We have an all night layover here with such an early
morning flight that it's impossible to make hotel accommodations,
and far beyond our budget. After touring the lavishly endowed
terminal we settle in for the night, encamping on the floor.

Sharing our little corner for the evening are a handful of
Vietnamese returning for their first visit to their native land. Most
are in their early thirties and had escaped by boat as teenagers.

Phuoc has just been laid off from a factory in Kansas City and is
using all of his savings to return to his hometown, a small village
north of Saigon. His parents, brothers and sisters all drowned when
their boat was attacked by pirates from Thailand. Phuoc and three
other young men were the only survivors out of nearly fifty refugees
on that ill-fated craft.

Phuoc speaks fearfully of his expectations. He wants only to
revisit his town and see if he can find some old friends and an uncle
who might still reside there. He has been afraid to write of his
family's fate and is unsure of the reception he will meet in the

village, but his heart is compelling him to return. He was drafted into the army of South Vietnam at seventeen and imprisoned in a re-education camp for two years by the communists. He has no idea what faces him upon his return.

Alternately effusive and withdrawn, his mood swings are dramatic and bring Minh out of the melancholia enveloping her thus far on the trip. She becomes animated, trying to lighten the young man's burden of fear. In so doing she is transformed into the vivacious young bride I married, and my heart leaps for joy within me.

As we board the plane for the ninety minute flight to Saigon (we refuse to call it Ho Chi Minh City) we wish Phuoc good luck and Godspeed, and our own fears and doubts are rekindled.

Our fears are really awakened when we get a good look at the plane which will carry us on the final leg of our journey. The old twin propeller relic is everything we have been warned about. Air Vietnam does not have the best of reputations for safety, nor for comfort or cuisine.

The Vietnamese flight attendants are most attractive in their traditional "ao dais", the flowing gowns pinched at the waist and worn over matching baggy silk trousers. Unfortunately their attitudes don't match their appearance. They are cold to the few westerners on board and surly with anyone they identify as ex-patriate Vietnamese.

The loud nervous chatter among the returning "tourists" falls away to a hush of fear and intimidation. The realization that the plane is owned and flown by the communist Socialist Republic of Vietnam spreads a pall over the little group of passengers. This is no longer the free world. We are all in the grasp of one of the last communist states in the world, and each of us knows only too well how terrifying that can be. Minh and I switch our prayers from asking for a safe landing to asking protection for us and all of our fellow travelers during the days ahead.

It is hard to believe that we have formed such a close bond with these people during the night in Changi airport and now we share so many emotions with them. Dear Lord, I hope that you're listening closely to these prayers.

Suddenly, forty hours of sleepless traveling fall away as nothing when the Air Vietnam pilot announces the final approach to Ho Chi Minh City (his words). The shimmering South China Sea gives way to a green kaleidoscope of rice paddies and palm trees as we descend to Tan Son Nhut airport.

Mixed emotions churn violently within us. Minh worries that her family will not know our arrival date and time, though the travel company has promised to wire them for us. I am more concerned about baggage inspections and official hassles.

Both of our concerns are well-founded as we soon learn, but nothing can compare to the initial shock as we step off the plane into a sweltering sauna called Vietnam.

Fragments of black thunderheads linger ominously, testifying to the storm which has just boosted the humidity to one hundred percent. The temperature is one hundred five degrees and breathing is a chore in the suffocating atmosphere.

We are crammed into an ancient shuttle bus for a quick trip to the terminal. The bus driver is rude and deliberately closes the door on a young man who is trying to wrestle a large bag onto the bus. No one dares to rebuke the driver.

In the terminal we spend three nearly unbearable hours wilting in a long queue as entry papers and baggage are scrutinized. With only two planes landing all morning there is still mass confusion and inefficiency. Dozens of passengers complain of lost luggage and many more are pulled aside for intense questioning by security officials.

Minh's girl friend has several cassette tapes confiscated and destroyed before her eyes. "Contraband," declares a sneering officer.

With great trepidation, Minh suggests that I place a five dollar bill in our passport when it's our turn for luggage inspection. We nervously discuss the chances of being thrown in jail for bribery and, weigh them against the prospect of having all of the medicine and clothing confiscated. Luckily I am perspiring so freely in the oppressive heat that the nervous sweat is indistinguishable as I hand our passports to the officer.

I manage only a weak smile and thank you as he slips the bill into his pocket and waves us through after a cursory inspection.

Thank you, Lord!

With barely an hour of daylight remaining we are released to an outside holding pen, entirely fenced, and resembling a cattle chute. The promised travel representative never arrives and we feel like prisoners as we survey the barbed wire topping the surrounding fence. Minh's friends are finally released and leave by another gate. A crowd of people, ten-deep, presses against the outside of the fence, anxiously trying to spot relatives among the detainees.

A frantic shout of "Chi Ba" catches Minh's attention as her sister thrusts her hands through the fence to touch her long-lost sibling. She takes my hands as well and tears well in her eyes as she sobs her greetings.

Suddenly, more family appears from the jostling throng, crowded against the fence. With a baleful look a guard allows us to squeeze through a narrow side gate. Almost immediately I feel a hand in my pocket and another gently tugging at a camera strap. I know then that I am really back in "The 'Nam". Our baggage is at risk.

Within seconds a cohort of sisters, nieces, nephews and cousins surround us and our baggage, much like a circle of musk oxen protecting their young. Thoroughly drenched with sweat, we embrace and cry with our family, who have indeed not received any telegrams and have made the arduous trek to Saigon each of the past four days, hoping to catch our arrival.

A composed young man emerges from the giddy crowd of relatives and takes my hand. When he hugs me and says "Ba", Dad in Vietnamese, I recognize Tri. As he embraces his mother I finally lose control and tears of joy join the sweat staining my face. Twenty-two years of praying, dreaming and hoping are climaxed in that hug. God is good.

As a new storm rumbles closer a brother-in-law miraculously procures a rental van and we are off before dark, a time when travelers must take care.

The ride through Saigon is nerve-shattering. Streets are jammed with motorbikes and pedicabs, bicycles and pedestrians. Huge trucks billowing clouds of choking black smoke, and occasional cars, careen through the confusion, horns blaring, replacing signal lights. Flashing a devilish grin, our driver asks if I want to take the wheel. Hastily declining, I close my eyes to the constant near misses as we honk our way through at speeds far in excess of anything I consider safe.

For the next two and a half hours twelve cramped, sweaty passengers and their luggage bounce their way along the rutted country road, dodging potholes large enough to swallow a bicycle.

Oncoming traffic spreads out over the width of the road and right of way is determined by the size of the conveyance, leading to innumerable confrontations, known in the States as playing chicken.

The solid knot in my stomach from the Air Vietnam lunch (probably the pungent crab meat balls) and the exhaust fumes, dust and oppressive heat and humidity are overwhelming. I am fighting for each breath as my stomach threatens to leap to my mouth at every bump. Impervious to all the joyous babble around me, I consider that if we ever reach Tam Vu alive I will likely die of food poisoning or heat stroke before morning.

But reach it we do, I survive the night and the adventure continues.

Chapter Thirty-two

The roosters begin crowing at 4:00 a.m. in Tam Vu. The one in the neighbor's yard would have been enough to wake us but those in the next room and under the window are a bit much.

A dawn meal of spicy chicken and rice soup accompanied by steaming hot tea settles the stomach problems of the previous night. I secretly hope that the next morning's broth will be thickened with a certain rooster or two.

We are staying in the home of Minh's mother deep in the flat, rice-growing Mekong Delta region. The house is made of bamboo and thatched palm leaves. The two large rooms have very high ceilings with vents to dissipate the heat. I couldn't tell if they were working. The small room at the rear serves as kitchen and chicken coop. Cooking fuel is furnished by dried coconut hulls and their aroma while burning is less than fragrant.

The beds are flat, HARD tables with ridged, HARD bamboo sleeping mats. Mosquito netting hangs down from a frame above the beds. With the netting rolled up the beds become couches by day. After the second night acquiring bruised hips I plan to send a card to Dr. Sam, my chiropractor, with a whole new meaning for the old saw, "wish you were here."

Water from a nearby well, constructed by the American Army in the mid-nineteen sixties, is carried to the house to supplement rain water stored in fifty gallon earthen jugs. Only repeated, concentrated chemical treatment renders small quantities potable for our American stomachs. Thirst is a constant in this sweltering tropical environment.

The house is one of a few in the area with electricity, supplied by a large local generator. Service averages about six hours a day .... and is sporadic at best. With no refrigeration, daily trips to the market are essential to insure fresh staples for the days meals.

We soon learn that none of the money we sent over the years reached Minh's family. Somehow we always received letters thanking us which bore signatures we recognized. At any rate, our disappointment turns to utter dismay when we learn that Minh's Dad might have lived had our money been available to purchase medicine. Additionally, the house Minh lived in here in Tam Vu which had a clean concrete floor and plaster walls had to be sold for money to buy food.

Minh's mother and sister and her family are often chided for having to live in a rude dwelling when they have a daughter/sister living in America where everyone is rich. Minh's sister mentions that there was a small family scandal in which a relative in Saigon apparently intercepted some of our aid packages, including money, and used them for personal gain. Thus the family was at least aware that we had tried to help them. The family also understood that Suus strong anti-communist stance and past work for the army were likely the reasons they were unable to obtain exit visas, despite all of our assistance.

Settling in, we find the next week at Tam Vu hot, humid and very dry. The temperature is in the hundreds each day while the humidity remains above eighty percent. At night, sleeping temperatures drop all the way to ninety. The uncharacteristic drought in the monsoon season is threatening the rice crop and has everyone worried. And for the entire week our bodies steadfastly refuse to acclimate.

Despite the primitive conditions, (the bathroom is a roofless platform suspended above the nearby fish pond and bathing consists of pouring basins of water over ones head) the family reunion is joyous and extended.

No American has been in Tam Vu since 1968 and we are the objects of continual stares, doubletakes and gatherings of curious onlookers. The expected retinues of children materialize and our gum is soon exhausted. There are so many people stopping to peer in the windows and doors we feel like fish in a very conspicuous bowl. The people, though, are open, friendly and very eager to talk with us.

Most of the locals are farmers and fishermen, but every household has been touched by the tragedy of war. There are dozens of stories of relatives killed or still missing. Daily we encounter people with missing limbs and hear of the terrible tragedy of birth

260

defects from chemicals used during the war so many years ago.

We spy the death certificates and pictures of Minh's two brothers on the wall of her mother's house. For the first time we learn what happened to them. Hoai, who became a Buddhist monk, was taken prisoner along with several fellow monks and nuns. They were forced to walk in front of Vietcong troops as they attacked a village. Hoai and all of his companions were killed.

Her youngest brother, Duc, was drafted into the army at sixteen. He was seriously wounded at seventeen and became addicted to morphine during his convalescence. Branded as a drug user, he was sent to the front line in an area of heavy fighting and was killed a few days later at the age of nineteen.

During these first days in Tam Vu, our emotions are running their full gamut; from wild joy to complete depression. It's so hard to maintain an even composure when living conditions are so different and each hour seems to bring a new revelation.

There is always talk of politics and repression as frustrated citizens unburden their pent-up feelings to an outsider. Minh's pleasure in seeing her mother and family again is constantly shattered as she moves through the abject poverty surrounding her. The suitcases of clothing and medicine which seemed so burdensome while traveling are mere drops in a leaky bucket as more relatives arrive each day. Nearly two hundred pounds of second hand clothing are gone in a matter of minutes.

Tot is indescribably happy to see her daughter again and no references are made to any previous hostility between them. Somehow a balance is struck between heartache and happiness and the visit settles into a routine. Can it remain so peaceful for the next month?

Mekong Delta mosquitoes are the stuff of legends .... and the flat, watery habitat surrounding Tam Vu surely qualifies for legendary status. Even the use of mosquito netting must be bolstered by liberal applications of Avon "Skin so Soft", a truly heroic insect repellent. We find it impossible to remain outside after dark.

The dirt track through Tam Vu is one of the very few roads in this region of the Delta. The vast farming district around this hamlet is nestled among hundreds of miles of interlacing streams, swamps and the mighty Mekong River itself. The area is traversed by narrow lanes and paths along paddy dikes, just wide enough, and sometimes smooth enough, to accommodate motorbikes and bicycles. Negotiating these paths is a daily enterprise as we visit family scattered throughout the area.

Most of our travel is on foot and we are constantly soaked with perspiration. Against family advice, we insist on walking four miles into the jungle to visit the grave of Minh's father. Her sisters explain that there could be bandits attracted by an American in the area or Vietcong who would try to exact revenge. We insist, however, and the trek to the grave finds us literally surrounded by family and neighbors and picking up more and more as we walk farther from the village past isolated homes in jungle clearings.

At the grave we pray and cry. Upon leaving we stop to visit Minh's aunts who lived with her on the old plantation. Aunt Phai, who was kidnapped and tortured by the Vietcong, is on her deathbed, hastened by her injuries. Tiet is still a ball of energy, bustling about and making sure we are well taken care of. It's a typical bittersweet reunion, but one we are becoming accustomed to.

We have wept at Suu's grave and now we laugh with Minh's sisters at a pre-wedding party for a cousin. We encounter Minh's best friend as a child in Tam Vu and are very pleased to see her for Minh had received word that she had been killed years ago.

Through all the sweaty treks along slippery, muddy paths we need hugh quantities of fluids to stave off dehydration, and with water and ice taboo, ... hurrah for the coconut!

We drink gallons of juice from freshly-cut nuts and eat the soft pulp remaining. In addition, fruits of all descriptions are in season and available for the picking. If only I knew their English names I would extol them here.

As poor as the countryside is the hospitality afforded at the meanest palm hut belies the dirt floor and lack of worldly goods. We are offered tea in every home and share, with some reluctance, home-brewed rice whiskey, and we eat rice soup until we burst. But the blessed Godsend, our staple refresher - is the coconut.

We will always remember the genuine warmth and spirit of hospitality we found at Tam Vu. And I will never forget my feelings as I walk the paths and explore the river where Minh grew up; the river she described to me where she and her family outran the hail of bullets fired by pursuing communists. As Minh shows me the rotting hulk of the old family boat the hair on my head stands straight up.   During all of those long evening interviews as I gathered material for the book I never expected to see the places and meet the people I was writing about.

The expected problems when we encounter the communist flag and official hassles have yet to surface. We see the required picture of Ho Chi Minh in every home but the residents pay it less heed than we, and soon it becomes invisible.

We are always accompanied by a contingent of relatives and extended family and have no fear of the specter of bandits, though we hear a few grim stories. Neither have we encountered hostility from former (and still active) Vietcong.

We frequently share food and drink with some of our former enemy, who are more than eager to identify themselves. Most of our family and new friends here grudgingly forgive us for these brief interludes but let us know that their feelings run deeply.

Both Minh and I realize that while we have tried to put the war behind us, it has been easier to do so far removed in America where reminders are fewer and farther between.

We find memories stirring restlessly when we meet an amputee or see so many good people kept from decent jobs or displaced from their homes because of their past loyalties. The urge to join whispered conversations is increasingly strong .... and whispered they must, be for the walls still have ears.

Minh's mother's home in Tam Vu - 1992

Minh with her mom and sisters - Tam Vu 1992

The author and Minh's sister Tuong - Tam Vu 1992

Tri, Minh, Hoa & Hieu on the former site
of the 36th Evac - Vung Tau 1992

Chapter Thirty-three

Hello Vung Tau .... where it all began twenty-four years ago.

We have hired a car and driver to bring us here from the verdant, sweltering closeness of Tam Vu; here to the broad sandy beaches; here to the refreshing ocean breezes; here where we met half a lifetime ago.

The small city of Vung Tau has changed. The peninsula on which it rests still juts proudly into the South China Sea but the barrier beach sand dunes have been leveled and a flock of hotels is growing where jungle growth once reigned, and a familiar theme is heard - the Japanese are buying up the seashore.

The scenery is still as breathtaking as we remember and the children are still as charming. The dogs are still as gaunt and salt spray still as alluring. There are no traces of the rusted old French tanks or American bunkers which used to clutter the beaches and dunes. On top of the mountain overlooking the point of the peninsula is a towering statue of Jesus, built by the Americans in 1974. His outstretched arms could be calming the waters or bidding peace to a troubled land.

We have chosen a small hotel overlooking the beach, renting rooms for Minh's mother and sisters and for ourselves. Their room is four American dollars per night, but my American face costs us eight dollars, after all, we are filthy rich tourists, aren't we?

Our mother's health improves daily as she breathes the clean salt air and takes short walks along the seaside. We soon feel comfortable leaving her with the family and strike out to find the site of the hospital where we met, unsure of the memories we may evoke. Using the distinctive outline of the mountain as a guide we are able to locate the site quite readily. Nothing remains.

There is a hollow feeling of disappointment as we walk through the scattering of houses and huts where the 36th Evac. once

264

dominated our lives. We cannot recapture enough of a memory to picture the former U.S. base. Perhaps it's just as well.

Walking along the streets of Vung Tau quickly rekindles the memories which were so hazy at the foot of the mountain. The sounds and smells and sights wash over us and we turn to one another simultaneously and smile. Our fingers entwine and suddenly we're thrust back in time. As we walk hand in hand it is impossible to ignore the stares of everyone we meet. There is astonishment, curiosity and anger in these faces. Only when we hear a derisive "Lien so" do we realize that I have been mistaken for a Russian!

There is a small enclave of Russian workers in the city from a petroleum plant which has eleven years remaining on a lease with the government. The Russians are disliked by most Vietnamese for their former support of the communist invaders and for their overbearing, disdainful attitudes and parsimonious habits.

As soon as I explain that I'm American the mood changes dramatically. I feel like General MacArthur must have felt on his return to the Philippines. Everyone is eager to talk with this returning G.I.. It would appear that city dwellers are as anxious to offer their hospitality as the farmers and fishermen of the countryside.

Tri, his wife Hoa and their son Hieu are with us every day, providing rides on borrowed motorbikes throughout the city and beyond as we try to absorb our surroundings through every pore. For me, the travels are a totally new experience since I rarely had a chance to move about during the war. I delight in surprising vendors and passersby with my rudimentary grasp of their language. As I remembered from the past, even poor attempts to converse in Vietnamese are greatly appreciated and draw enthusiastic responses.

With the exception of the proprietors of the government-operated souvenir shops along the front beach and government officials, we are not treated as tourists or "Viet Kieu", expatriates. It is impossible to move about the small city without encountering beggars. Most seem to have some physical disabilities and are invariably accompanied by a grimy waif with a haunting, forlorn expression. We still can't refuse any of these unfortunates but soon learn that we are easy marks due to my Caucasian looks. We finally avoid certain locales where there are large collections of beggars who sometimes jostle one another and us in their desperate attempts to cadge enough money for a meal.

While I am enjoying the attention we attract - and the unaccustomed sensation of being the tallest person around - Minh is disappointed to find that she has forgotten so much. The city has changed somewhat, but her bewilderment goes beyond mere confusion over new street names and numbers. There is a different atmosphere .... an air of poverty, frustration and malaise that is much different from the time she once lived here.

Hard times and broken promises .... such a sadly appropriate epitaph for so many dreams that have died in these muddy streets following the war.

After the unusual rainless week in the Mekong Delta, daily storms hit Vung Tau with a vengeance. Unfortunately, for our two Americanized bodies the temperature remains in the nineties with the humidity at the saturation level. Minh and I both suffer from this feature of the country which we had apparently been so willing to forget.

As we continue to explore the city, searching for old friends and landmarks, we are surprised by the candid and often vehement outpourings of frustration and hatred concerning the communist government. With no encouragement on our part, citizens stop us everywhere we roam to describe over and over again how they have been removed from their homes, businesses and jobs after the takeover in 1975. Communists from the north were given these jobs and homes and are still holding them, though somewhat uneasily of late.

After just a few days here we can feel the tension, and gain a sense of changes that might be on the horizon. Churches are open now, with Catholics and Buddhists alike freely practicing their religions. Free enterprise is not limited to back alley black market transactions, but thriving along every street. Many of the shops and businesses are communist-owned but far more are run by South Vietnamese who are striving to regain some of their former independence.

In an open-air cafe we meet an old gentleman who insists that we join him for tea. He speaks five languages fluently and is starving for the opportunity to speak English with an American. His story is short and typical. A few of his family members successfully escaped from the country on a boat while others were lost at sea. But for an

266

illness he would have attempted to leave himself. He asks our help in sending a letter to his brother in America. His plea is repeated by many others we encounter. They haven't enough money to buy a stamp.

Emboldened by my rapidly improving conversational Vietnamese and a lack of negative contacts, I begin striking out on my own for early morning strolls on the beach -- where I can mingle with the fishermen -- or downtown among the street vendors and townsfolk. My relatives are horrified when they discover these solo jaunts and make me promise not to go anywhere without some of them along. I am naive, they explain, if I think everything is safe here. They relate tales of murders and disappearances and other stories of gloom. Unfortunately, the stories are corroborated by many of the people I have met. I reluctantly agree to cease my solitary explorations.

Minh and I continue to share the beauty of Vung Tau with her mother and the rest of the family but a feeling of uneasiness has been imposed on us and we feel it will remain for the rest of the trip.

Our family's warnings light close to home when I am asked to help a friendly teacher with English classes for some employees of our hotel. He is a delightful man with a perfect command of English. I help him twice at classes, enjoying myself thoroughly conversing with his students, some of whom will never threaten his job. But now his friendly overtures have climaxed with an invitation to me to accompany him on his rounds throughout Vung Tau and the surrounding area. He is insistent that I come alone .... no room on his Honda for Minh and no need for any of the family to come along either.

Though I'm inclined to go with him, my family is adamant that I decline. I feel they are over-reacting - unduly suspicious of a harmless invitation - but they insist that I not leave alone with this teacher, who is obviously a communist despite his winning ways. The deciding vote is cast when two maids from the hotel warn Minh and my sister-in-law not to let me go. They can't elaborate but they are sincere in their warning.

I don't leave with the teacher and I will never know what might have transpired.

While in Tam Vu we obtained a travel pass valid for the entire country. A pack of cigarettes and a five dollar bill easily procured this invaluable document from a second cousin of Minh who supported the Vietcong and was rewarded with a government job. Now we will make good use of the prized pass. We are leaving on a side trip to the city of Dalat in the mountainous central highlands two hundred miles to the north. Minh's family has never traveled anywhere in the country before and neither Minh nor I had been north either.

We again rent a small Toyota mini-bus and draw the same amiable drivers who brought us up from Tam Vu. All vans and mini-buses operated by the travel company must have a second driver to watch the rear and assist in maneuvering along the dangerous highways.

Fifteen of us somehow crowd into the narrow vehicle and we are off. As we climb into the mountains there is a striking difference in the type of crops grown. Coffee and tea plantations supplant the coconut palm. Lettuce, broccoli and other cooler weather vegetables replace many of the fruit trees of the south. Entire mountainsides are cleared here and covered by banana plantations. Flat land for growing rice is at a premium.

The travel pass proves invaluable at the numerous military and police checkpoints. Our drivers are impressed with our ability to obtain this eagerly sought-after document. We are impressed, unfavorably so, by the breakneck speed our flat-land drivers achieve on these winding mountain roads. It's not unusual to spin through a hairpin turn on slippery red clay while gaping at a seven hundred foot sheer drop just off the road shoulder, which has no guard rail. The lack of seat belts in the van heightens our thinly disguised anxiety. There is no doubt that our greatest danger over here is on the highway and not from robbers, although the microbes in the water, food and air run a close second.

We finally arrive in Dalat in a blinding thunderstorm, a daily occurrence now that the monsoons are really here. We search in vain for a hotel that will accommodate all of us. It seems that there are only two small hotels approved (read safe) for foreigners in the entire city. Reluctantly Minh and I split from our family. Entering the hotel we silently watch as the door is barred behind us.

At 2:00 a.m. we are sitting bolt upright in bed.

"Minhoi," Minh whispers, "what is going on?"

"I don't know, Hon," I reply, "but it doesn't sound good."

From the street four stories below it sounds like a riot is in progress. Easing over to the window I cautiously peer out. The scene below chills my blood. In the light of flames shooting from a pile of debris I can see six or eight men shaking the barred doors to the hotel and throwing bottles against them. They are shouting angrily. For the next hour we scarcely dare breathe. We haven't a clue as to the nature of this disturbance but it does not bode well.

By 3:00 a.m. silence again reigns. The men have disappeared. We sleep little for the rest of the night. In the morning we learn that there are national elections today, and the men outside were just drunk and probably protesting foreigners being lodged in the hotel. Nevertheless, we are warned, it would be a good day to stay off the streets.

We pick up Minh's family early for a meal in a downtown cafe and set off a vicious fight between adjacent competing proprietors. Business is slow and foreigners are both rare and highly desired.

Ignoring the early morning advice not to travel, we set out to explore the city and surroundings. The city proper is built on a series of hills, much like Ithaca, New York. There are even a number of waterfalls serving as tourist attractions nearby. Many of the larger buildings are of French origin, and indeed, we meet three Frenchmen in the city. Other than a handful of Russians in Vung Tau, they are the only westerners we have encountered.

Dalat is a tourist attraction for many Vietnamese, and was called the second Paris by the French during their occupation here. The population is much more heterogeneous than we have noted in the south. People are taller and a strong Chinese influence can be found. There are also many hill tribes of wandering farmers and Montagnards in evidence.

We soon discover that the friendly, more spontaneous attitude of the people in the south is lacking here. Many of the original inhabitants of the city have been forced to move south and the influence of northern communists is pervasive. Communist flags fly on street corners and from dozens of buildings, a sight we never encountered anywhere in the south. There are sour expressions on so many faces and an unwillingness to speak with us.

The cold atmosphere is also reflected by the weather. Dalat is cold - a mere sixty-five degrees Fahrenheit. Minh and her Mom catch colds and pick up stomach viruses. Their tour of the small city is much abbreviated and we decide to leave after only three days.

The trip back down through the mountains is more exciting than any roller coaster ride I have ever experienced. The tension created by the realization that our drivers are not used to steep mountain roads is almost unbearable. We have barely missed several large buses and many smaller vehicles and once again our lives are in deadly peril. We all give silent thanks when we safely reach Vung Tau once more.

We have passed over the bridge near Baria where my bus was held up by a fire-fight between the Vietcong and South Vietnamese army regulars in 1970 when I returned to bring Minh out. The memory of that close call gives me goose bumps and I take Minh's hand in mine. She remembers as well and shakes her head resignedly. We have been so lucky.

A few more days in Vung Tau ends now with a final trip back to the Delta and Tam Vu. Our friends were able to visit us for two days in Vung Tau and we make arrangements to meet them in Saigon the day before our departure. Time is flying by and I don't know if we will ever get to see and do all we had hoped to.

It is probably fortunate that our trip is nearly over. Minh is quite ill with stomach cramps and diarrhea while my American digestive system is still holding up well. We are making a list of all the relatives with various illnesses and special medical needs. Perhaps someday we can provide some specific help, but for now we must be content with dispensing broad spectrum antibiotics, anti-bacterial creams and Tylenol.

Tam Vu - 9:00 a.m., the day before we depart for Saigon.

"If I had had a rifle I would have killed you. And at fifty meters I wouldn't have missed."

So spoke the attractive middle-aged widow sitting in the chair beside me.

We are sitting in Minh's mother's house in Tam Vu and the woman has stopped by to chat. She has just told me that she saw me filming three weeks ago near her home, some three miles distant over paddy dikes and through uncleared jungle, and that seeing her first American in twenty-four years produced an overwhelming urge to kill him/me.

Her husband and children were killed by Americans in the war and her initial reaction to seeing me was one of vengeance. She speaks proudly of being a loyal Vietcong, even today. My family moves nearer to us, stunned by her outburst, but ever protective.

As we talk further she mellows, admitting that her first urge has faded, but that she isn't the only one who lost family and still harbors strong feelings against her former enemy. I try to explain that many American families were also torn asunder by the war but she counters with the far greater numbers of Vietnamese who died or were wounded. She reveals that she and the other local Vietcong fought hard to prevent the Americans from colonizing her land. That was what she had been given as our reason for coming to Southeast Asia.

She expressed bitterness at her abandonment by the party once the war was over. A tiny pension and no land grant did not compensate adequately for her sacrifices, she brooded. When I asked what pensions or grants the millions of South Vietnamese received she snorted derisively, "They lost the war. Why should they receive anything?"

Following another half hour of discussion we reached a stalemate and both of us spoke of burying the dead and getting on with life ... life with peace. Minh's family and some neighbors who were visiting shook their heads. There can only be peace when we own our country again and the communists depart, they averred.

As the woman left I found myself shaken by her revelation. I had expected to find such resentment here, but the month of travel had not revealed any until this moment. Now I understood somewhat why my family here was so protective. I also understood why Minh and I have been under such a strain for most of the trip.

When we first entered the country we risked offering a bribe to the communist soldier-official inspecting papers and baggage. From then on we were never sure how each official would treat such an offer but were resigned that it was how the country operated today.

In addition to the stress of continually watching our backs, deciding who and how much to bribe, avoiding serious illnesses and injuries, equitably sharing our gifts without offending family members, and considering where and where not to film, there is a constant physical drain coping with weather, time change (exactly 12 hours opposite from the U.S.) and a major change in diet. We will surely have much to reflect on when our journey is completed.

For two days prior to our departure Minh's mother alternately

271

cries and hugs us. She repeats over and over that she will never see us again before she dies and couldn't we stay longer. It is hard to leave her and the good people of Tam Vu. Very hard.

Our final two nights in Vietnam are spent in Saigon. We want to be sure our plane tickets and papers are in order and try for a good nights sleep before the long journey home. We visit the police station to have our video tapes approved, not wishing to lose the precious memories we have captured. When we are told that there will be a two week wait before the tapes can be inspected, Minh manages to stick ten dollars between the tapes. The money represents a month's income for the official and an hour later, with no inspection, the tapes are packaged and officially sealed for us.

At the hotel, Tri, Hoa and our grandson Hieu stay with us and dream of the day they will join us in America. We may have expedited that hope by some of the contacts we made on the trip, and by the grease we applied to the skids.

All of Minh's sisters and their families join us at Tan Son Nhut to say goodbye. Twice I have left Minh behind at an airfield in Vietnam in uncertain circumstances and our parting was as sad as any parting can possibly be. But now, as we depart together from this beautiful family, I am so choked with emotion that I cannot speak. The desire to get home to be with our children in Cortland is pulling us, making our leave-taking all the more difficult.

Minh tearfully embraces everyone in sight while I take care of the final departure arrangements. As we strain to see through the cloudy windows in the rising plane we are rewarded with a final glimpse of the family, waving farewell. Minh and I are silent for most of the trip to Singapore. Only when we taxi in to Changi airport are we fully aroused. A large group of Vietnamese who had been visiting their former homeland, and are U.S. bound, send up a rousing cheer. No more communists!

The remainder of the trip home is beyond arduous. From the time we arrive at Tan Son Nhut airfield to the time we reach Cortland, over sixty hours have elapsed, including a freezing eleven hour wait in the air-conditioned Changi airport which feels like the North Pole to us this time through. At Kennedy airport the plane adjacent to ours crashes on takeoff. The fact that it is the same airline we are to use between New York and Syracuse makes a significant impression. Eventually we manage to grab a taxi to La

Guardia and barely make the last night flight to Syracuse.

Our journey has been eventful, fruitful and inspiring. Less than three months after our return we receive news that Tri, Hoa and Hieu have received their exit documents from Vietnam. Seventeen years of vain attempts to reunite our family may soon be over. We have never been this close before.

We have seen poverty and generosity that will forever remind us of the real values in this life. Our fervent hope is to return to Vietnam with all of our children, but for now they will have to be content to rely on our videos and memories to teach them of the Asian half of their dual heritage. Perhaps someday the world will realize that all peoples are alike in so many ways and that the artificial differences of language, color and customs are truly insignificant.

And so Minhoi, you have your book - your legacy as you say. But I say your real legacy is shining brightly in all of the lives you have touched here on earth. I pray that your life is long and touches many more lives, especially mine.

Marie, Mike Jr., Mike
Marty, Maureen, Minh

273

Suu and Tot, Minh's parents - c 1955

Thu and Mike Jr. - 1970